BC SPACE

MYTHING IN ACTION

Dedicated to the memory of Jerry Burchfield
and in honor of Mark, Jerry and BC Space

Grand Central Press

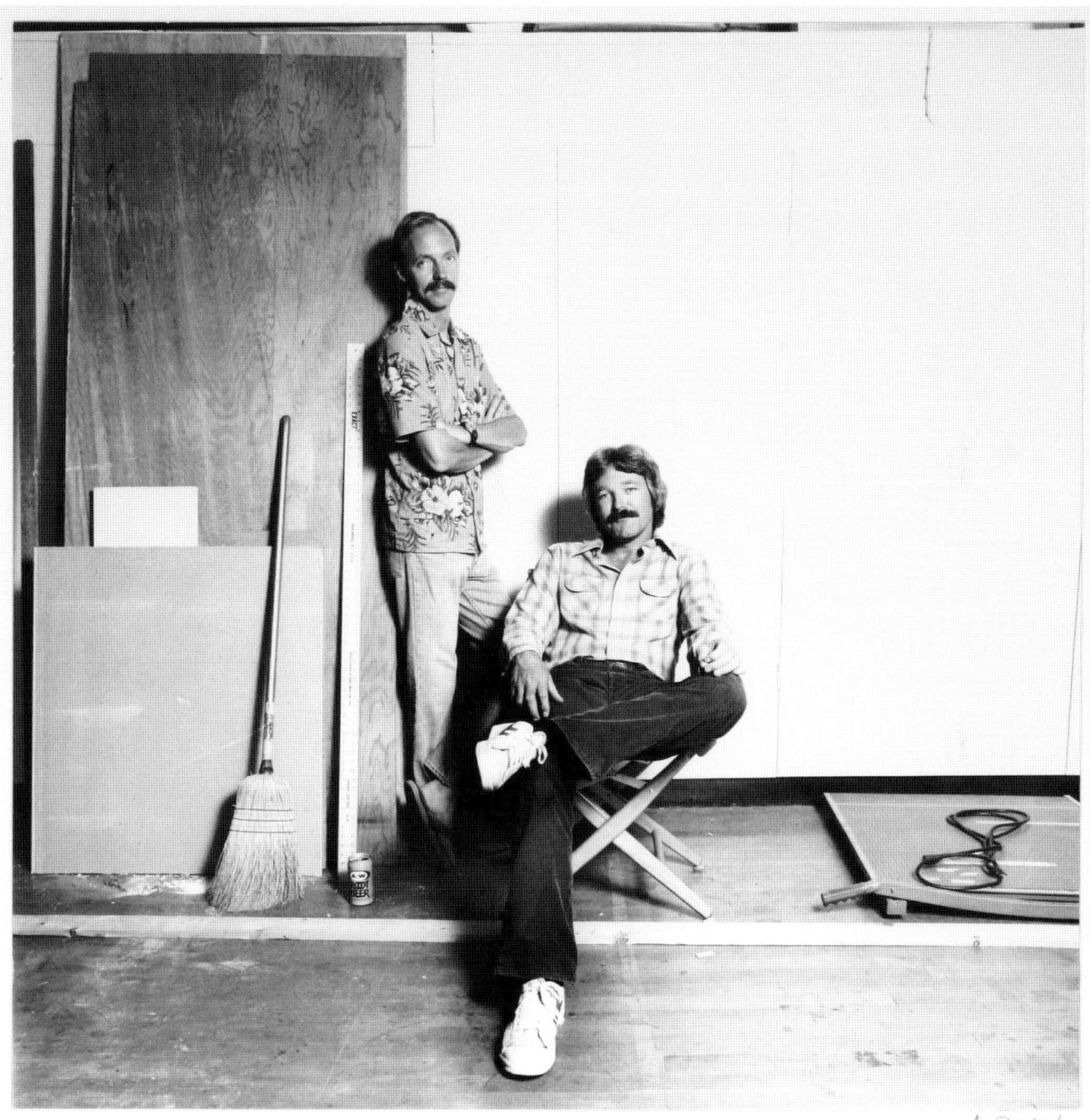

Mark Chamberlain and Jerry Burchfield, BC Portrait, 1975
Photo by Al Belson

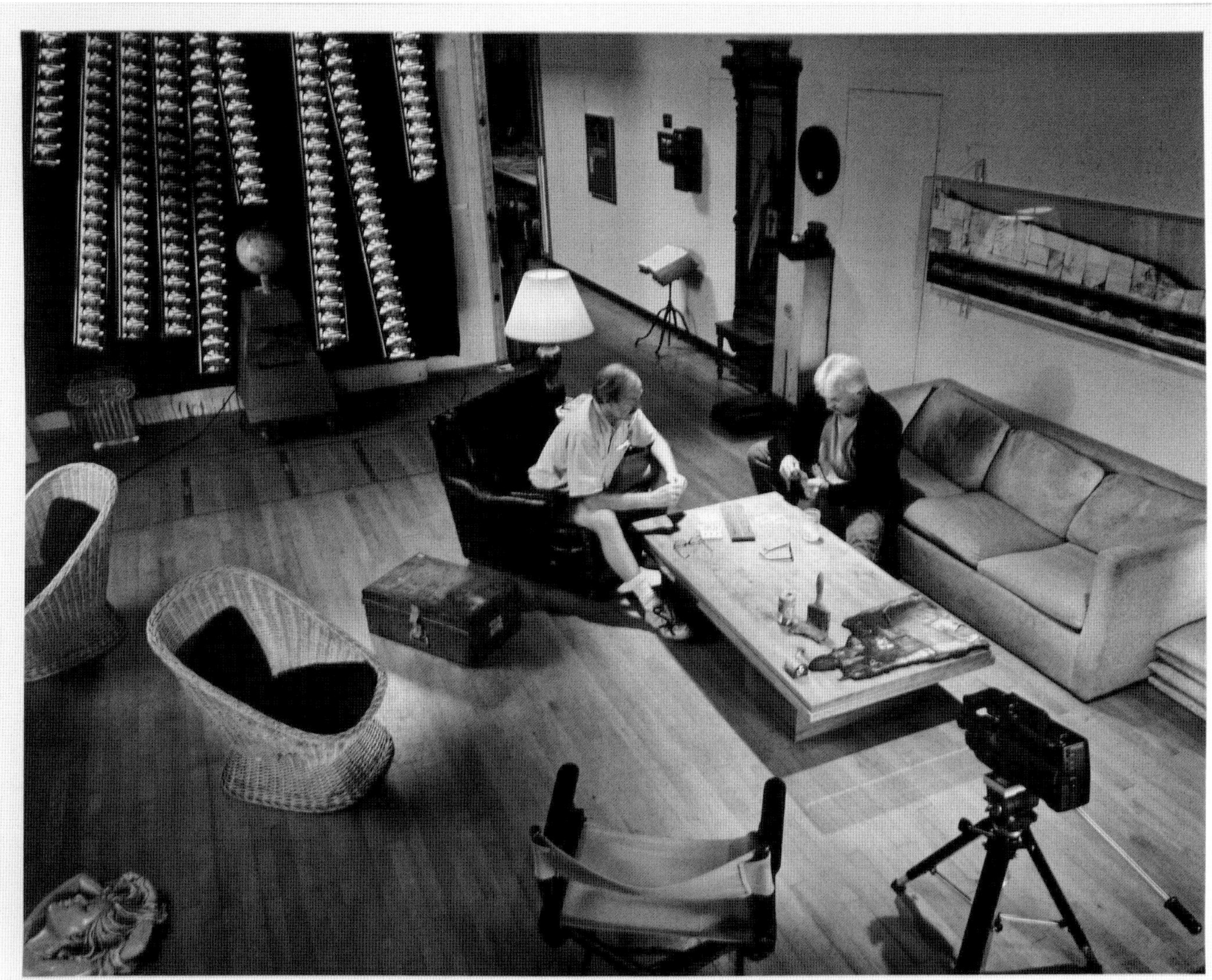

Mark Chamberlain and Jerry Burchfield
BC Portrait, 1996
Photo by Neil Chapman

Jerry Burchfield
Truth the First Casualty, 1992
Mixed media

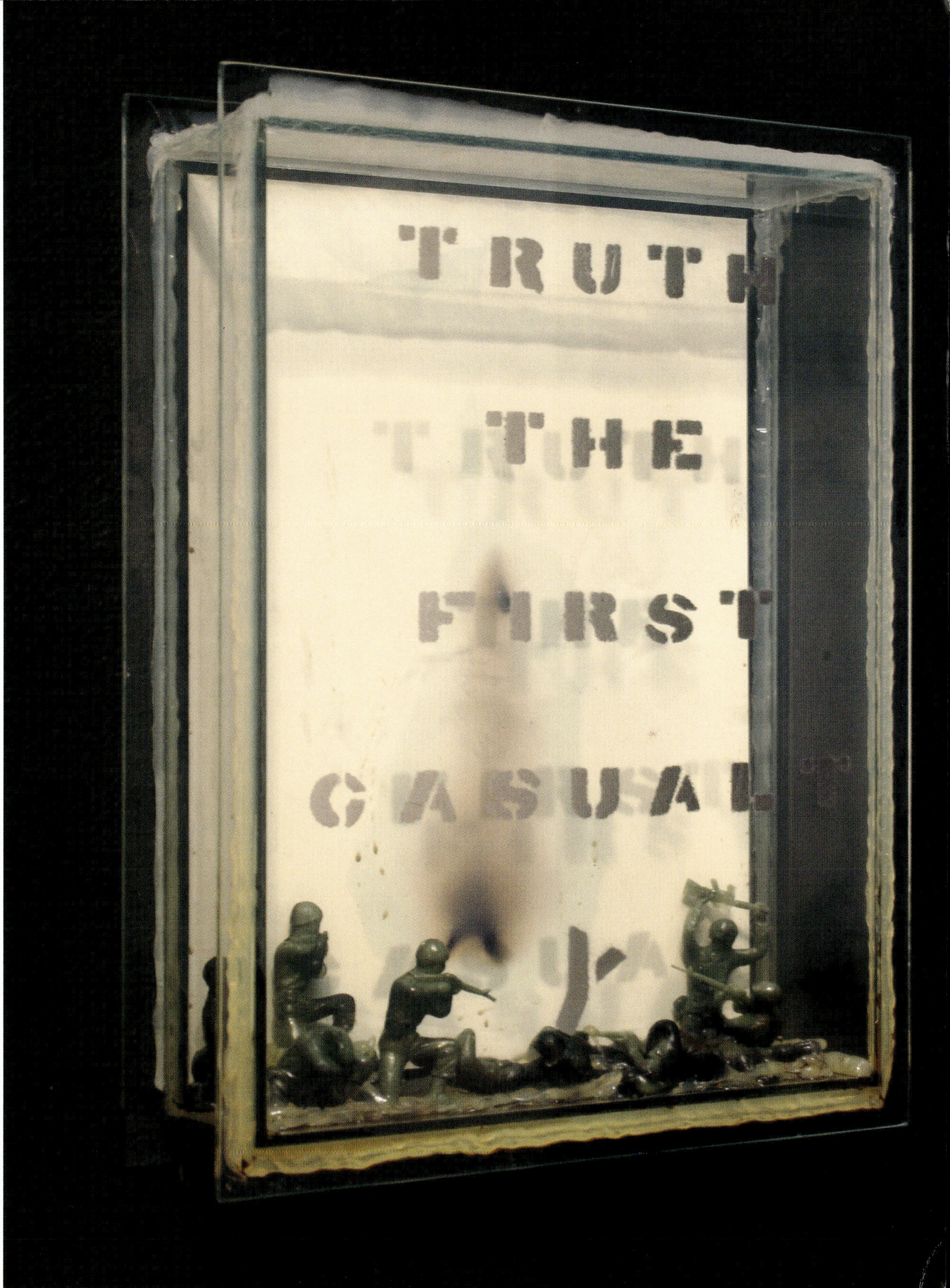

TRUTH

THE

FIRST

CASUAL

BC Space: Mything in Action
by Liz Goldner

The art of photography is a dynamic process of giving form to ideas and explaining man to man," wrote photographer/curator Edward Steichen in 1955. He was referring to the Museum of Modern Art exhibition *The Family of Man*.

Despite selected photographic exhibitions in a few visionary museums and galleries, photography back then was commonly perceived as an adjunct to other art forms, Mark Chamberlain, BC Space Gallery co-founder, explains.

By the early 1970s, museums and universities recognized the growing allure of photography as art. Yet few art galleries would exhibit this medium in the front room. Mark Chamberlain and art partner Jerry Burchfield resolved to help change this state of affairs. They opened BC Space in Laguna Beach, "both to generate income and to provide the tools needed to explore our own photographic art," Chamberlain says. "With proceeds from these activities, we were free to exhibit contemporary work based solely on merit, not salability."

Today, this contemporary fine art photography gallery, one of the longest running venues of its kind nationwide, has dramatically influenced our appreciation for photographic art. The history of BC Space presented in this book is truly a story of myth making in action.

Viet Nam's Influence
In the late 1960s, images from Viet Nam published around the world transformed our understanding of photography as art. "Think of the naked little girl running with napalm burning her skin," Chamberlain explains. "The power and poignancy of that and other images touched the human psyche in dramatic ways and helped change the course of history."

Mark Chamberlain's military tour during the American War in Viet Nam changed his life's trajectory, from operating the family business to becoming a photographic artist, gallery owner, curator, and creator of large multimedia events.

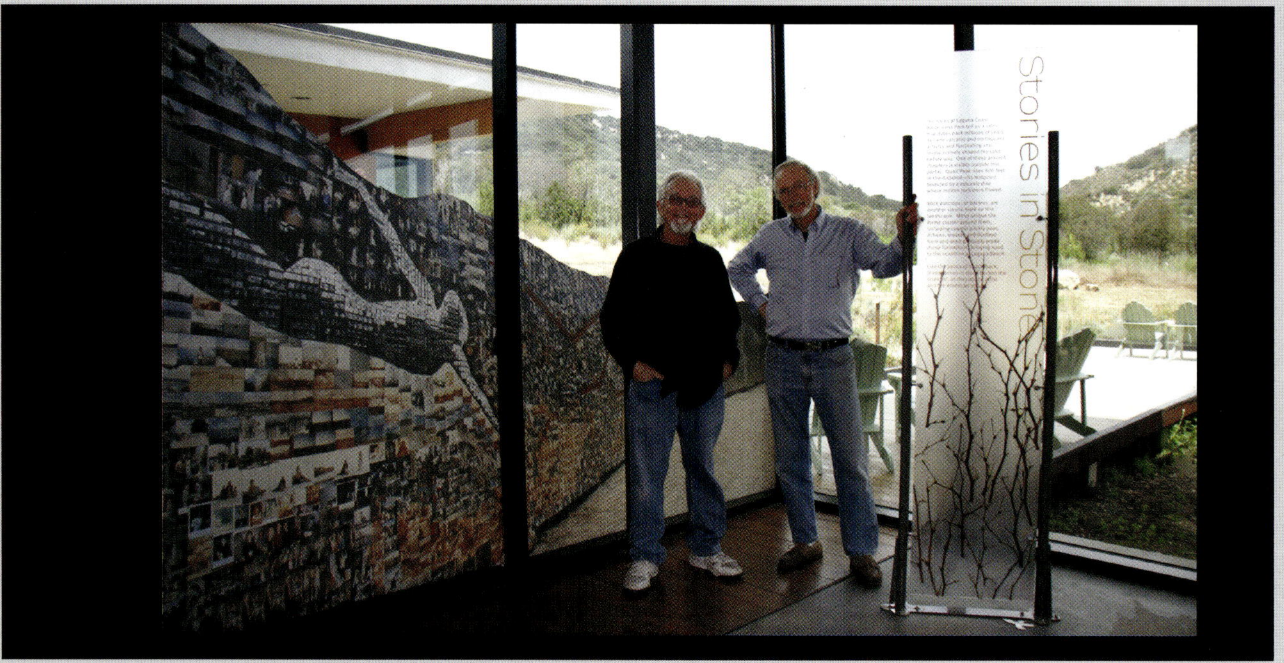

Jerry Burchfield and Mark Chamberlain
BC Portrait at Nix Nature Center
Gateway to Laguna Wilderness, Laguna Canyon, 2009
photo by Damon Nicholson, 2009

He grew up in Dubuque, Iowa, and received an exemplary college education with a bachelor's degree in political science and a master's in business administration. In February 1967, only two days after receiving his master's, he was drafted into the army. Narrowly avoiding jungle duty in Viet Nam, he ultimately served a one-year tour in South Korea. Often citing the Chinese concept that crisis presents opportunity, he views that military experience as a turning point. While not engaged in active combat, Chamberlain spent time with soldiers transitioning back from Viet Nam, regarding them as "broken people whose lives were changed forever."

"While stationed overseas, I picked up a camera primarily to keep my sanity and provide an outlet beyond the more common practices of drinking, whoring, and gambling. I also took classes in the Korean language and history and (very fortuitously) found a photography instructor attached to the military crafts program who saw talent in my work. Mr. Chae became a real mentor, teaching me darkroom techniques and forcing me to examine the deeper meanings in my photographs." Chamberlain often roamed the cities and countryside, conversing with the people while photographing their lifestyles."

"Returning home, I could not find the threads of my previous path, yet I had a growing desire to find an outlet for this newfound passion." In 1969, he packed up his MG Midget and headed to Los Angeles, aspiring to open a photographic art gallery.

When those plans fell through, he relocated to Laguna Beach, a community that seemed "like a safer haven than L.A., with a canyon road that reminded me of the Midwest." Along with photography, he supported himself as a housepainter, carpenter, electrician, and general handyman, developing skills he later employed to construct BC Space.

Creating BC Space
Jerry Burchfield was born in Chicago and grew up in San Diego with an illustrator/artist father who encouraged his son's studies in photography. While Jerry was deferred from the draft, he was deeply affected by the war and the maelstrom of antiwar protests. As a young man with a rebellious streak, he was on a quest to find deeper meaning for his life's work. In 1971, while attending college and working at a commercial photo studio, Burchfield met Chamberlain, discovering a brother/comrade who shared his enthusiasm for photography as fine art.

Burchfield recalled, "I met Mark when he was querying submissions for the Laguna Beach Winter Festival of Arts. We exhibited the first photographs ever at the Festival, including our own images, works by local photographers of merit, and prints by deceased Laguna notables such as Paul Outerbridge and William Mortensen."

Within two years of their meeting, Burchfield and Chamberlain decided to go into partnership. They raised funds, located the proper equipment, devised a business plan and officially opened BC (coined from their initials) Photography and Custom Lab Services on April 1, 1973.

In that 1,000-square-foot space (with expansion capabilities), Chamberlain and Burchfield initially shot and processed film for commercial clients. But they soon focused on shooting and printing for other galleries, museums, and artists.

They also presented informal photography exhibitions displaying a wide range of work, many infused with political, social and environmental messages. As word of their innovative shows spread throughout the region, BC exhibitions became standing-room-only events.

"Artist friends told us we were crazy to start a business like this in Laguna," Burchfield said, "and that we needed to be in Los Angeles where the action was. But we liked our cheap rent, working near the beach, and our upstairs studio space, a former Masonic Lodge that Mark stumbled onto."

"This was a time of great change," Chamberlain adds. "We were affected by the ongoing war and the undercurrent of protests. You could say that BC Space was forged in the cauldron of that contentious time period."

It is easy to visualize Burchfield and Chamberlain in 1973, their combined vision, insightful natures, penchant for working and playing hard, and their attractive, bohemian looks. They were a natural pair, destined to help change the prevailing perceptions of photography while addressing societal concerns in their art.

Aggressively Contemporary Work
Burchfield and Chamberlain built adjacent darkrooms to process and print for clients as well as for themselves. They often shouted through the wall between the rooms while working, until Mark cut a hole in the wall and hung a black curtain over it. They had many intense dialogues across that confessional black hole...about art, the environment, and

their own artwork.,
Soon BC was mounting monthly photography exhibitions, some attended by hundreds of people, many gaining coverage by local and national media. They gradually expanded the venue to 2,400 square feet, renaming it "BC Space" to reflect the open-ended character of their ambitions.

Burchfield explained, "We were a pioneering entity showing aggressively contemporary work by some of the most innovative photographers in the country. We ignored the tourist tradition of most Laguna galleries. As our audience was mainly artists and enthusiasts, not collectors, we often spent more money on exhibits than we took in."

In 1981, BC Space held their "Photography Auction Exhibition," published an extensive catalogue, and formally hung 245 works by little-known to famous photographers, including Ansel Adams, John Divola, and Brett Weston. They received great media attention, took in $18,000, but had spent everything on the show, a formal catalogue, and remodeling the space to accommodate the exhibition.

In 1982, artist Sheila Pinkel created *Thermonuclear Garden* in the newly expanded gallery space. The installation consisted of information sheets, maps, artworks, and take-out food containers listing major manufacturers selling weapons to foreign countries. The show attracted hundreds of viewers and extensive press, and subsequently evolved into 11 additional shows exhibited across the country. Pinkel was the first of several artists who lived at BC while building artworks there.

BC Space took another big plunge in 1983, purchasing a high-end Cibachrome print processor to create color images with vibrancy and archival qualities to meet museum standards. Photographic artists, many adding color to their palette, began commissioning BC to print their images. Chamberlain explains, "Unlike most custom labs, we had better understanding of their needs and goals and could speak their language."

In 1984, the *Orange County Register* commissioned BC Space to print their photographs of the Los Angeles Olympics. Employing Cibachrome, BC processed the prints and matted the images to museum standards, creating the work for which the *Register* won the Pulitzer Prize.

As BC Space grew in vision, complexity of exhibitions, and size, several hundred people joined its evolution.

These employees, volunteers, and artists helped construct the space, mount the shows, display work, and even perform there. The Space became a multidisciplinary venue, encompassing all visual media, including film and performance arts.

Laguna Canyon Project

The Laguna Canyon Project, a satellite BC venture, was a photographic documentation of the Canyon Road, the main access route to Laguna Beach and the Pacific Ocean from inland Orange County. "We wanted to document changes of the Canyon over time to create a broader awareness of regional and global environmental issues," Chamberlain says.

In 1984, the Project's *Time Machine for Moving Stills* displayed a 516-foot-long continuous photograph of sequential shots of the road. Chamberlain elaborates, "Larry Gill and I designed and built the device with assistance from several artist and engineer friends. *The Time Machine* gave a real presence to the Project, attracting the interest of museums throughout the country. We finally pulled the plug on it, since we needed to get on to other phases."

In 1988, Chamberlain wrote in *Journal of Orange County Studies*, "Local residents see the Canyon as a greenbelt buffer, while others view it as virgin territory ripe for development. But we felt it imperative to call into question prevailing conceptions of progress. We used photography, video, sculpture, performance, installations, and collaborative events to address these concerns."

The Project's largest and most dramatic Phase was *The Tell* photomural, constructed in 1989, seven miles into the canyon, across from the Irvine Company's proposed massive Laguna Laurel Housing Project.

The Tell

The name "Tell" comes from the archeological term for a mound of artifacts from prior civilizations, buried over by natural elements. A Tell was cited in James Michener's best-selling 1965 book, *The Source*, which deals with the evolution of civilization.

The Tell photomural was built as a small mountain, composed of hundreds of thousands of photographs, reflective of the people who donated their images.

It grew to 636 feet long and ranged from 36 feet high, dwindling down to the ground, undulating across the landscape, and diving back into the hillside. The installation resembled the voluptuous nature of the surrounding canyons, echoing a female figure in its shape, while its stylized Easter Island head was its physical and philosophical foundation.

People from across the country donated countless personal photographs. Several hundred volunteers helped build the installation and glued the pictures onto the framework, weaving the photos together like pixels in a pointillist painting by density, color, content, and type of material, and positioning specific storylines on the chakra points of the larger body of the mural. The stories related many tales of man, woman, and the land.

The Tell became the site of numerous demonstrations, as well as receiving coverage from CNN, *Life* magazine, and other national and local media. "On November 11, 1989, we coordinated with environmental groups to host a Walk and Demonstration to the mural. It was attended by an estimated 11,000 people," Chamberlain explains. "As a consequence, the land was released for public acquisition. The Canyon is now a key part of the Laguna Wilderness Park."

"Those rambling darkroom dialogues with Jerry over what we could do to protect a valuable piece of countryside evolved into a project that actually helped preserve that land," Chamberlain adds. "Although encroachment is still a threat, the road and its surrounding hills are designated to remain undeveloped forever."

The Tell was taken down for storage in 1990. While most sections were destroyed in the Laguna wildfire of 1993, it became a part of local folklore. One wall-size photograph documenting *The Tell* is incorporated into the Nix Interpretive Center (across from the installation site), the gateway to the 6,200-acre Laguna Wilderness Park.

Agonizing Breakup
Jerry Burchfield passed away on September 11, 2009. A few months before his passing, he talked about the painful breakup of his business partnership with Chamberlain in 1987 (even though he continued supporting BC projects). "We tried to represent artists whose work we admired, but as artists ourselves, not sales people, we sold very little. Everything changed when I became a parent and financial reality hit home. We struggled over how to make BC Space more lucrative, but everything we came up with would have ruined it.

"I left the gallery to better support my family and child, turning to full-time teaching [utilizing a master of fine art degree earned while at BC]. It was the most agonizing decision I have ever dealt with." In time, teaching gave Burchfield a new perspective, as he mentored numerous photographers toward more creative expression.

"In BC fashion, we exhibited "The Art of the Matter" about the breakup; [it was] an evolving, expanding dialogue on the role of the artist in American society. We have remained great friends and continue to collaborate on art projects...and Mark kept the B in BC Space."

Expanded Perspectives
After Chamberlain assumed sole ownership of BC Space, he gradually expanded the gallery's perspectives, exhibiting other visual and performance media on an equal footing with photography. "Ideas and issues expressed through art became more important to me than just one medium," he explains. "Besides, photography had gained its place in the art world."

He continues to explore issues: art as an expression of our deepest yearnings; the shamelessness of healthy sexuality; societal evolution; politics and economics; the hell and hypocrisy of war; and environmental concerns.

BC Space exhibitions since 1988 include "Inside Out" (1988), about mental illness; "Just War" (1991), about the first gulf War; "Cities of Chance, LA/NY" (1998), contrasting coastal life styles; "Pretty Lies, Dirty Truths" (2003), opening two months before the second Gulf War; "For Shame" (2004), a reaction to a politician's prohibition of nudity in art; "Come Hell and High Water" (2007), a scathing photographic essay on Hurricane Katrina; "My Father's Party is Busted," opening before the 2008 presidential election; and "Capital Crime$" (2012.)

The Legacy Project
The Legacy Project was a natural outgrowth of the Laguna Canyon Project. Its intent was to chronicle photographically the transformation of the former El Toro Marine Air Station into the Orange County Great Park.
By 2000, the decommissioning of the El Toro air base

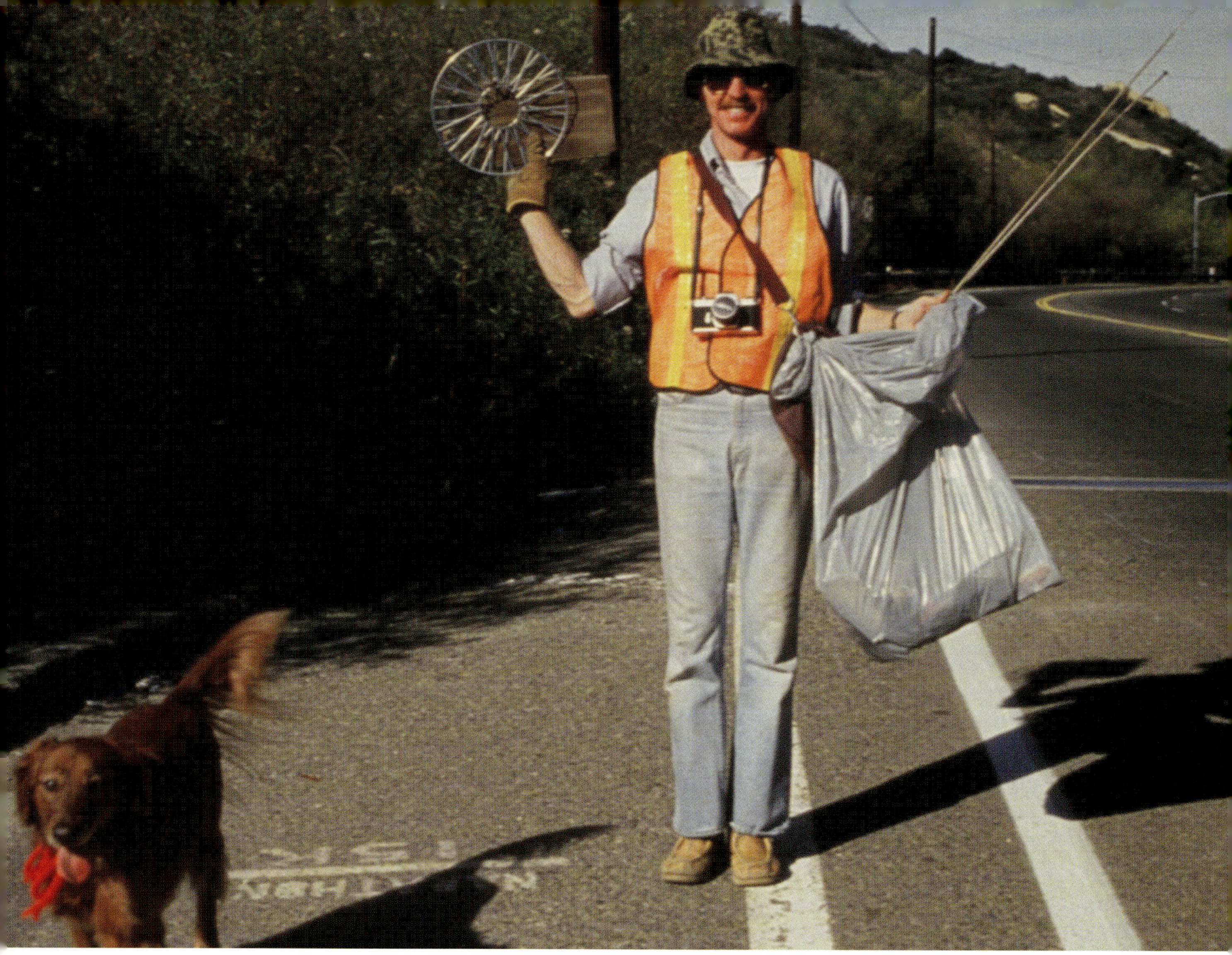

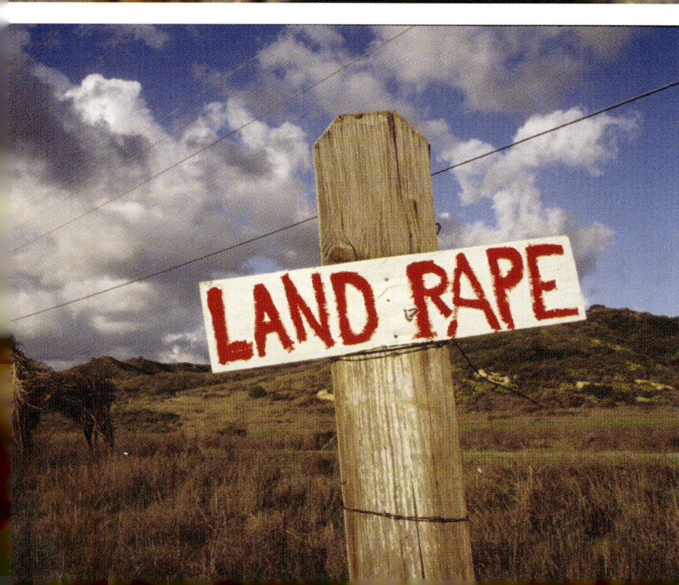

LAND RAPE

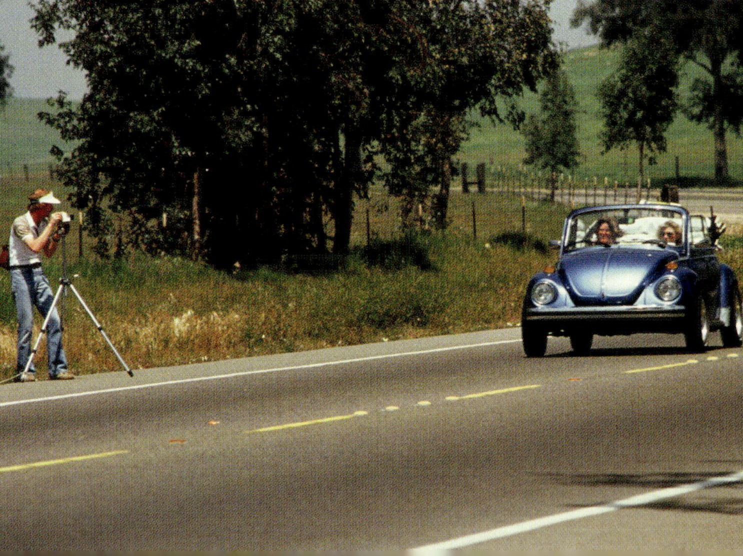

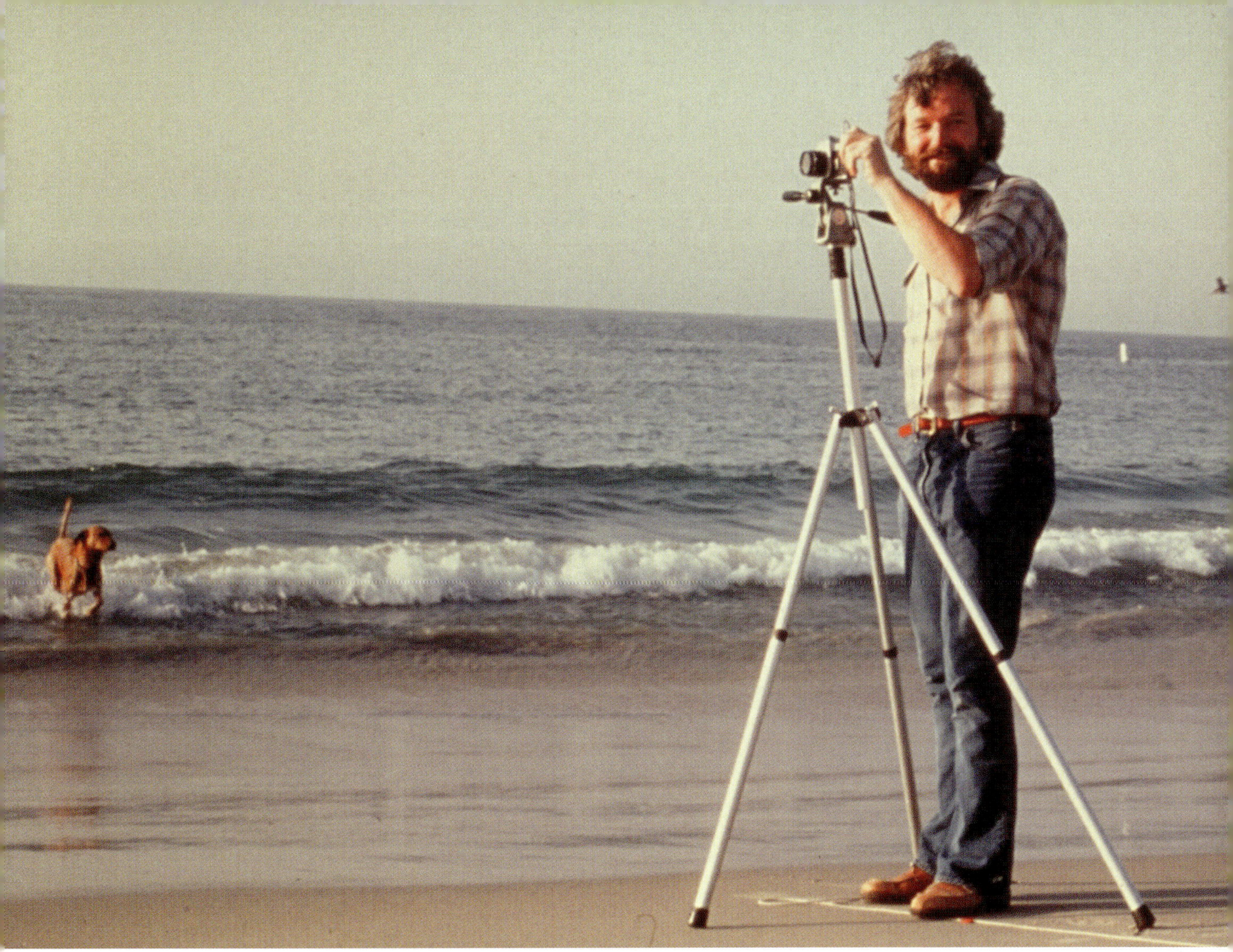

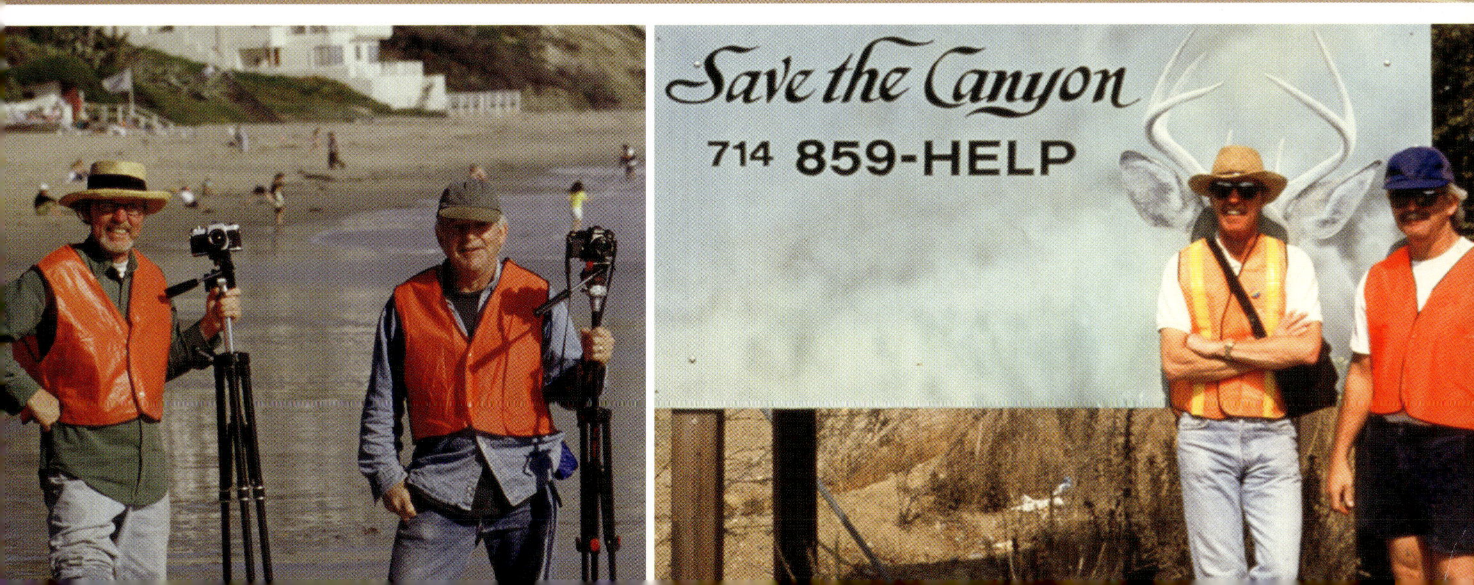
Save the Canyon
714 859-HELP

in Irvine, California had become a topic of contention. One faction favored turning the 4,700-acre site into an international airport. Chamberlain, Burchfield and a huge contingent of Orange County residents and environmentalists preferred a public park. They expressed their desire that the proposed park would connect with the Laguna Wilderness Park, providing a natural corridor from the San Bernardino Mountains to the Pacific Ocean. In 2005, the Orange County Great Park proponents prevailed and plans for reconstruction began.

In 2002, before that decision was reached, Burchfield, Chamberlain and fellow Cypress College instructors Rob Johnson and Clayton Spada escorted a photography class to the base.

"We felt like archeologists entering a ghost town when we first explored the air station," Burchfield commented. "While prowling the base and shooting the officers' homes, backyards, and playgrounds, we had a strong sense of the families who had lived there. We saw barbecues, furniture, and children's shoes, and could almost hear the sounds of the people who had worked and played there. Our images from that time period depict a hallowed past and a presence of life."

Subsequently, fellow photographers Jacques Garnier and Doug McCulloh were invited to join the undertaking, which was renamed The Legacy Project and dedicated to documenting the evolution of the Great Park over the next decade.

The six Project members have already amassed hundreds of thousands of photographs of homes, schools, churches, theaters, and playgrounds of the city within a city, which had been occupied by Marines and their families since the early 1940s. The photographers have also shot runways, hangars, and distant mountain ranges of the shuttered base to document its transition into a park.

Today, as Great Park grand plans are being re-evaluated, Legacy Project members remain committed to their 15-year goal to document its evolution. They have erected a room-size camera obscura in the artist-in-residence building, and conduct workshops to help maintain public interest in what could still be the largest urban park in the nation.

The Great Picture

In July 2006, The Legacy Project created the world's largest photograph. Project members along with 400 volunteers converted an F-18 jet maintenance hangar at the base into a giant camera obscura. After months of preparation and testing, a 35-minute exposure was made through a six-millimeter pinhole lens onto a single seamless muslin canvas that was coated with gelatin silver emulsion. The photograph, dubbed The Great Picture was then processed in an Olympic-pool-sized developing tray constructed on site.

The resulting 3,375-square-foot photo is 3 stories high by 11 stories wide and portrays the control tower structures and tarmac of the former air base with the San Joaquin Hills as a backdrop. This heart of the air station is designated to be a central region of the Great Park.

In 2007, The Guinness Book of Records certified the Project's Camera Obscura as the largest ever recorded. *The Great Picture* has been exhibited in four venues to date, including the Central Academy of Fine Arts, Beijing, China. It is currently slated for display at the New Orleans Photo Alliance, Fall 2013, and at the Smithsonian Institution, in conjunction with PhotoDC, Spring 2014.

Gallery Ambience

In downtown Laguna, a Frisbee's throw from the ocean, there's an innocuous steel door with a discreet sign. Open that 90-year-old door, climb a steep, narrow stairway to a large, bright entryway lined with artworks. Walk into two well-lit galleries, the second with a skylight and black ceiling. Continue into a large open area, the combined studio/entertainment/performance area. Accoutrements include a small stage from the original Masonic Lodge, a first-rate sound system, a projection screen, and large glass doors facing a quiet lane.

When Mark Chamberlain is alone, shooting and printing images, BC Space is a sanctuary and respite from the boutique-, gallery-, and restaurant-lined street below. The tall, slender, professorial proprietor, accompanied by his blue heeler, Po, graciously welcomes clients, artists, and friends who often stop by. Engage Mark in conversation and you'll witness his expansive knowledge, confidence, and wit. One favored discussion topic is the philosophy of inventor Buckminster Fuller.

When BC has an art exhibition, poetry reading, folk concert, or play, the space fills up with people of all ages, races, and backgrounds, all delighted to be part of this vibrant scene.

One significant exhibition, "Capital Crime$" (2012-2013), addressed how, "The power of concentrated money has subverted professions, destroyed small investors, wrecked the regulatory state, corrupted legislators en mass, and repeatedly put the economy through the wringer." (Quote by historian Thomas Frank!) Chamberlain asked artists, "Do you have anything to say about this dire economic situation and would you like to add your voice to the debate?" More than 60 responded with paintings, sculpture, collage, assemblage, mixed media, installation, photographs and video. Chamberlain wove these works together to create a powerful indictment on the abuses of money in our culture.

Looking Forward

BC Space is not a foundation and does not solicit donations to support its escalating rent and cost of exhibitions. Located in a commercial area on Forest Avenue, Mark Chamberlain continues to support the gallery through his Photographic Art Services. Within that space, he devotes much of his time to working as a mentor, curator of the work of others, and creator of multimedia events. Here, he also explores his personal artwork, free of the need for commercial conformity. "Years ago, I learned that the camera is just another tool to create art." He has used that powerful tool for decades, exploring its endless possibilities, creating *River Tales, Dream Sequences, Future Fossils,* and other dynamic series. He has taught in several colleges, attributing his vast knowledge of photography and its history to the need to teach it.

Chamberlain calls himself an "arteologist," an artist exploring life unfettered by convention. "While actively engaged in the present, shooting pictures or curating, I am often referencing the past and hope my work will allude to the future."

Today, BC remains firmly ensconced in the building in which it was launched. It has kept pace with the dramatic changes from film to digital image making, while also presenting exhibitions of painting, sculpture, installations, and video, as well as film, music, theatre, and dance events.

For Mark Chamberlain, BC Space—presenting innovative and courageous work that often challenges the status quo—is his passion, his bliss and his mistress.

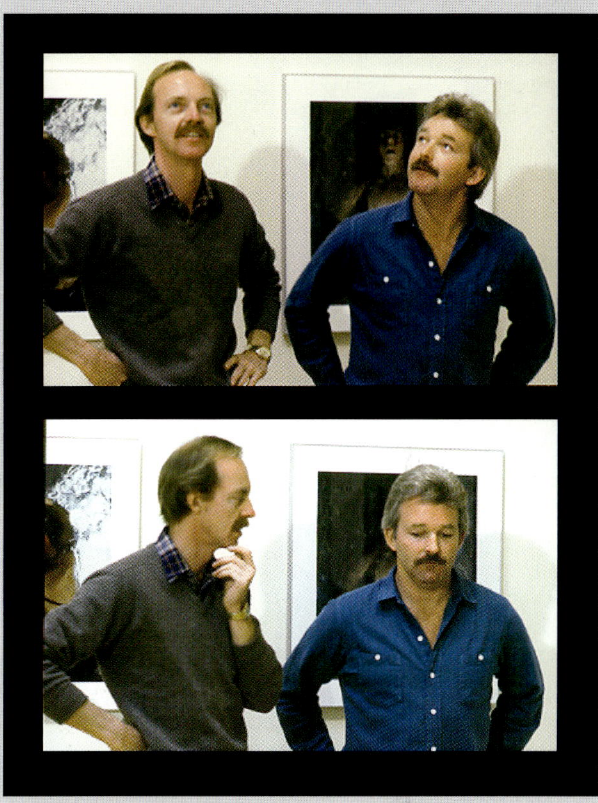

Mark Chamberlain and Jerry Burchfield, 1976
Photos by Mark Johnstone

(previous page)
Outtakes from the Laguna Canyon Project.
Top left: Mark & Sophie on Phase VII, Surface Collection of Found Objects, 1988.
Top right: Jerry on Final Shot of Phase I, 1980.
Bottom left to right: Aftermath of Toll Road Battle, 1996; Mark in Canyon on Phase I, 1980; Jerry & Mark on Completion of Phase XIV, 2000; Mark & Jerry in Preparation for Phase VIII, 1989.

Liz Goldner is an art reviewer operating out of Orange County, CA. She is a regular contributor to Art Scene, Art Ltd, Artillery magazine and the Huffington Post among others. She is a member of the International Association of Art Critics.

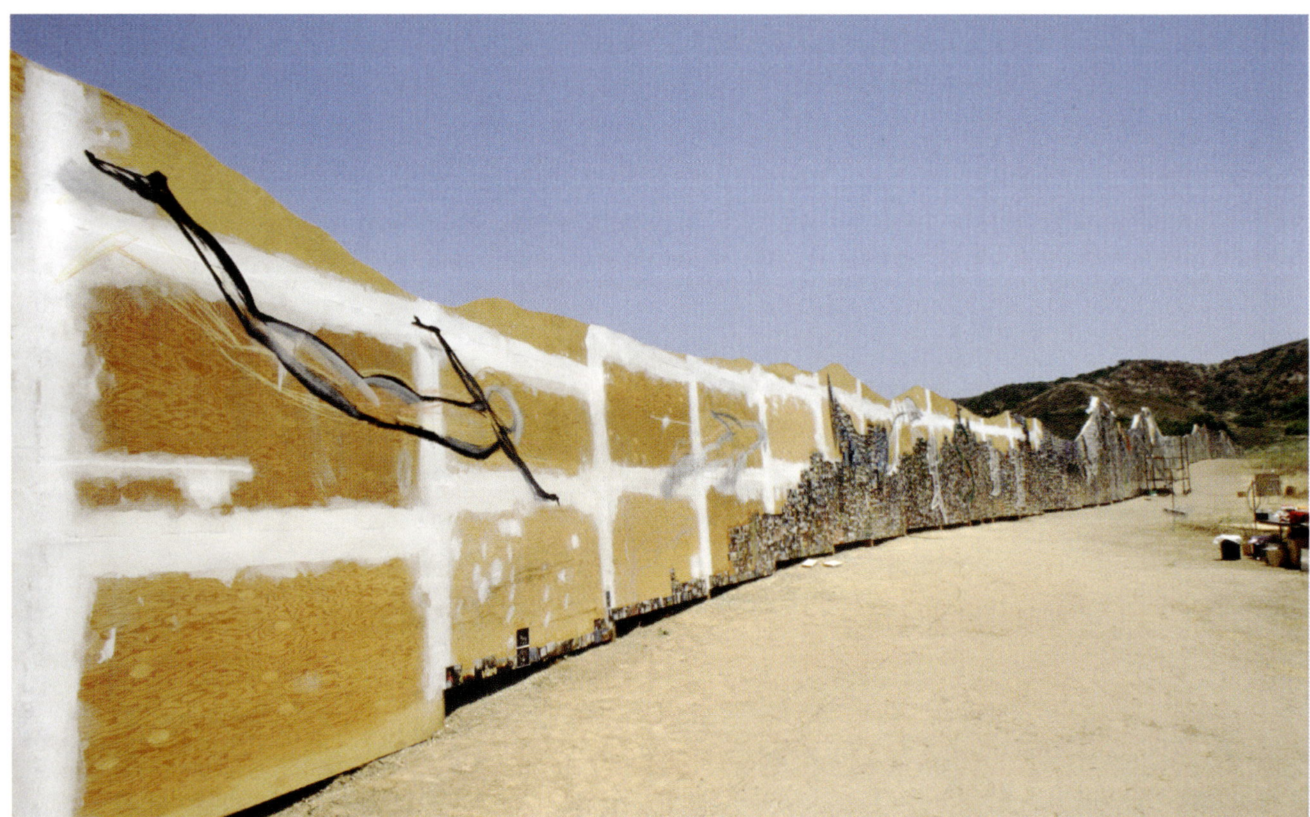

"One of the most challenging aspects of The Tell was how to deal with the inevitable fading of the photographs when exposed to the desert climate of Laguna Canyon. We originally struggled with how to prevent or retard the fading, but all the potential solutions were toxic and antithetic to the environmental goals of the project. After two years of testing, however, we were delighted to discover that the prints we were most likely to collect would predictably fade to a sepia cast that mimicked the changes the canyon itself went through as it evolved from the vibrant colors of spring into the pale brown hues of fall. What we had initially considered a handicap became a great advantage.

"This revelation allowed us to incorporate an evolutionary quality into the mural, by making specific components out of longer-lived photographs that would endure over time. Once the elements played their role, the mural slowly changed to reveal a carefully constructed tale of our collective relationships to the land, as the individual stories of contributors' lives gradually receded into the background. Telling their life stories was why people participated, and what compelled them to come to see the results, but it was the collective story of Mankind that ultimately prevailed."

Mark Chamberlain

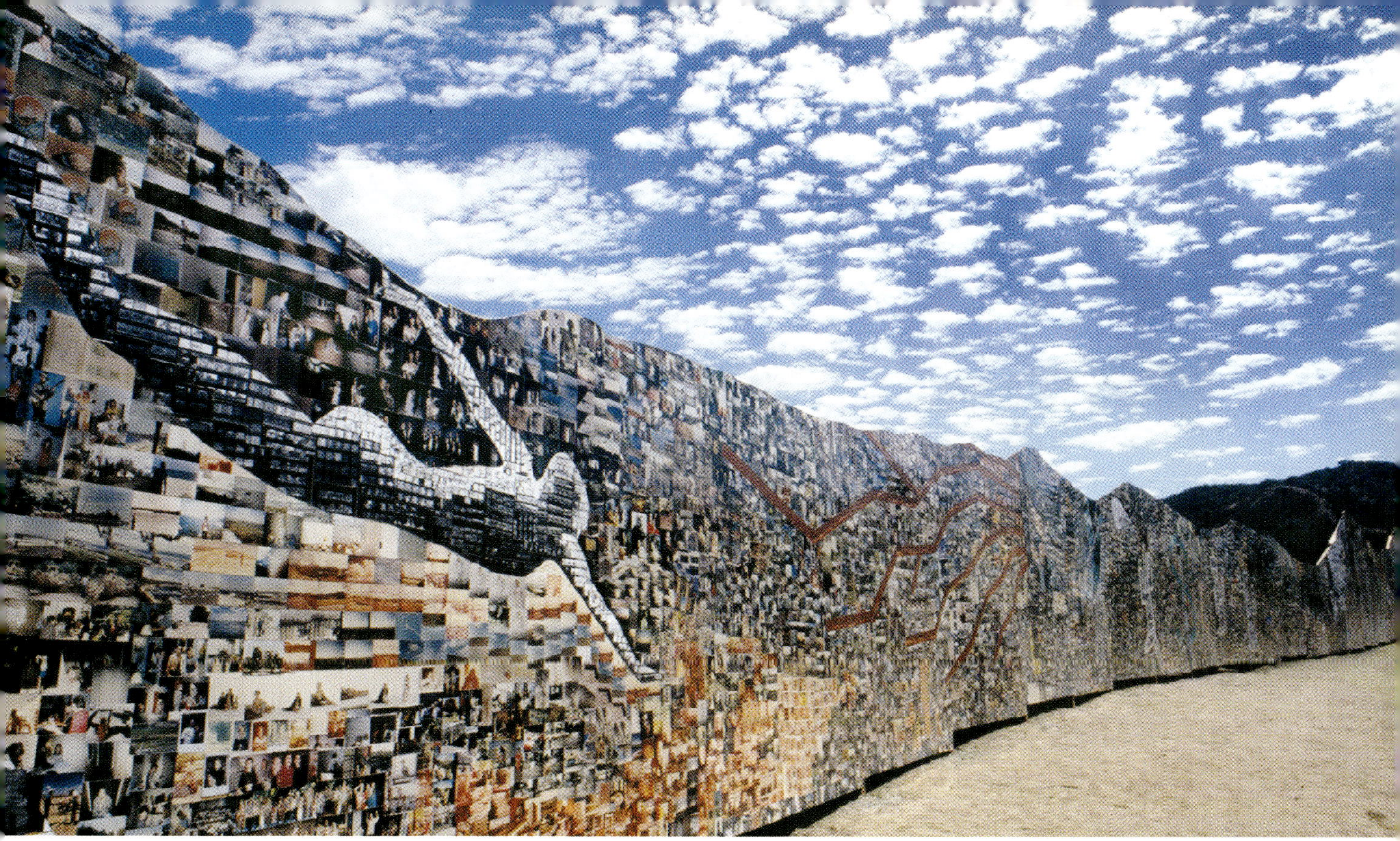

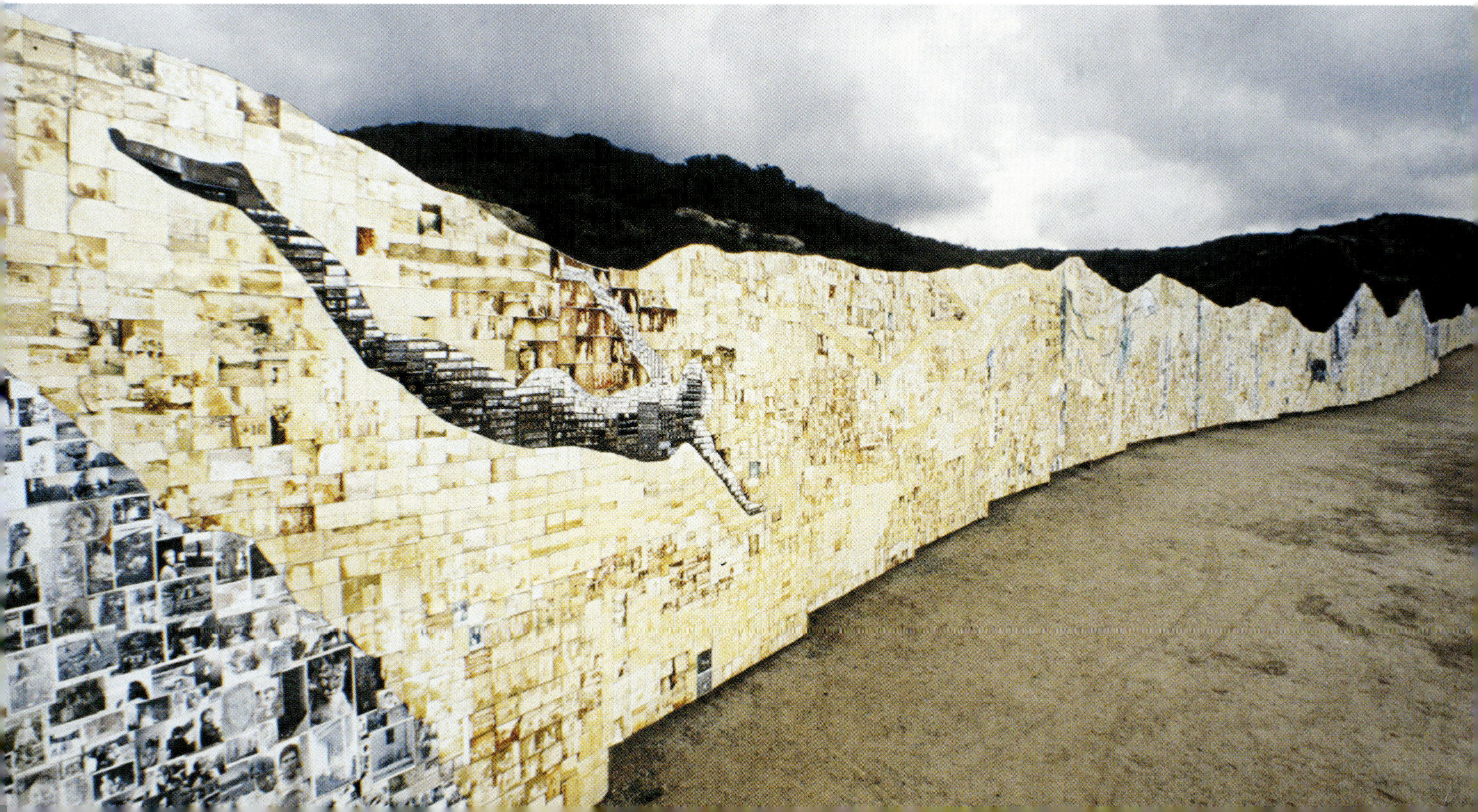

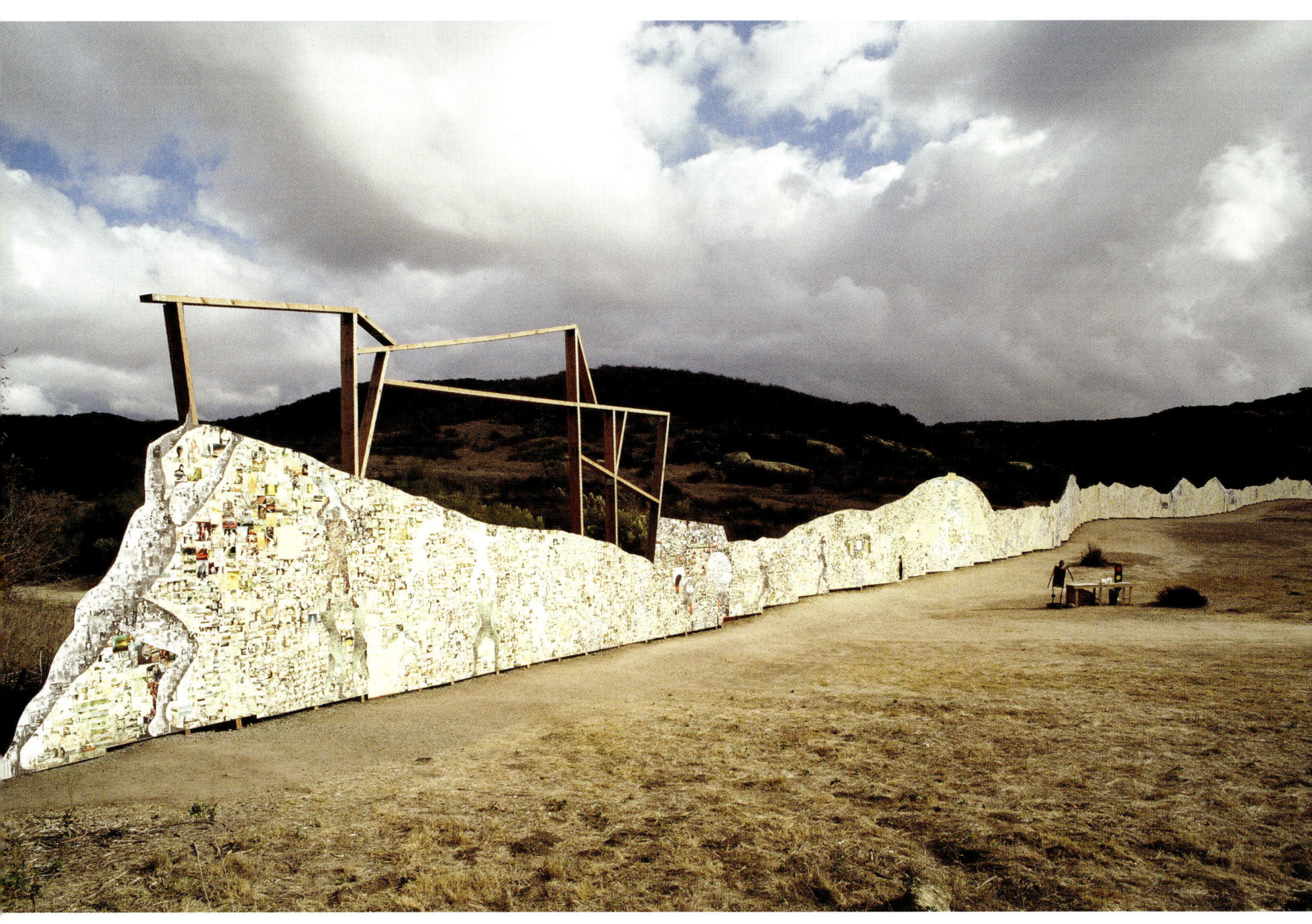

(previous page)
Mark Chamberlain and Jerry Burchfield
Community Collaboration
Diving Figure" from Tell Mural, early stage
and later stage, spring, 1989
Courtesy of BC Space

Tell Mural, later stages, January, 1990
Courtesy of BC Space

right: left side: (top) Signs at the Walk; (middle) Viewers at Walk;
(bottom) May Day Beginning Assembling images, May1, 1989
Courtesy of BC Space

right: right side: (top) Coyote Door, mid stage; (middle) Dedication
Day, Aug 19, 1989, with Mayors and Vice Mayors of Irvine &
Laguna; (bottom) Working on Green Man, May 1, 1989
Courtesy of BC Space

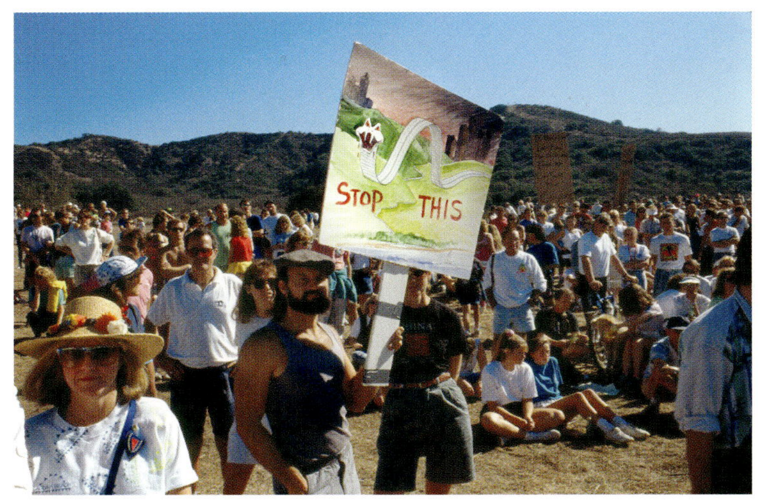
STOP THIS

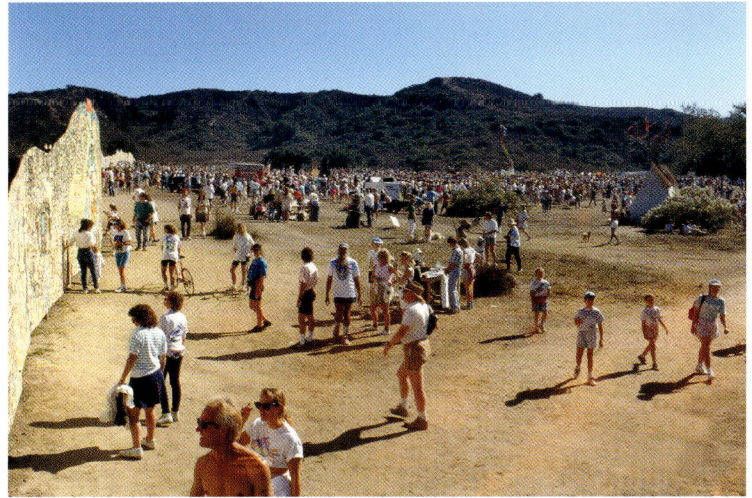

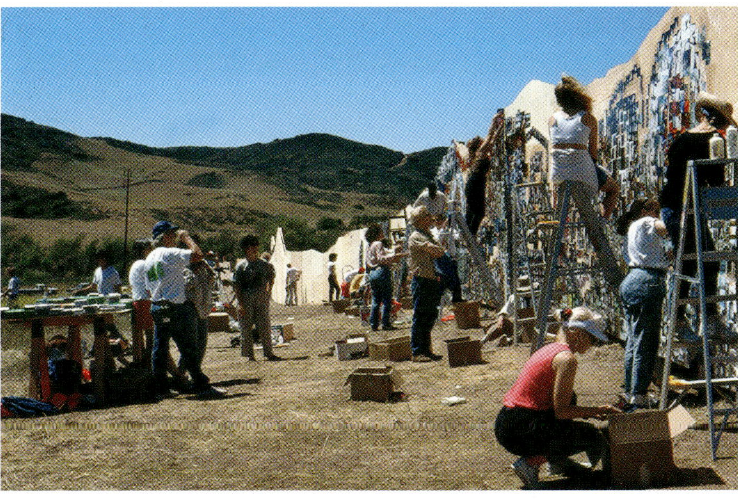

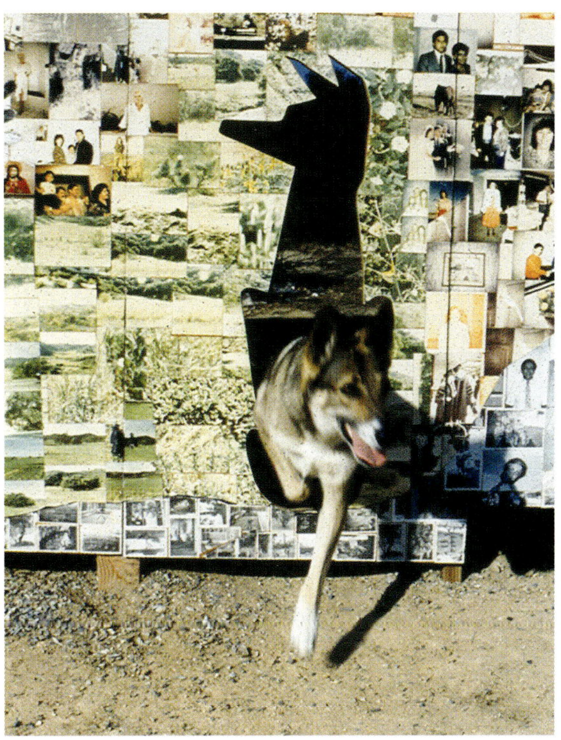

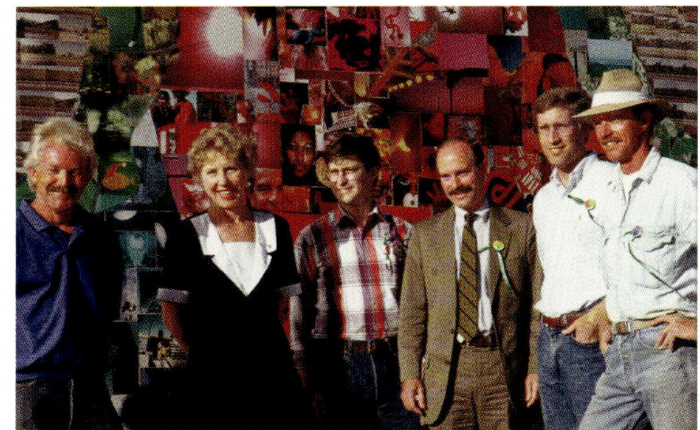

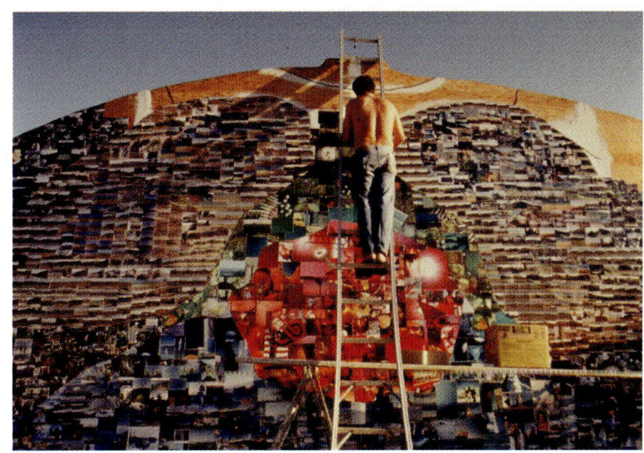

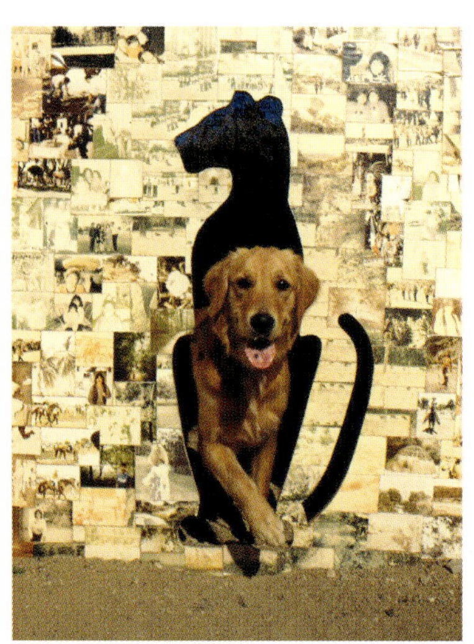
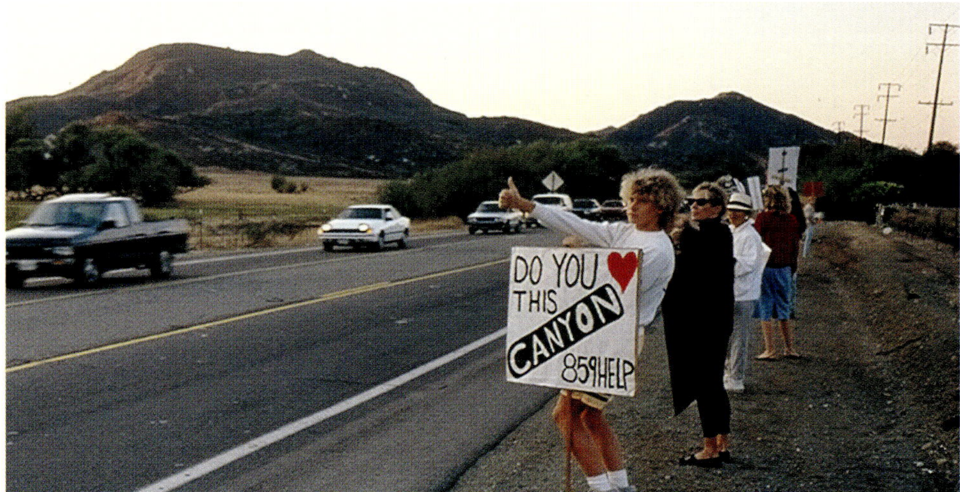

DO YOU ♥ THIS CANYON
859 HELP

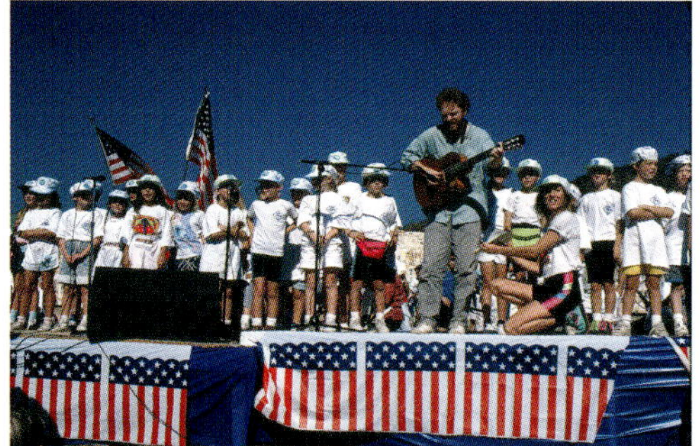
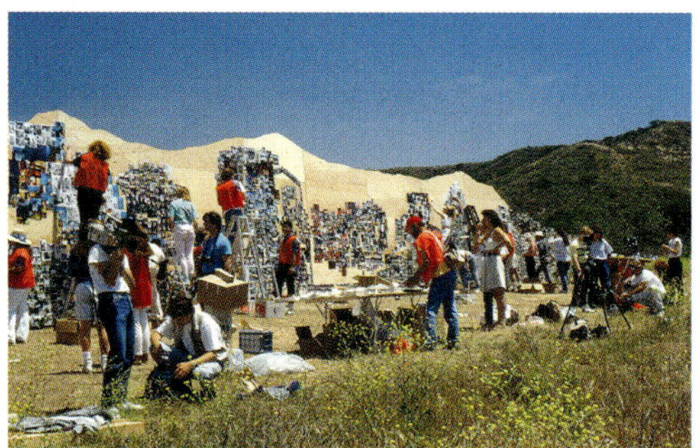
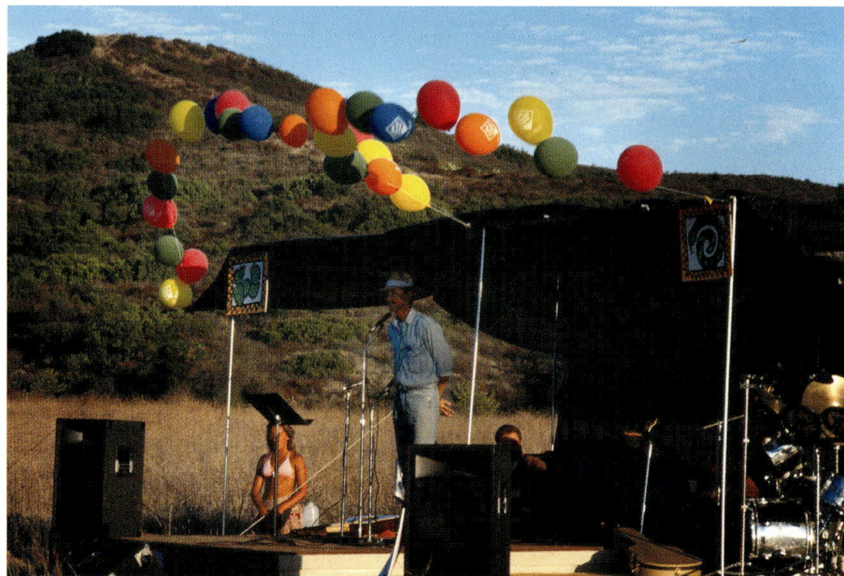
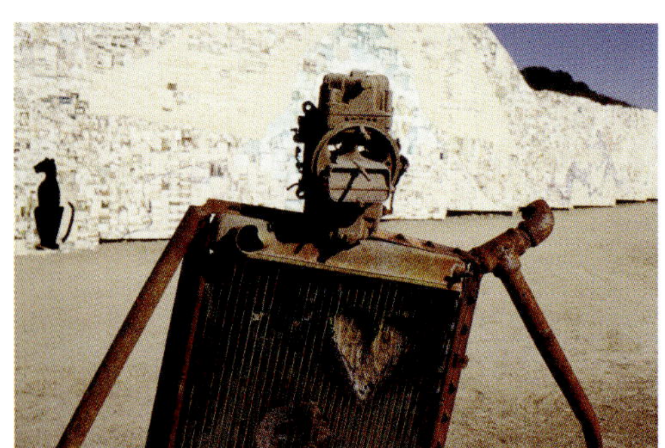
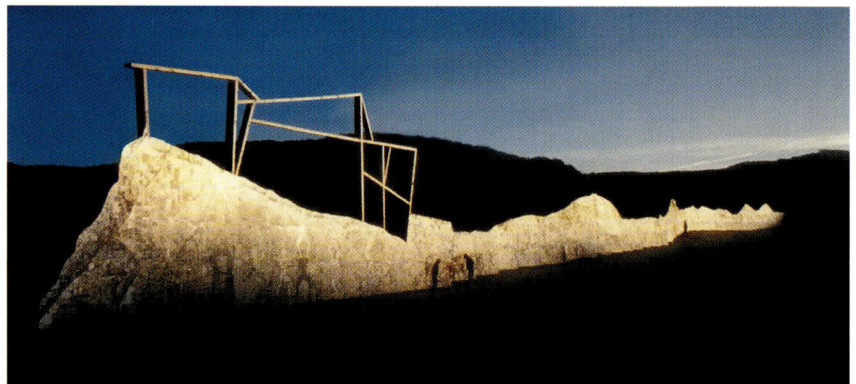

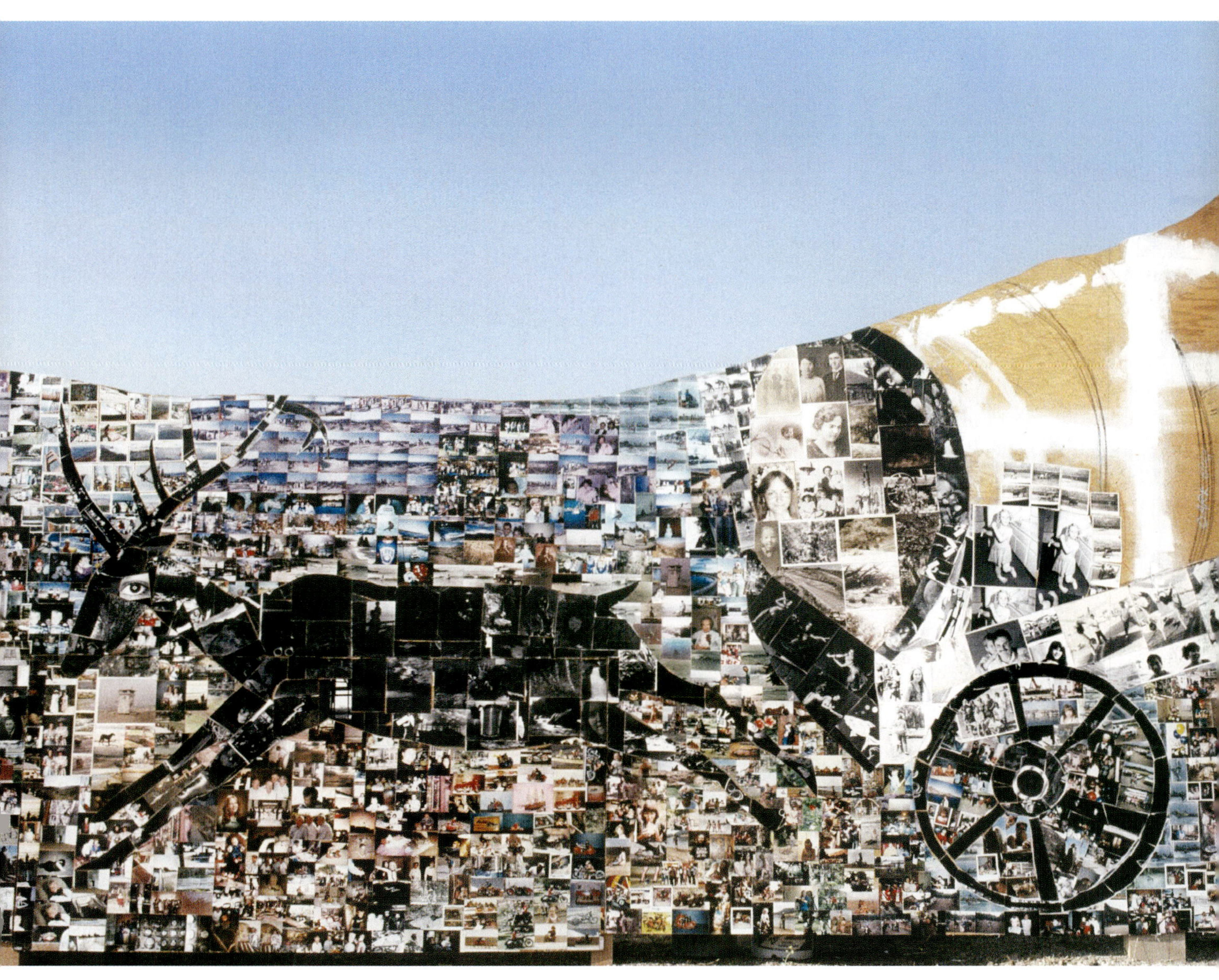

left: left side: ((top left) Mountain Lion cutout late stage; (top rt)
Picketers frequently lined the highway near the Tell; (middle
left) Mark Turnbull performs at Tell for Walk; (middle left lower)
May Day Assembling; Private Property stands guard late
stages; (middle right) Dedication Day Ceremony (Aug. 19, 1989);
Tell View Final Sunrise, Jan. 1990

Deer Under Construction, May, 1989
Courtesy of BC Space

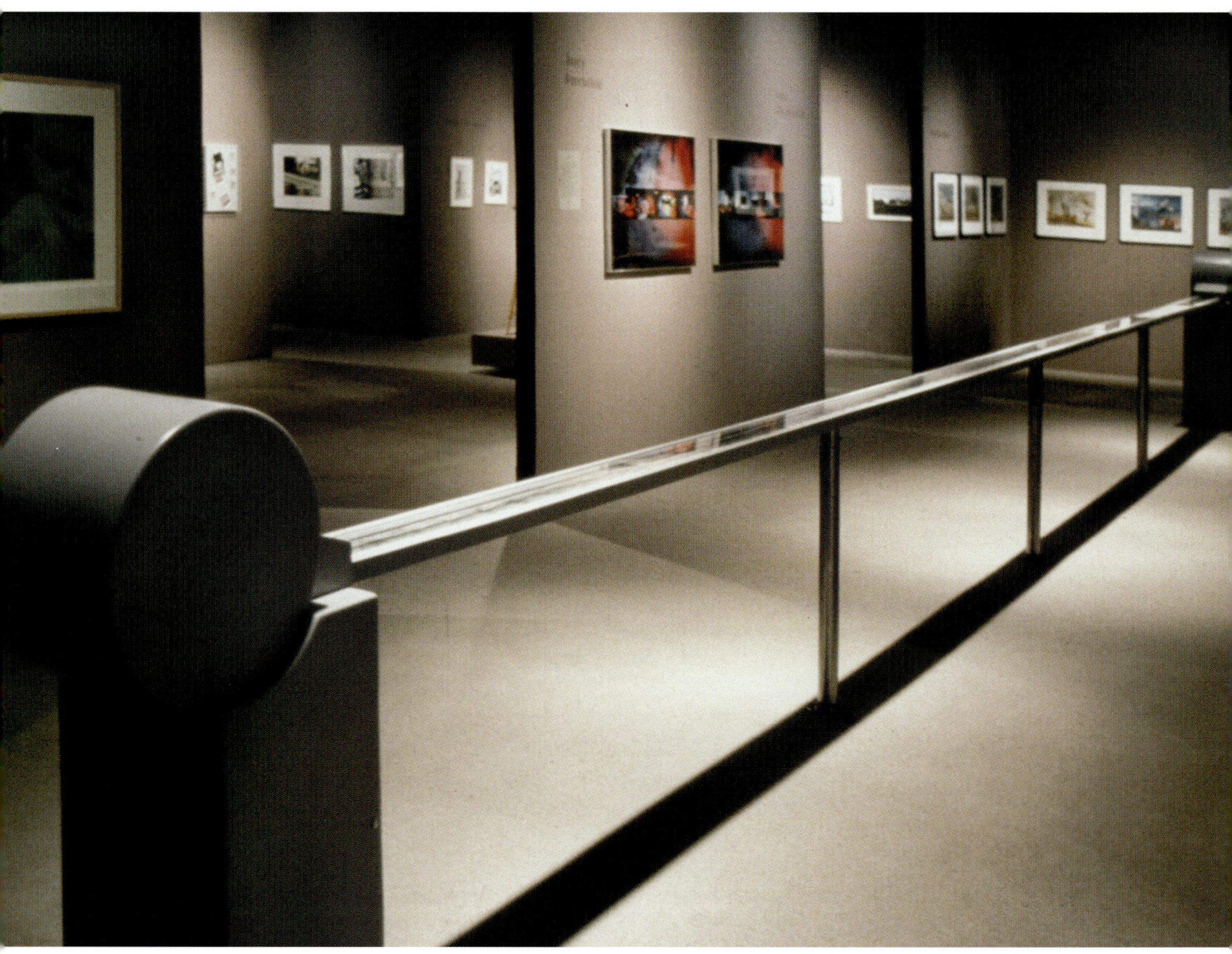

Mark Chamberlain and Jerry Burchfield
Time Machine For Moving Stills, Bowers Museum Installation, Summer, 1984
Courtesy of BC Space

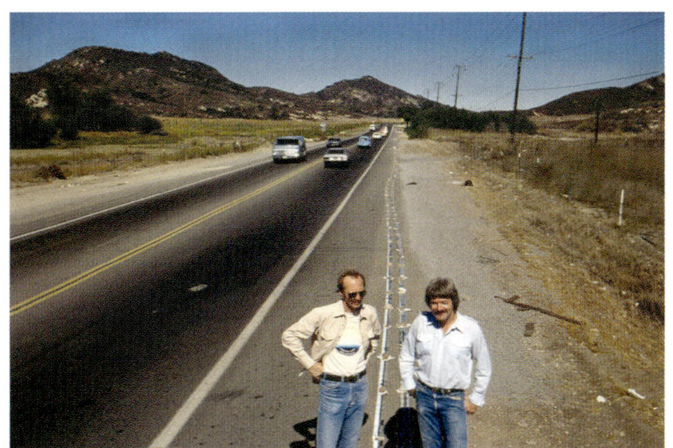

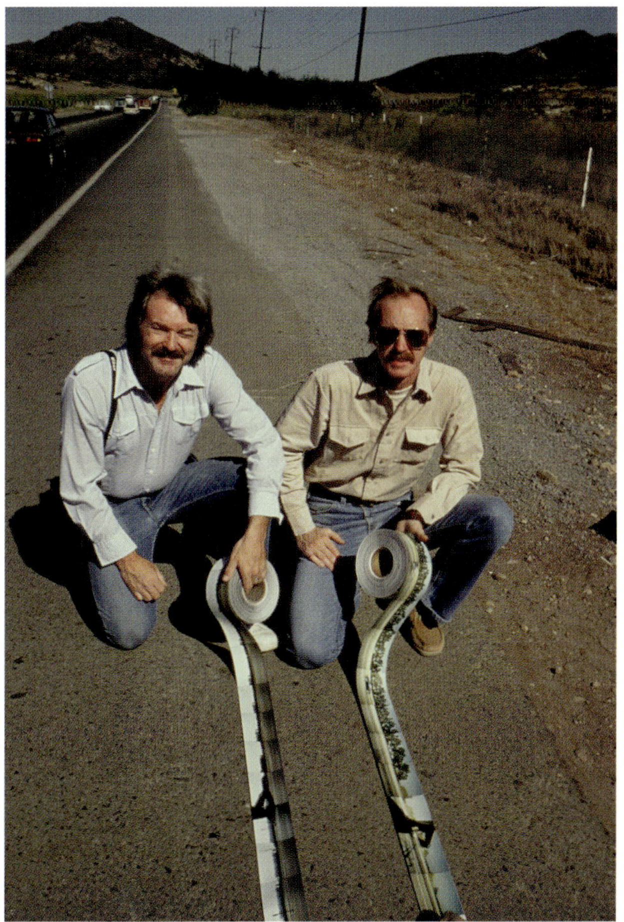

Mark Chamberlain and Jerry Burchfield
in Laguna Canyon with Phase II prints, 1980
Courtesy of BC Space

BC SPACE—A TRIBUTE

It's widely understood these days that in the past half century—maybe a little more—the institution of the art gallery has succeeded in commodifying and commercializing the work of the artist into something that suits the purposes of high commerce and sometimes, regrettably, distorts the higher purposes of art. Big international galleries like Gagosian have become the Goldman Sachs of the cultural world, exerting a powerful and unhealthy influence on aesthetic values and concerns, and radically affecting the food chain that leads from the major galleries in art world capitals down to the thousands of smaller operations across the globe—and even, more toxically, to individual artists struggling to make a name and keep afloat financially.

All the more reason, then, to appreciate the vital work of alternatives to this system like BC Space, where the emphasis is not on commerce (at times, I'm sure, to the chagrin of those who would not object to the opportunity to turn an honest penny!) but on values like quality, intellectual challenge and social responsibility. There have been such spaces—for-profit and non-profit, both—that have opened their doors with much fanfare and unbridled optimism over the years I have been observing the art scene in Southern California; and many that have closed those same doors amid disappointment and frustration.

It requires vision, commitment, patience, dedication—and perhaps a certain bull-headedness!—to persist with such a space amid the commercial imperatives that govern our world today. Some of these are, of course, quite sensible: with the overhead costs involved in running a gallery space, few can afford to sit around and lose money year after year. Artists, too, want to sell their work as much as those who show their work, not just for the money—though even artists need to pay the bills—but for the act of communication that a sale implies: someone cared enough about the work to pay for it and place it in their home. Then, too, an artist needs to get stuff out of the studio (and her head) to clear space for something new.

Kudos, then, to BC Space, which has understood its task to be to support the vision of individual artists, particularly but not exclusively those working in the medium of photography; to promote the work they do; and to serve its community in significant and impactful ways. The intention with which Mark Chamberlain and Jerry Burchfield started out, now these many years ago, was even more ambitious: to change the world, one artwork at a time. They pursued this purpose not only with exhibitions but with ambitious public art projects and interventions involving artists, certainly, but also an entire community in creative endeavors. No better way for the lay person to understand the process and purpose of art than to be involved in its creation.

Equally important—and rare—is the consistency and longevity of BC Space's work. Despite all odds, it has outlasted a great number of comparable ventures and continues to thrive at its location on Forest Avenue in Laguna Beach. In territory many others would spurn amidst a plethora of commercial tourist galleries, BC Space persists in waving the flag of the new and the bold, and in sharing its vision of an art that unabashedly embraces the notion of creative freedom combined with social responsibility. Long may that flag wave!

Peter Clothier
February, 2012

Jerry Burchfield
Cypress Trees El Toro, Legacy Project, 2006
Archival pigemtent print
Courtesy of the artists

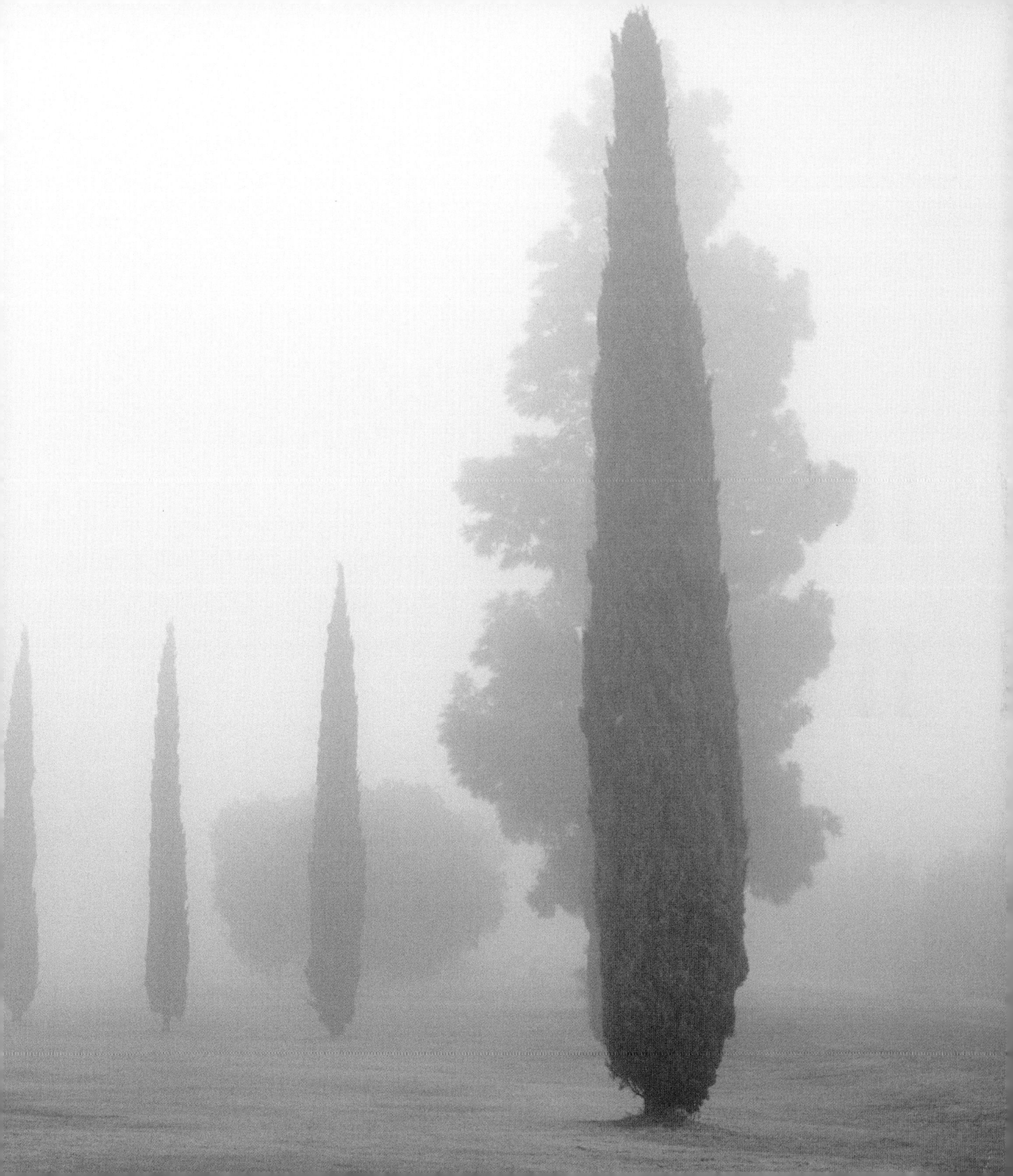

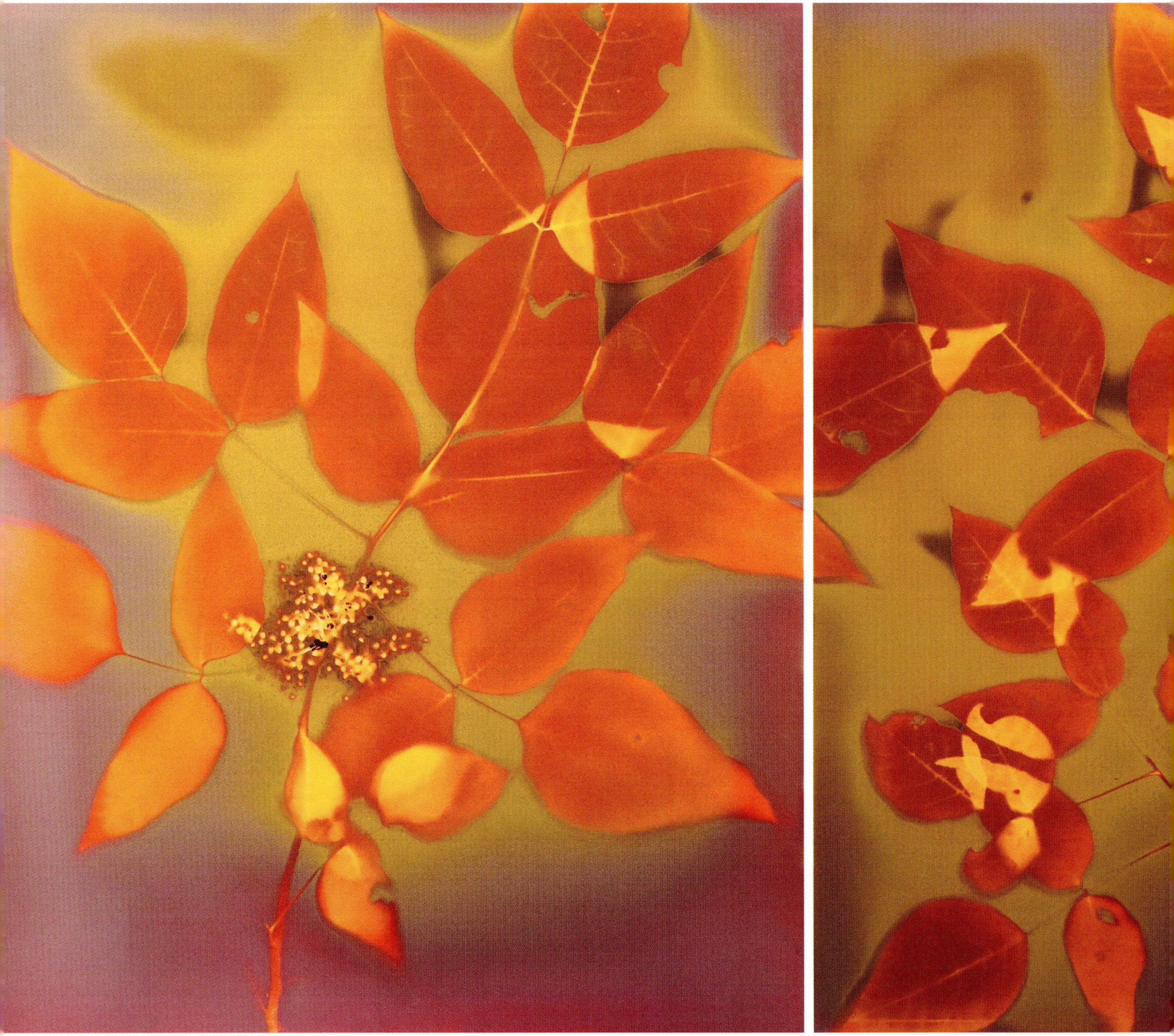

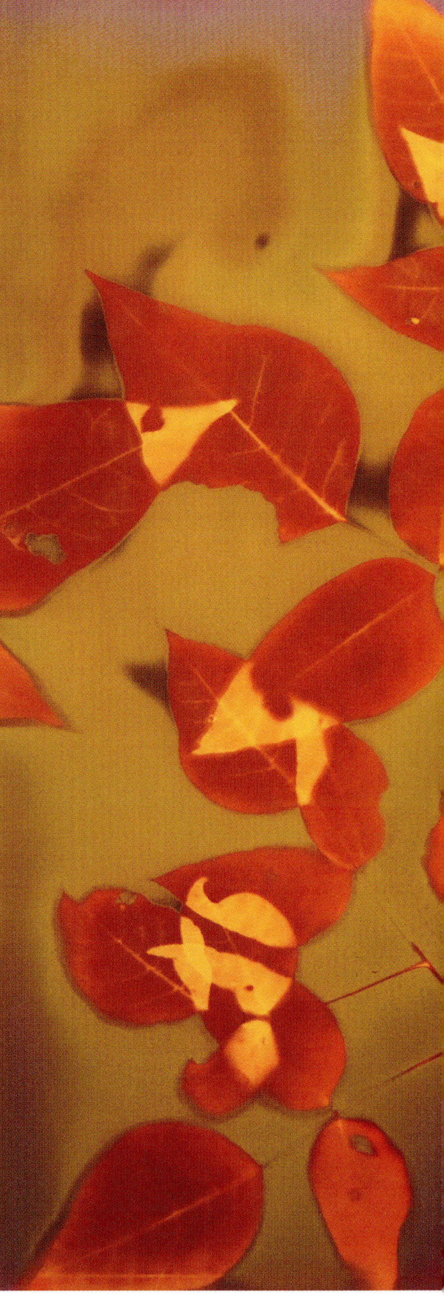

Jerry Burchfield
Toxicodendron radicons (Poison Ivy), 2008
Lumin print, black and white gelitin silver
Courtesy of the artists

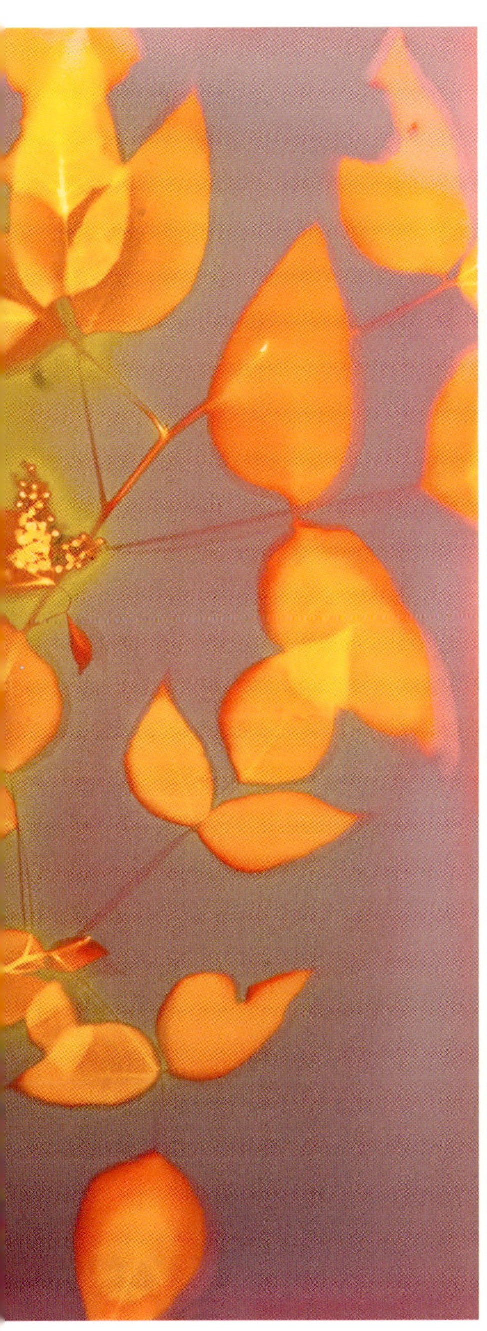

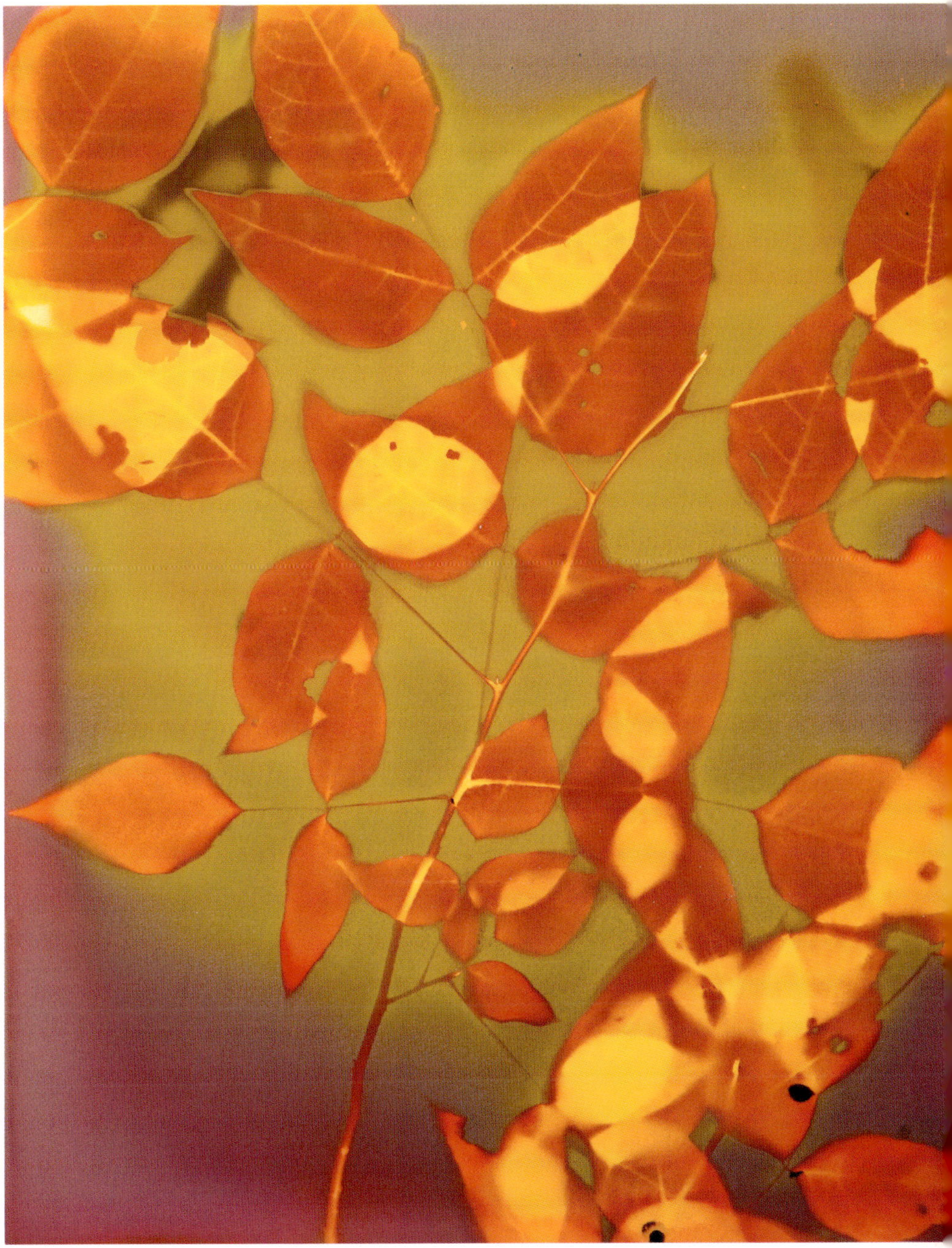

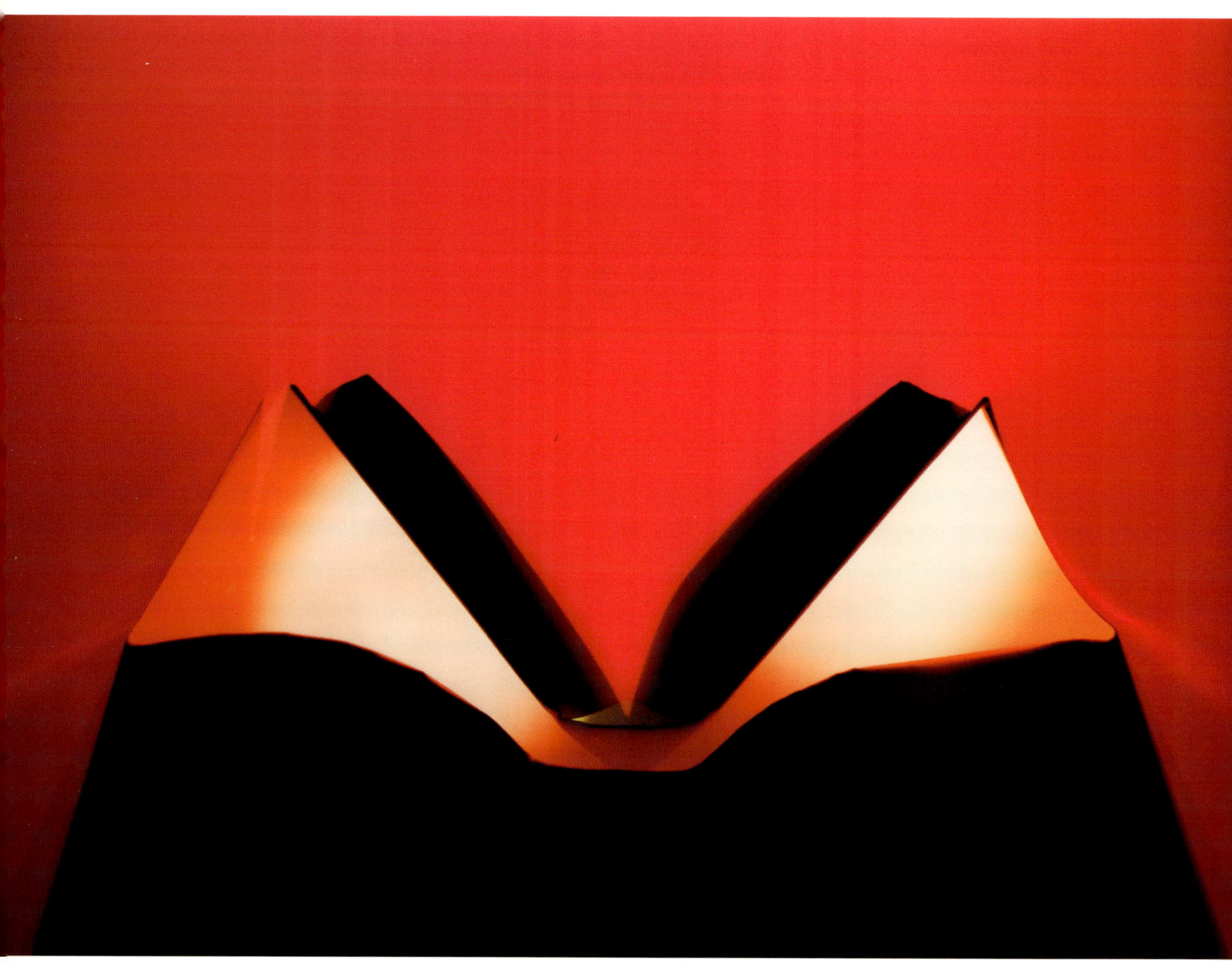

Jerry Burchfield
Voices of the Pages Series, 1993
Cibachrome photogram

Voices of the Pages Series, 1993
Cibachrome photogram
Courtesy of the artist

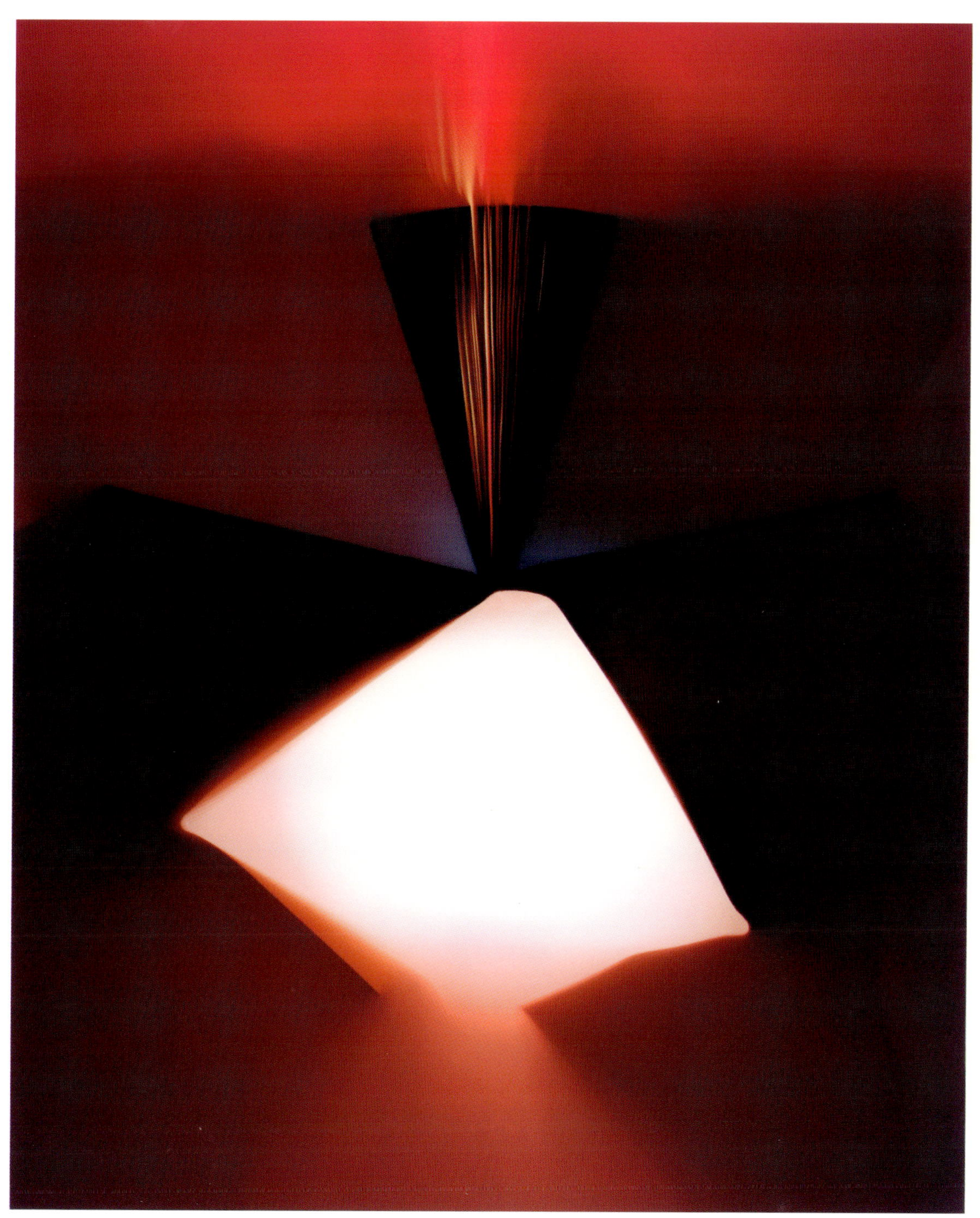

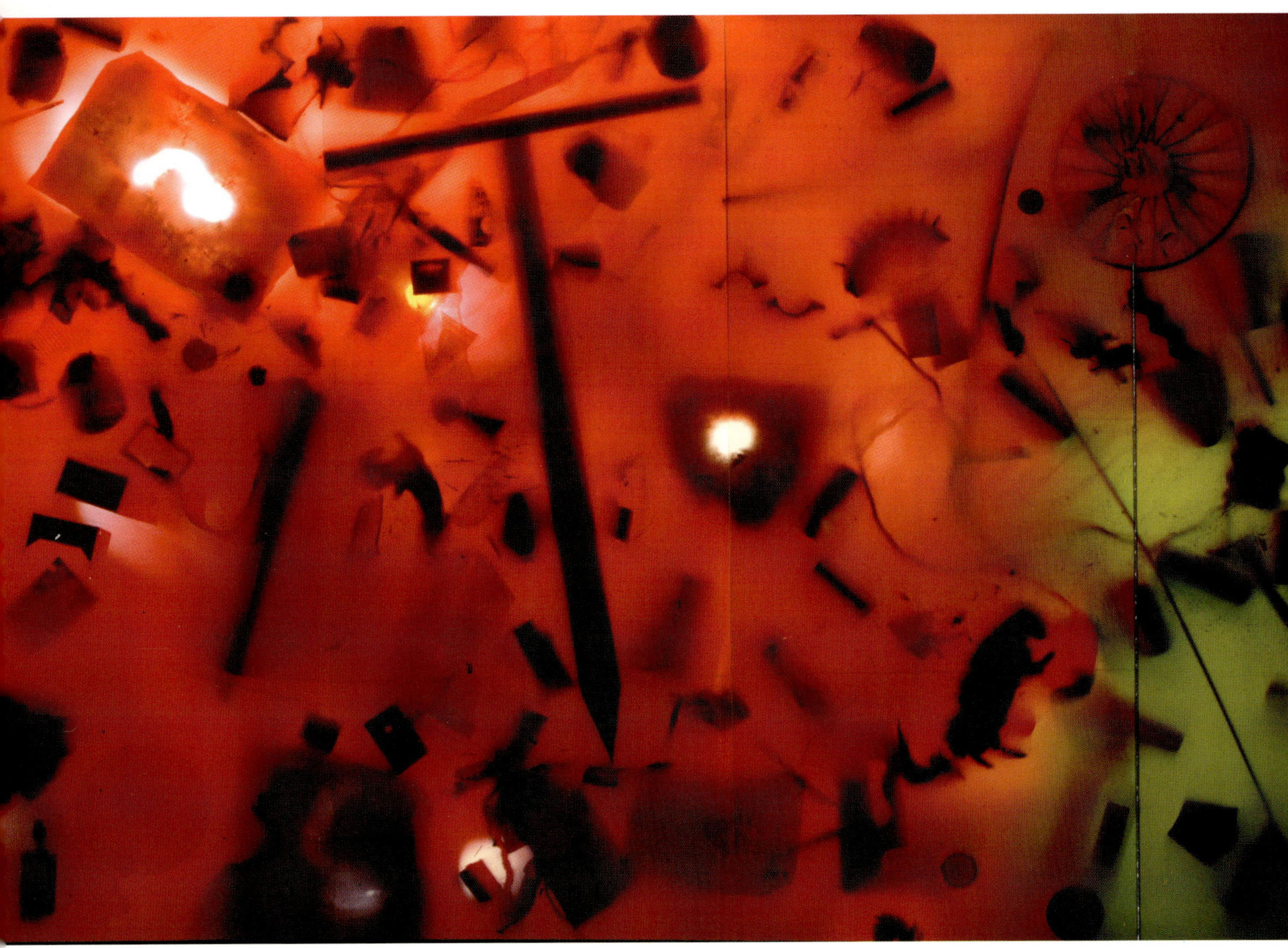

Jerry Burchfield and Mark Chamberlain
Dorothy's Dream, Tellgram from Phase VII, 1988
Cibachrome photogram
5' x 15' feet
Courtesy of BC Space

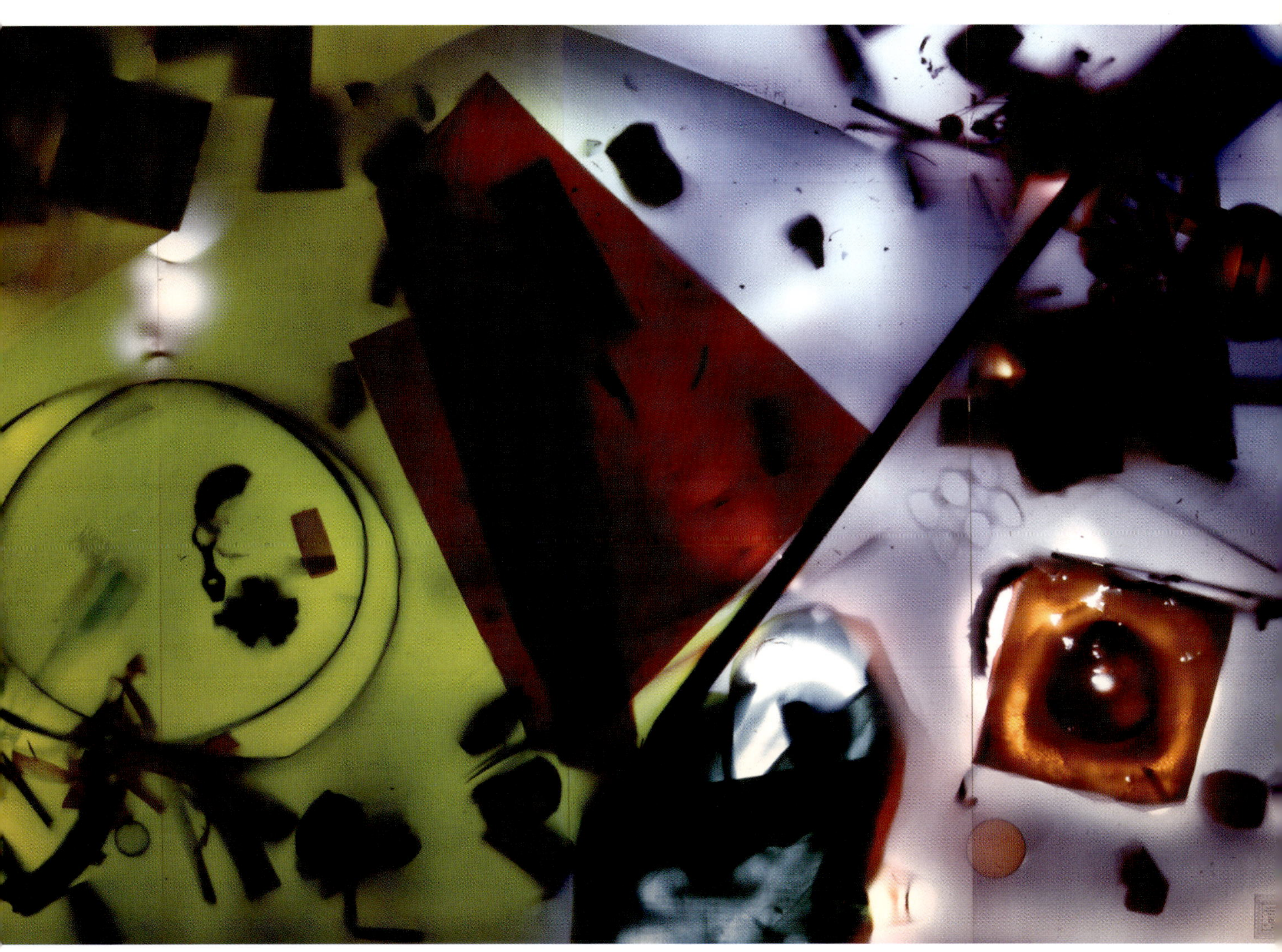

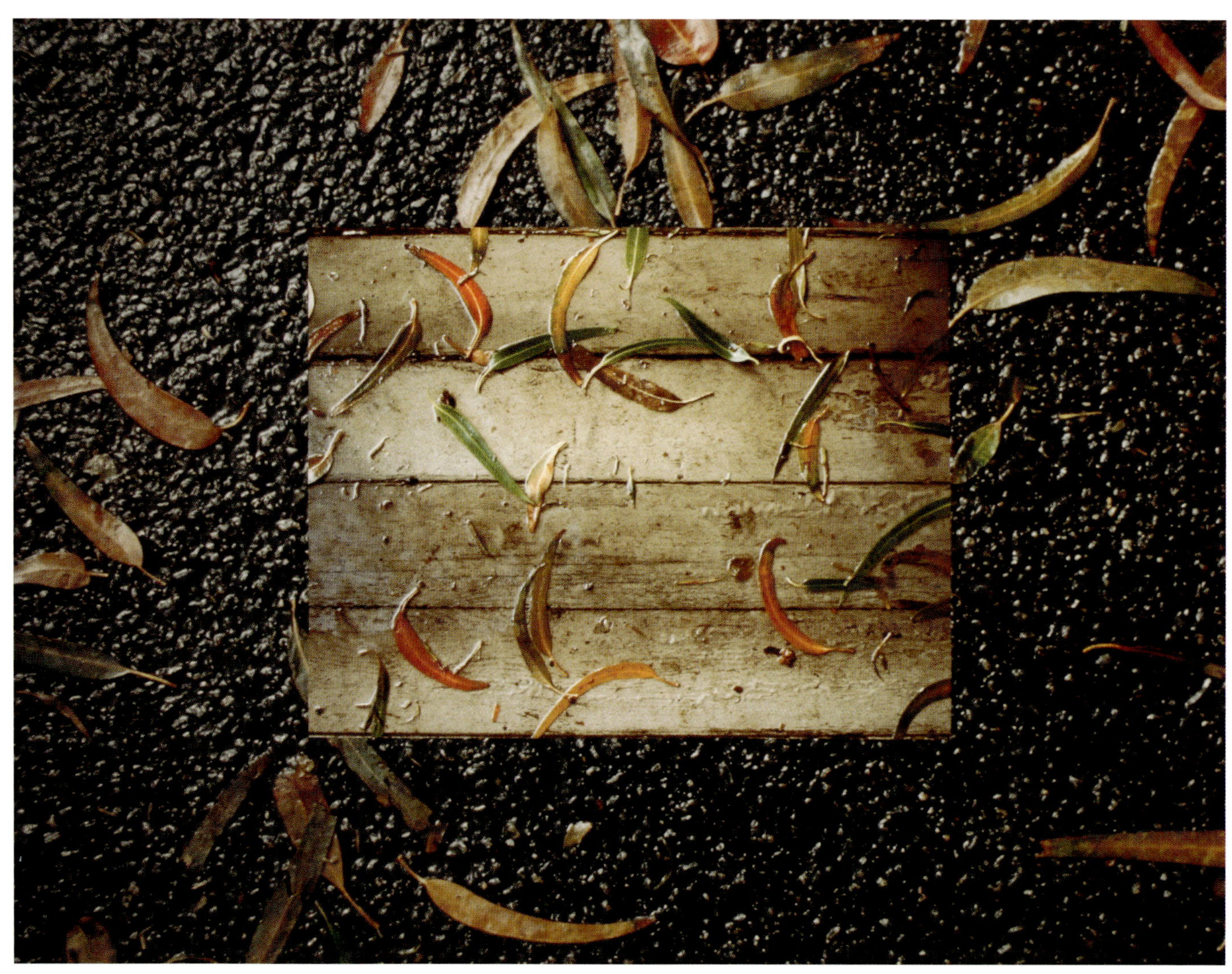

Jerry Burchfield
Untitled #1437 Leaf Series, 1975
Cibachrome prints

Untitled #1436 Leaf Series, 1975
Cibachrome prints
Courtesy of the artists

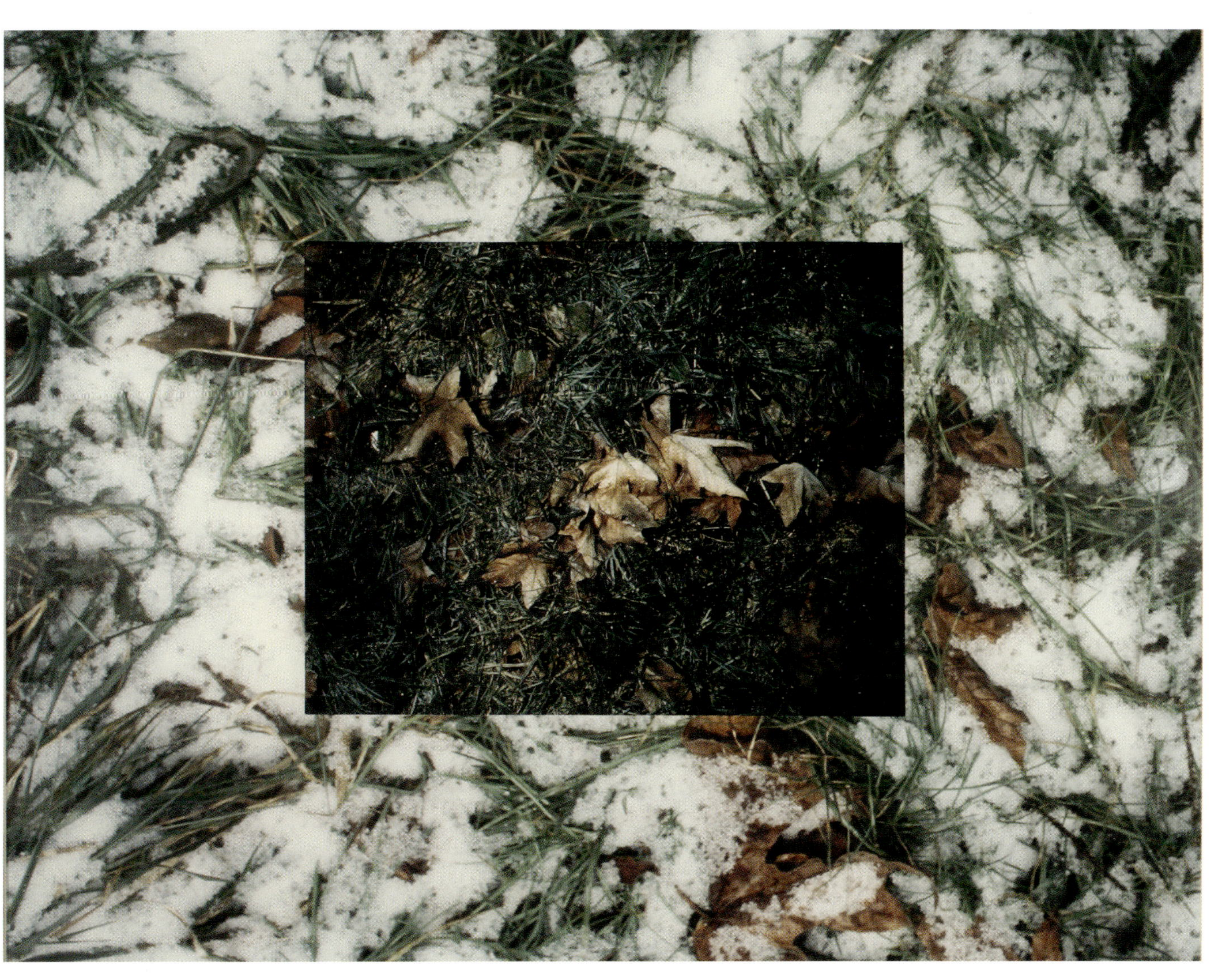

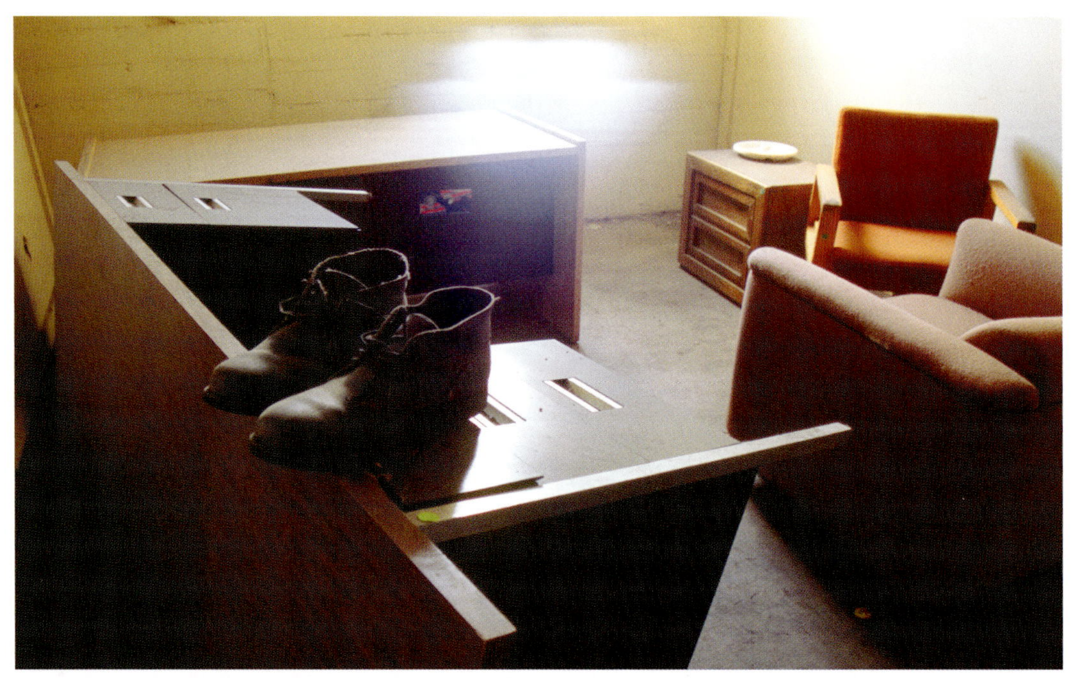

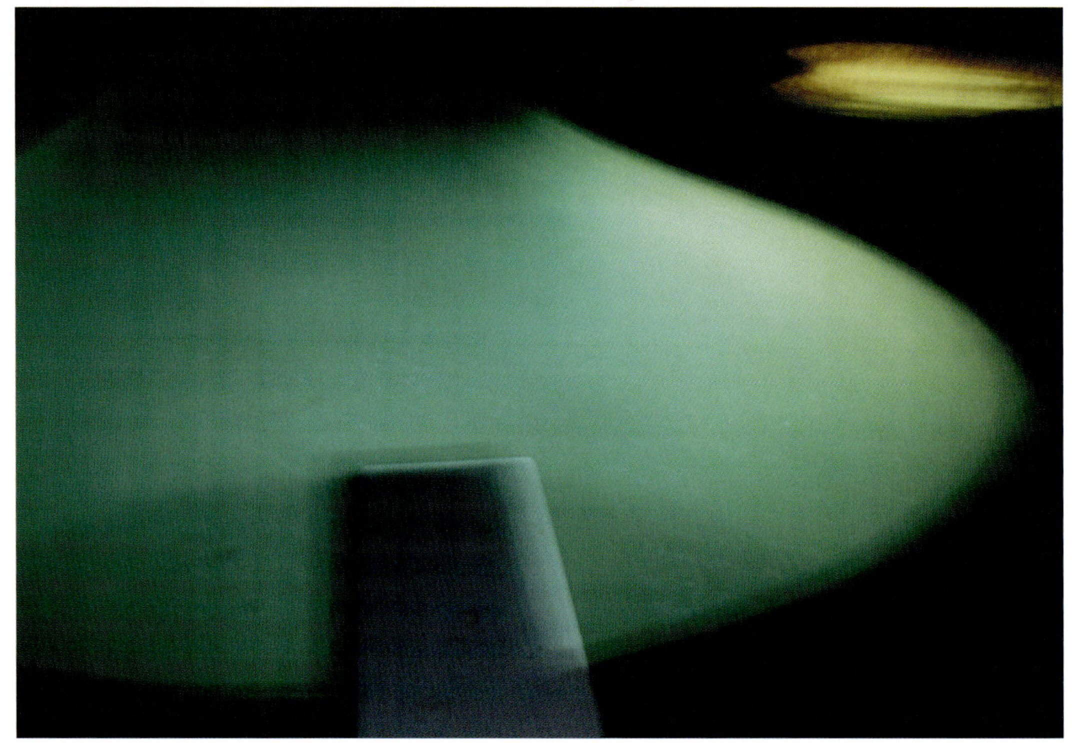

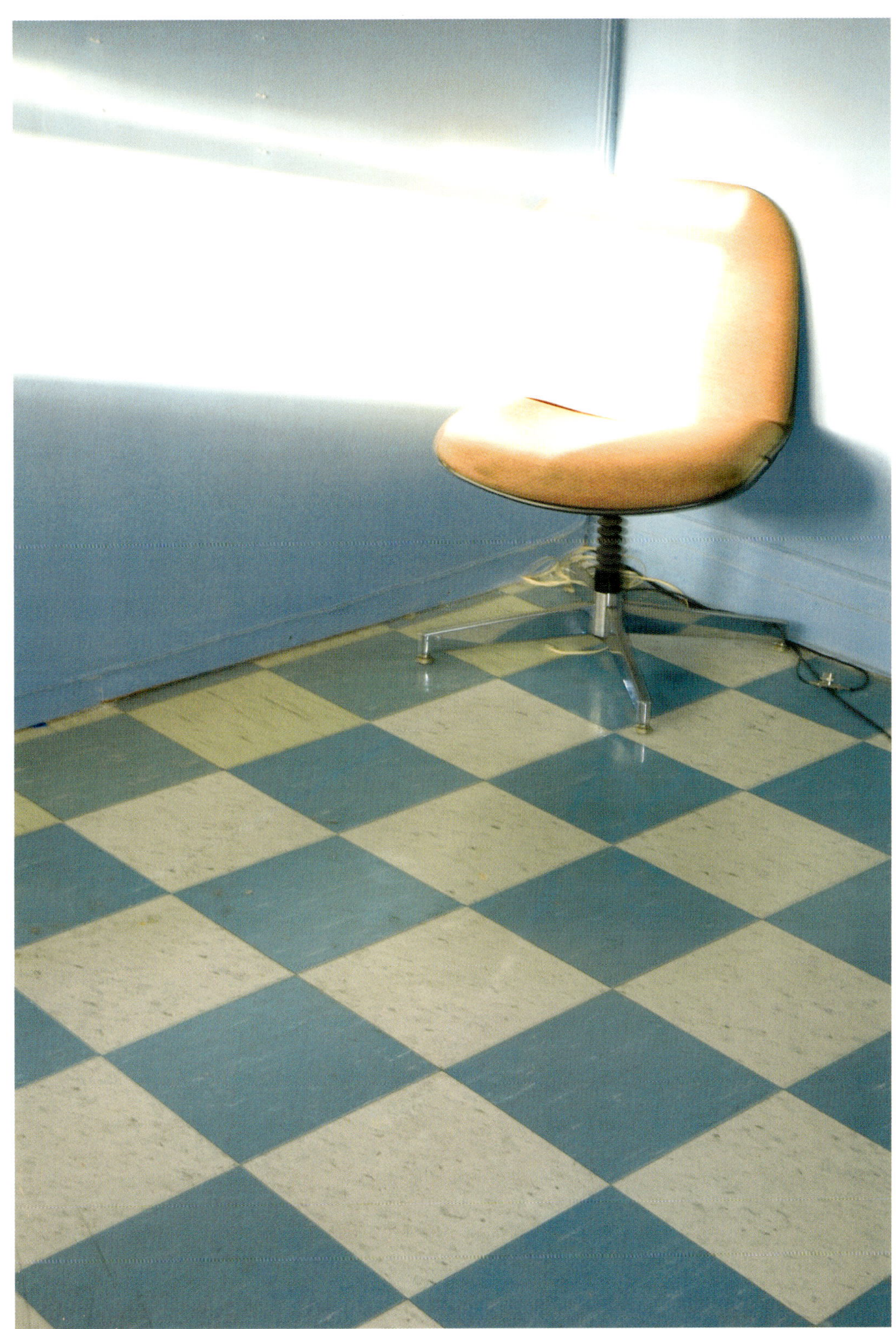

Jerry Burchfield
Interior With Shoes, Bldg #48, 2005
Pigmented archival print

Untitled # 1639
from the Night Walking Series, 1975
Cibachrome prints

Illuminated Chair, Billeting Bldg #58, 2005
Pigmented archival print
Courtesy of the artists

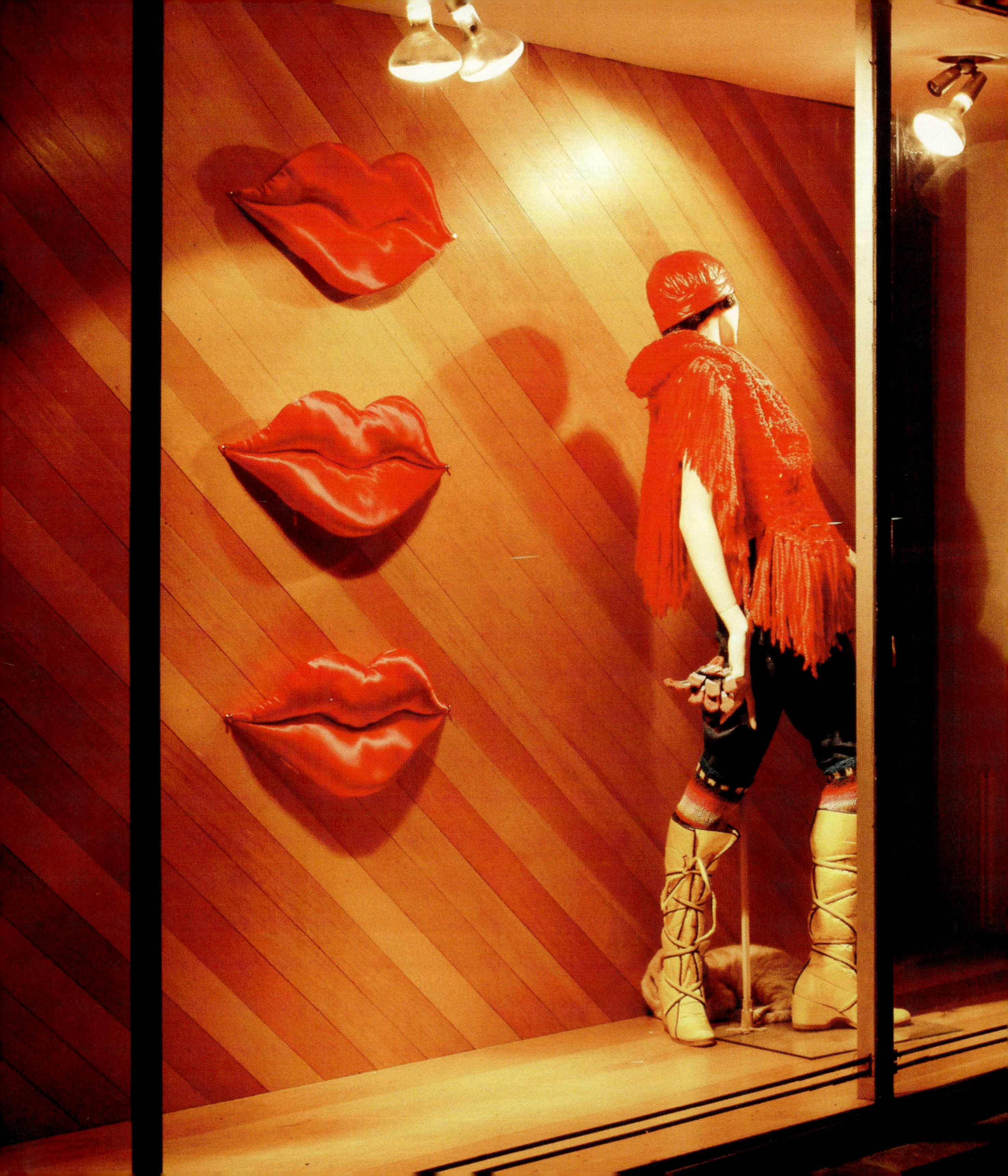

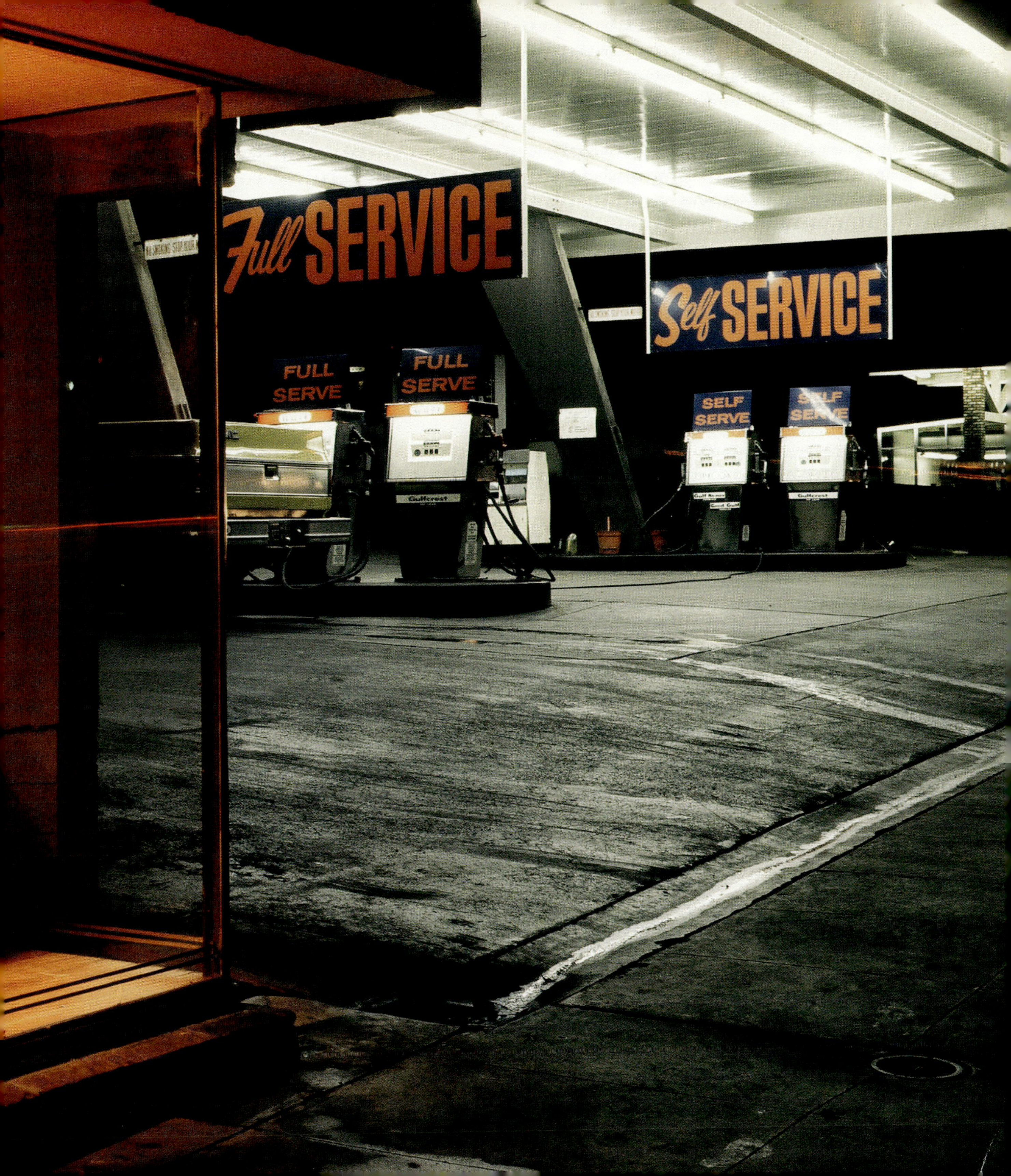
Full SERVICE
Self SERVICE
FULL SERVE
FULL SERVE
SELF SERVE
SELF SERVE
Gulfcrest
Gulfcrest

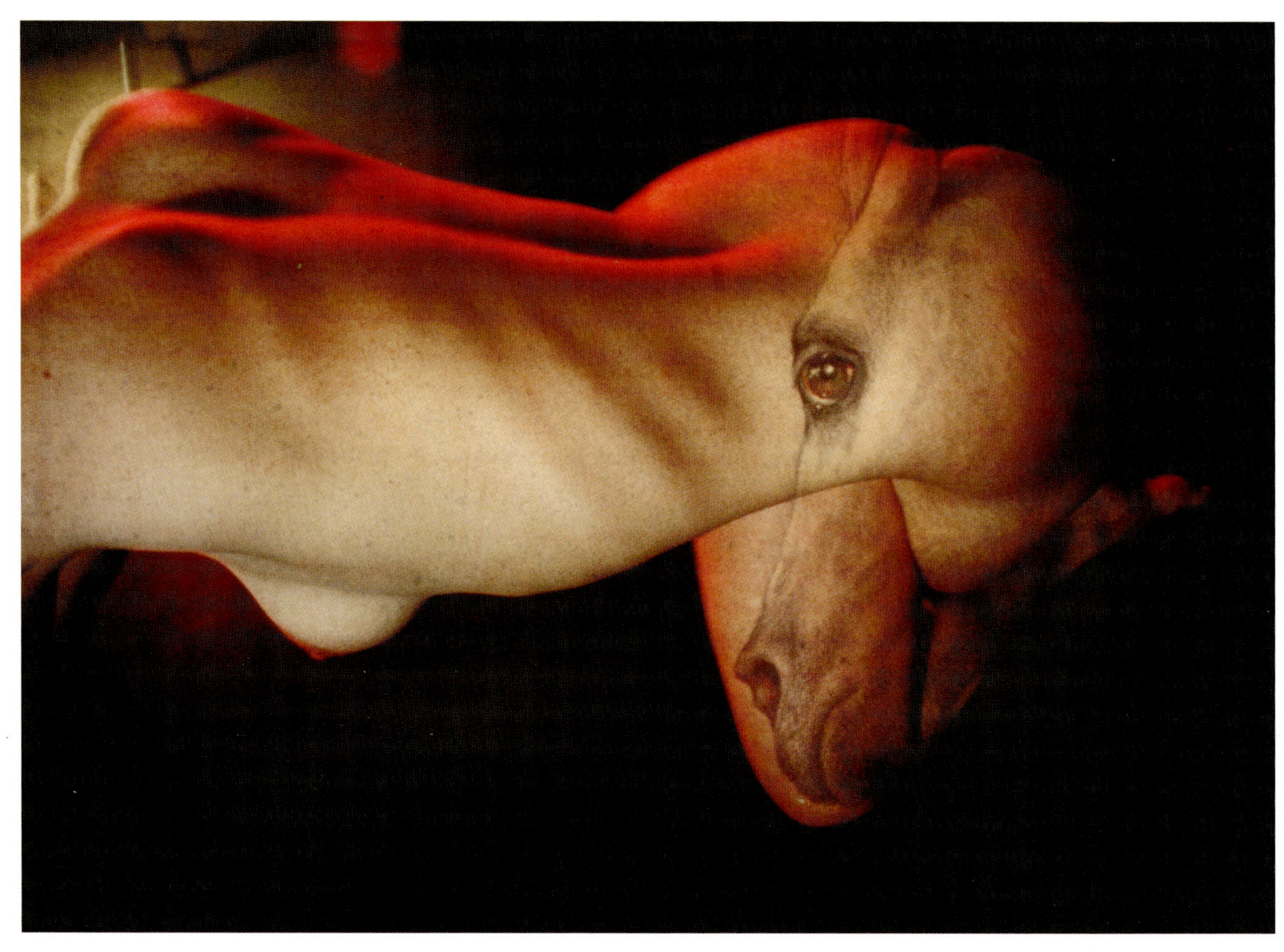

(previous page)
Mark Chamberlain
Lip Service from Future Fossils series, 1975
Chibachrome print

Mark Chamberlain
Bare Back Rider from Dream Sequences series, 1980
Chibachrome print

Untitled Dreams from Dreams Sequences series, 1982
Chibachrome print
Courtesy of the artist

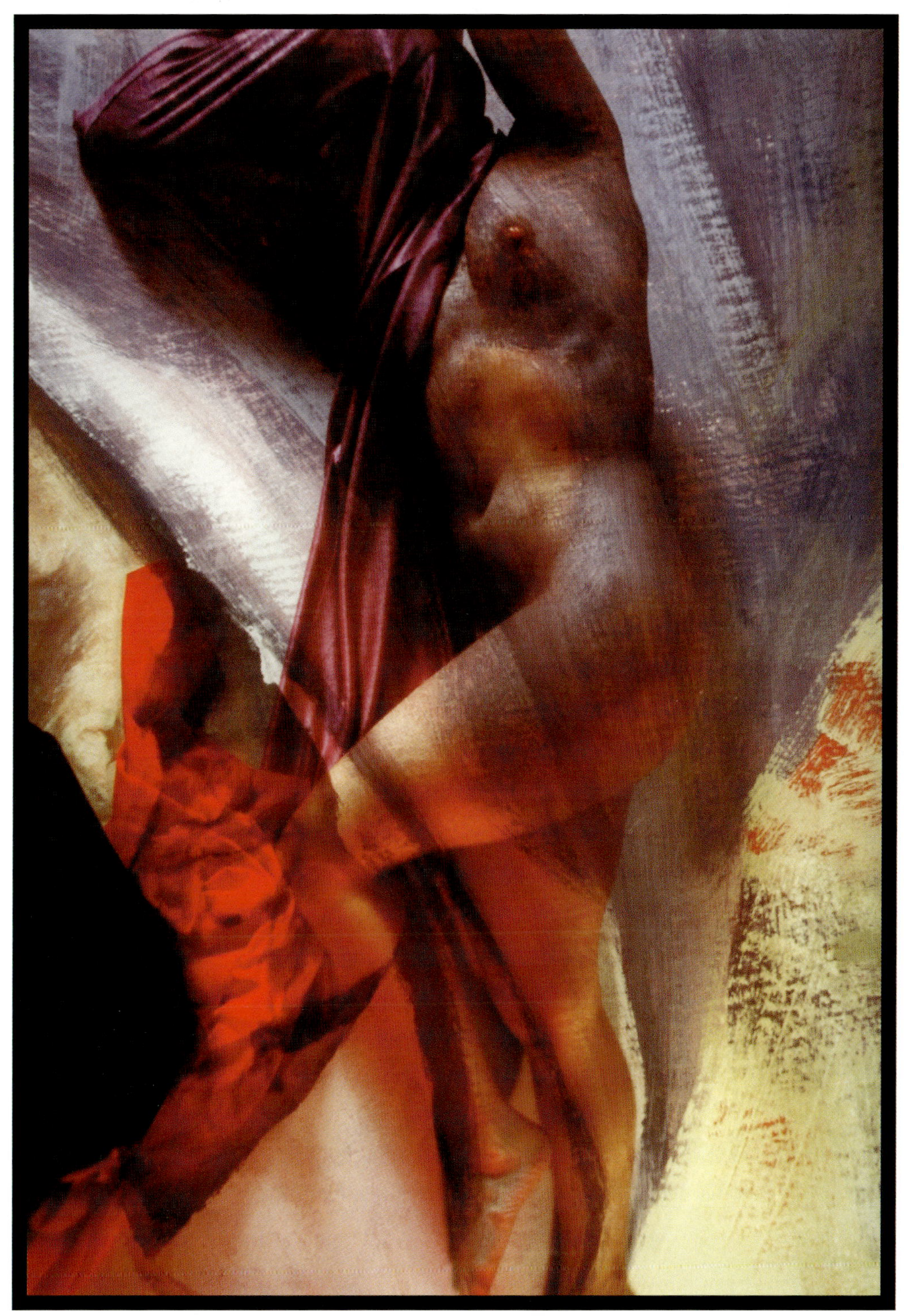

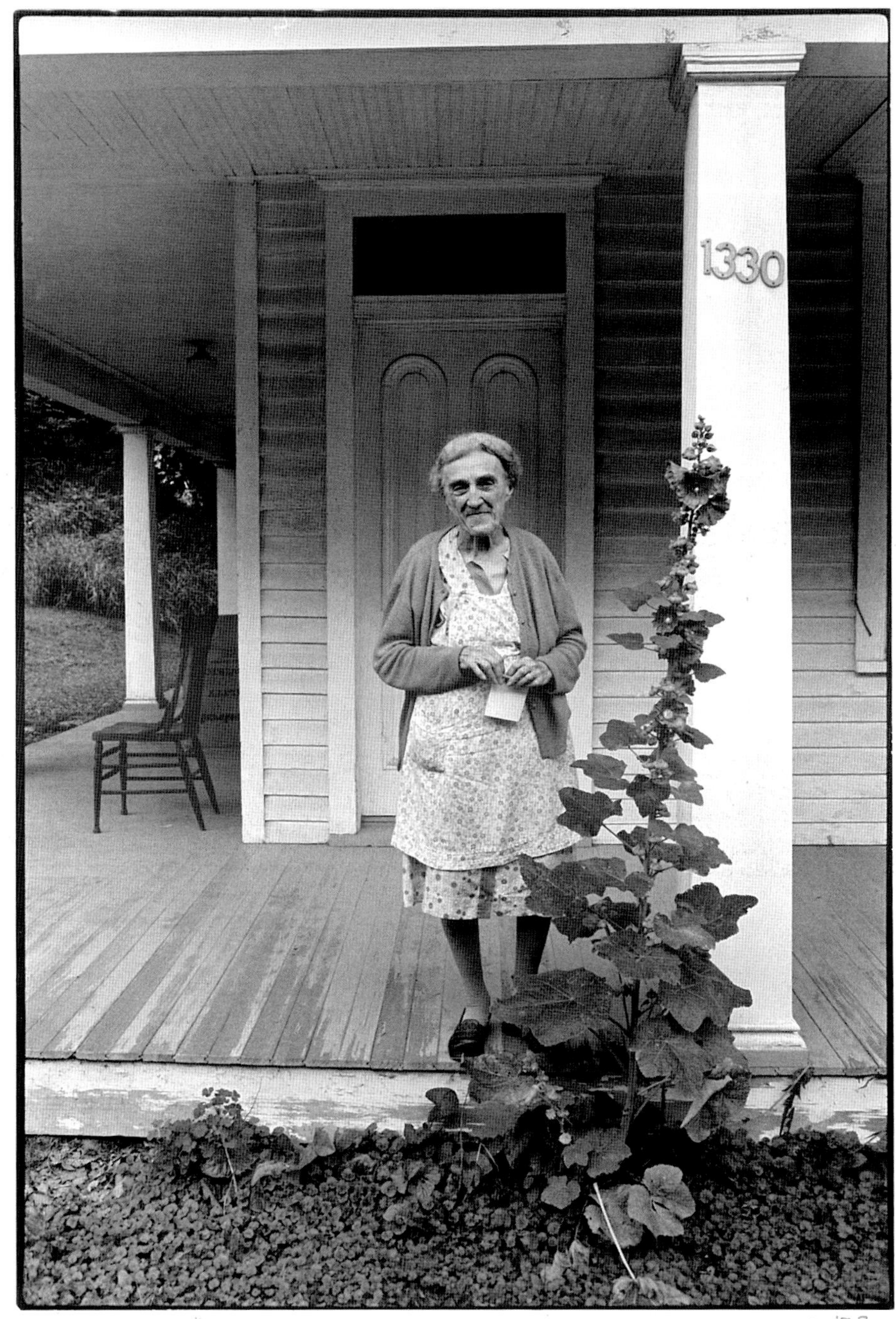

"MRS. DILLARD"   MC '73

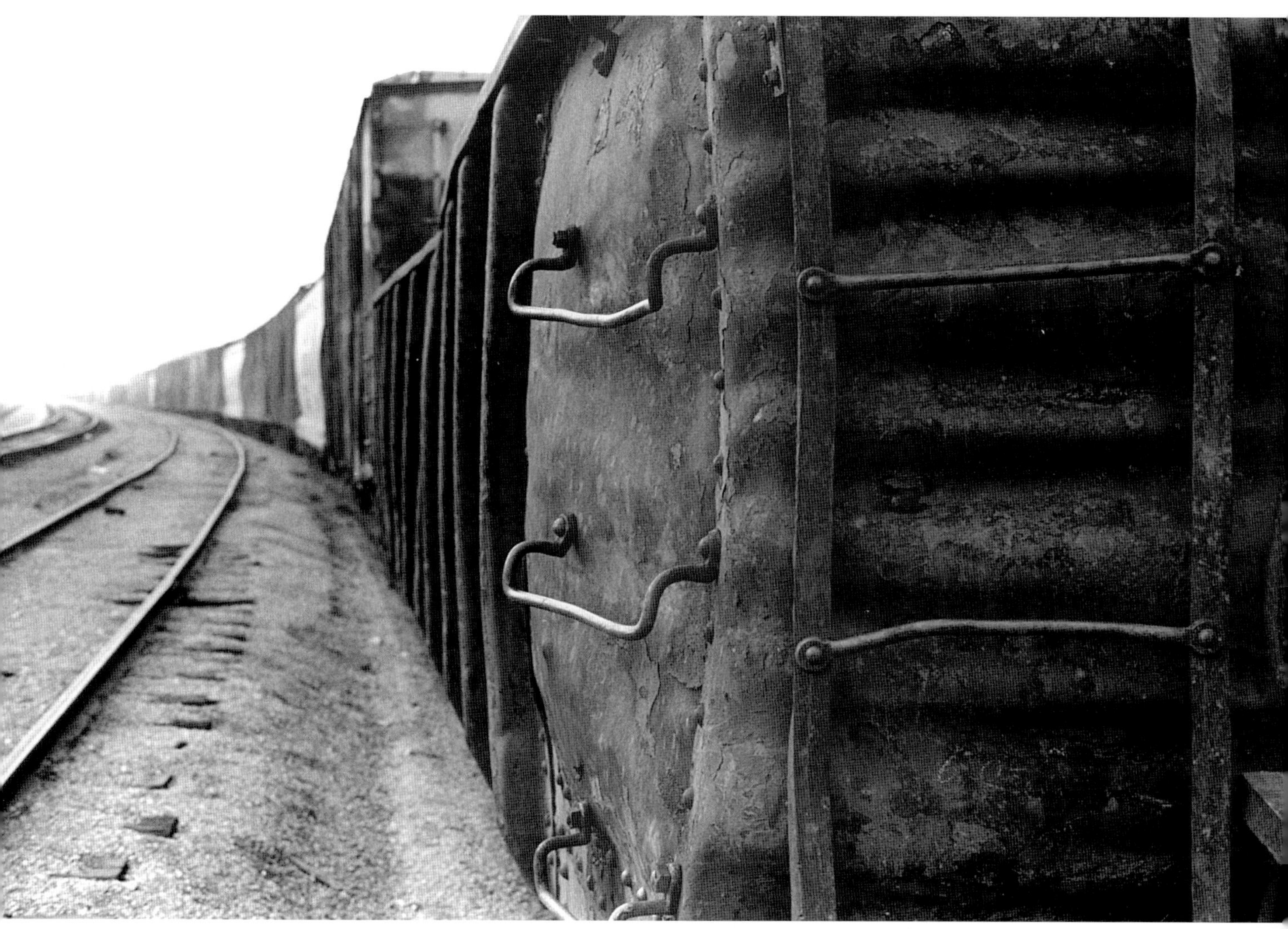

Mark Chamberlain
Mrs. Pillard, Dubuque Passages series, 1973
Black and white gelitin silver print

Last Boxcar to DBQ, Dubuque Passages series, 1974
Black and white gelitin silver print
Courtesy of the artists

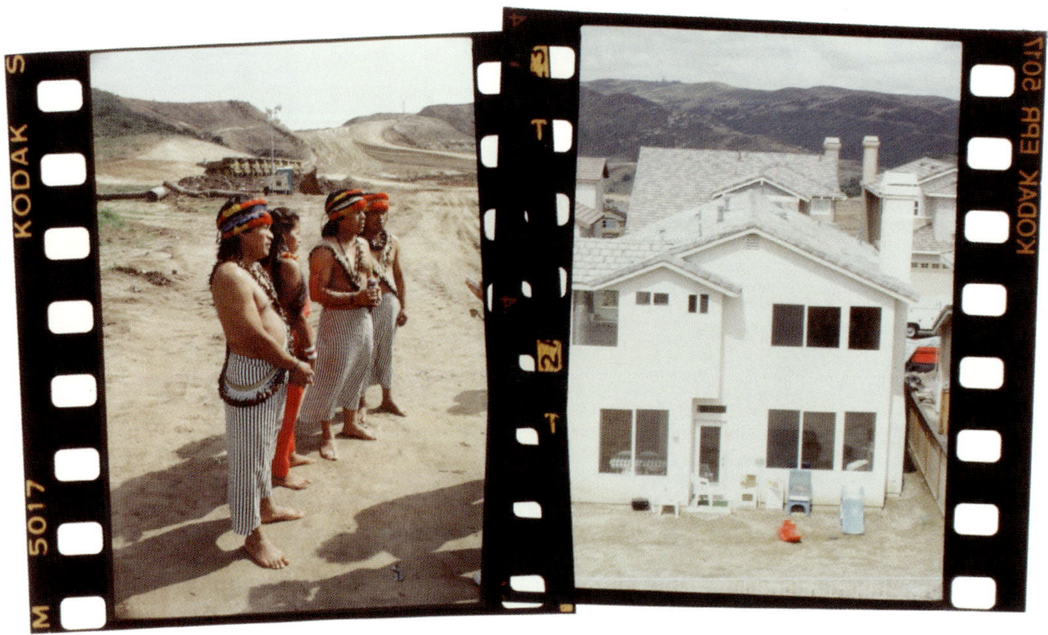

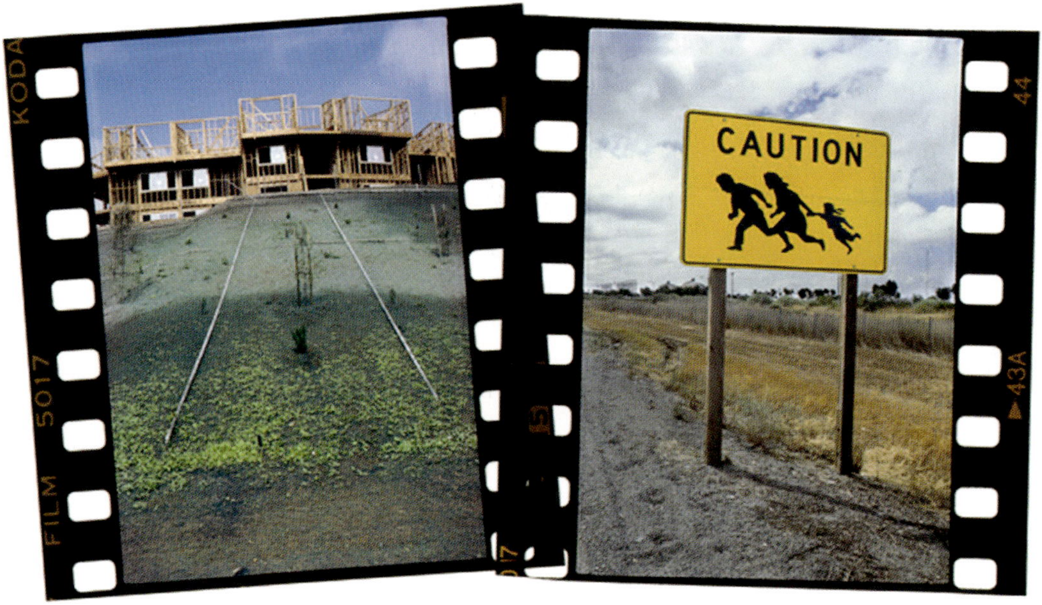

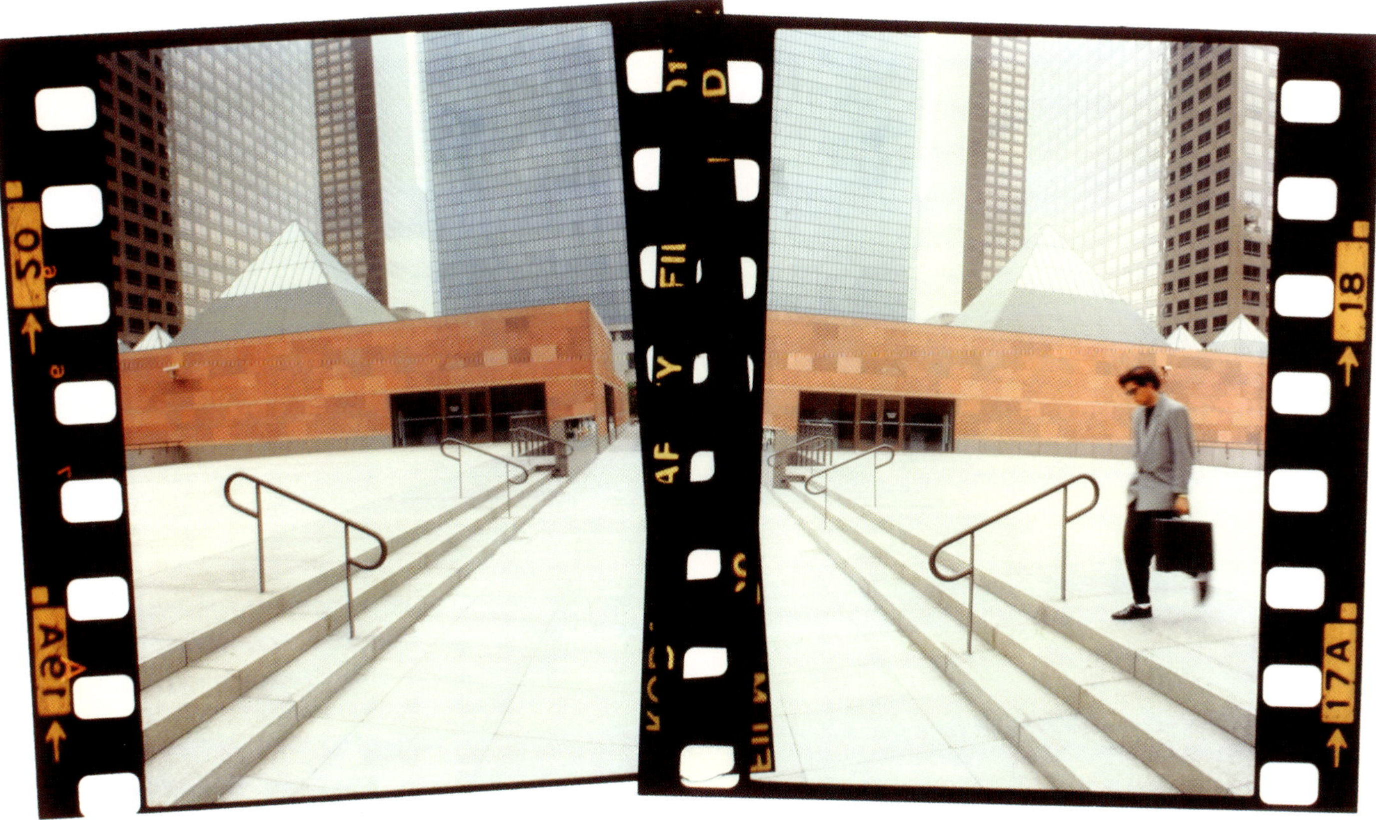

Mark Chamberlain
Looking for 2000 in Laguna Canyon (Grupo Charrip), 1996
Cibachrome prints

Looking for 2000 in Laguna Niguel (Caution Crossing), 1996
Cibachrome prints

Looking for 2000 at MOCA, 1996
Cibachrome prints
Courtesy of the BC Space

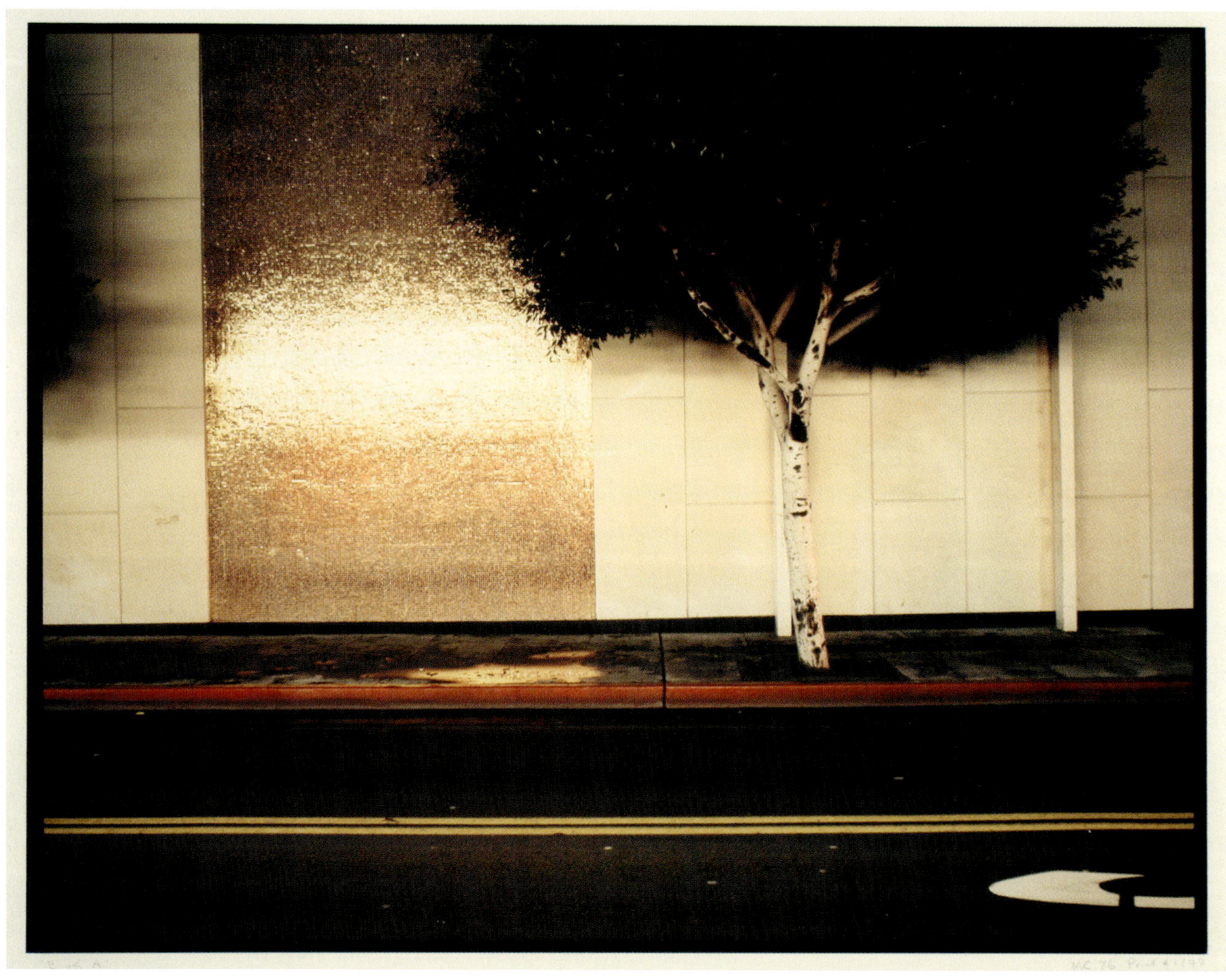

Mark Chamberlain
All That Glitters, 1975
Cibachrome print

Think I Can, 1975
Chibachrome print
Courtesy of the artists

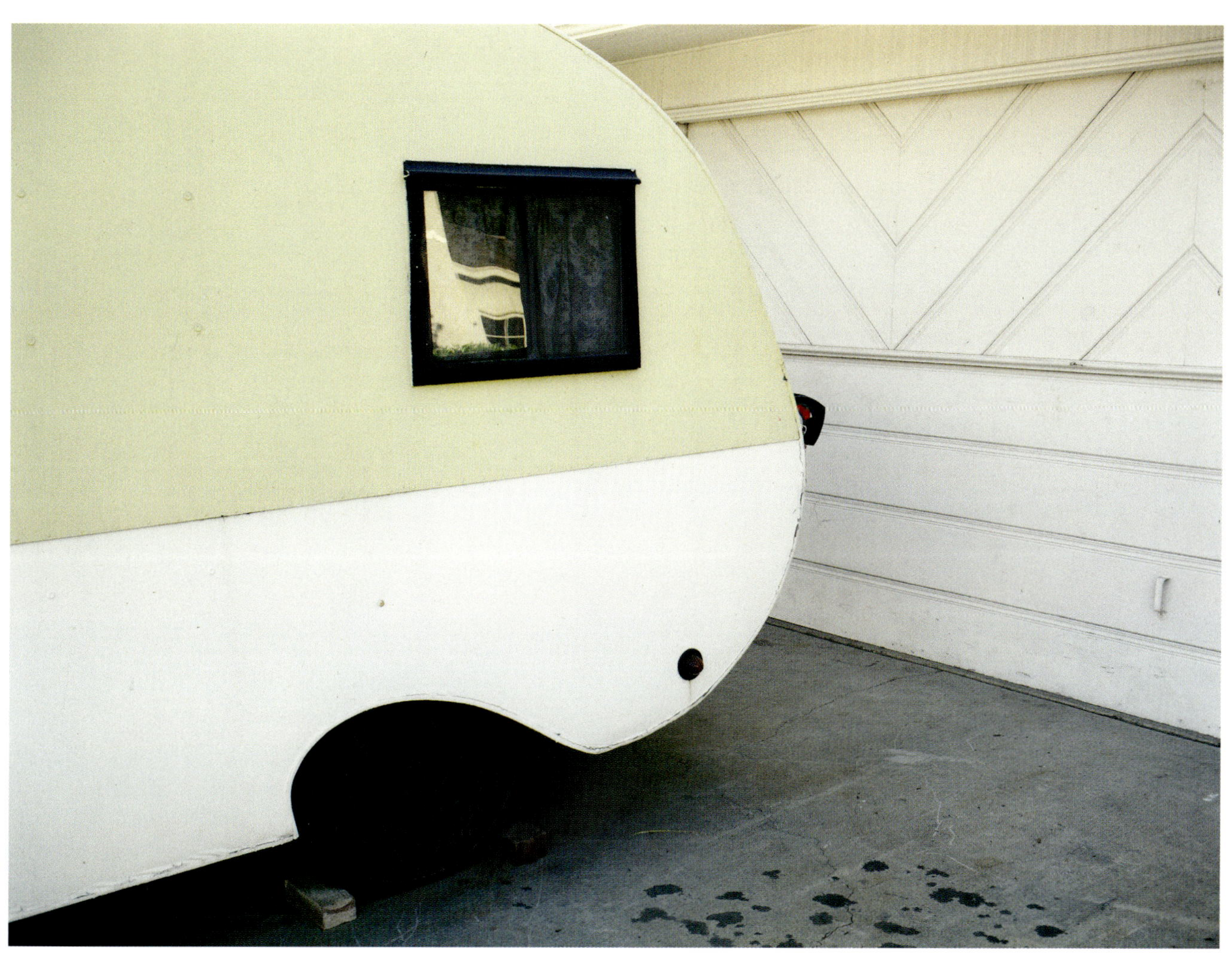

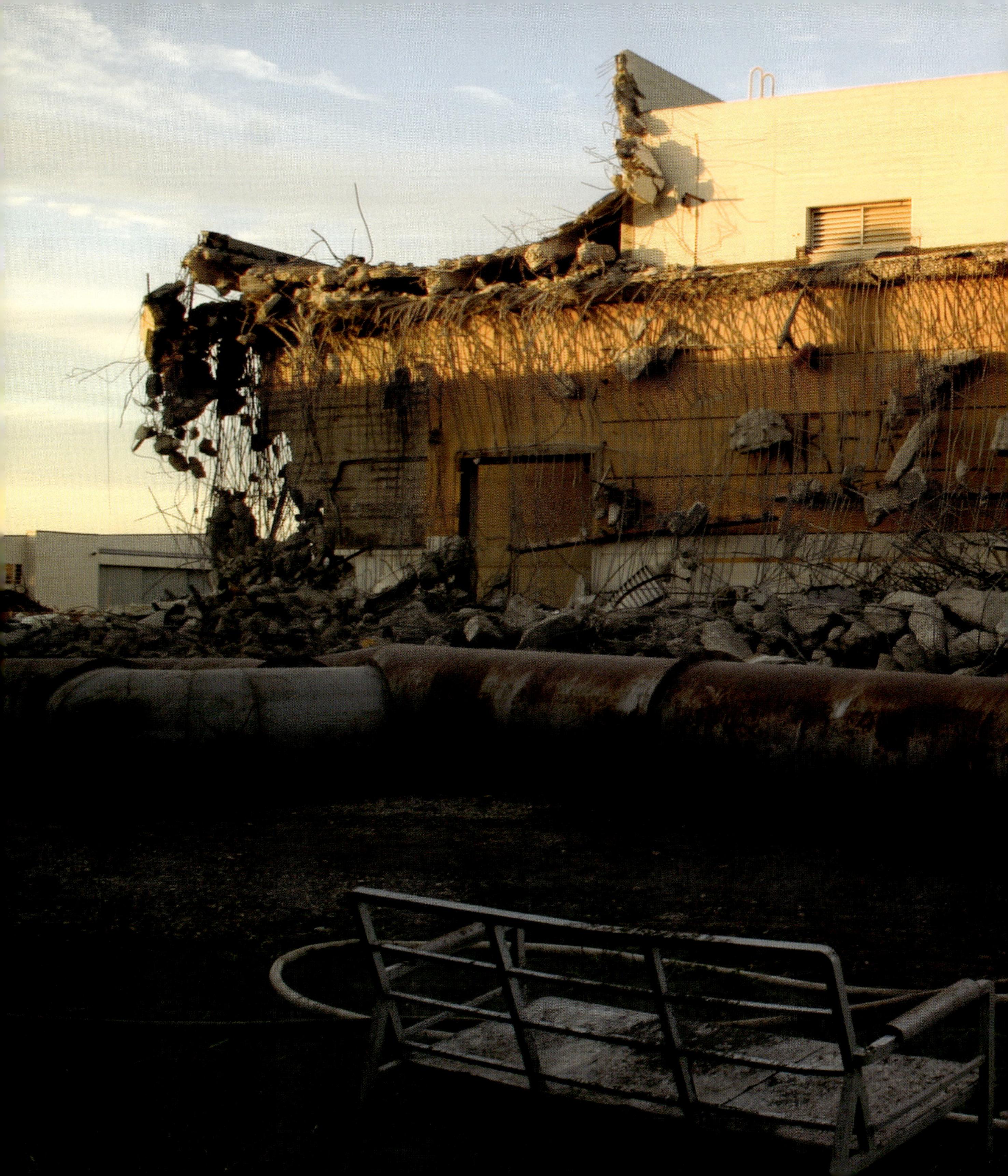

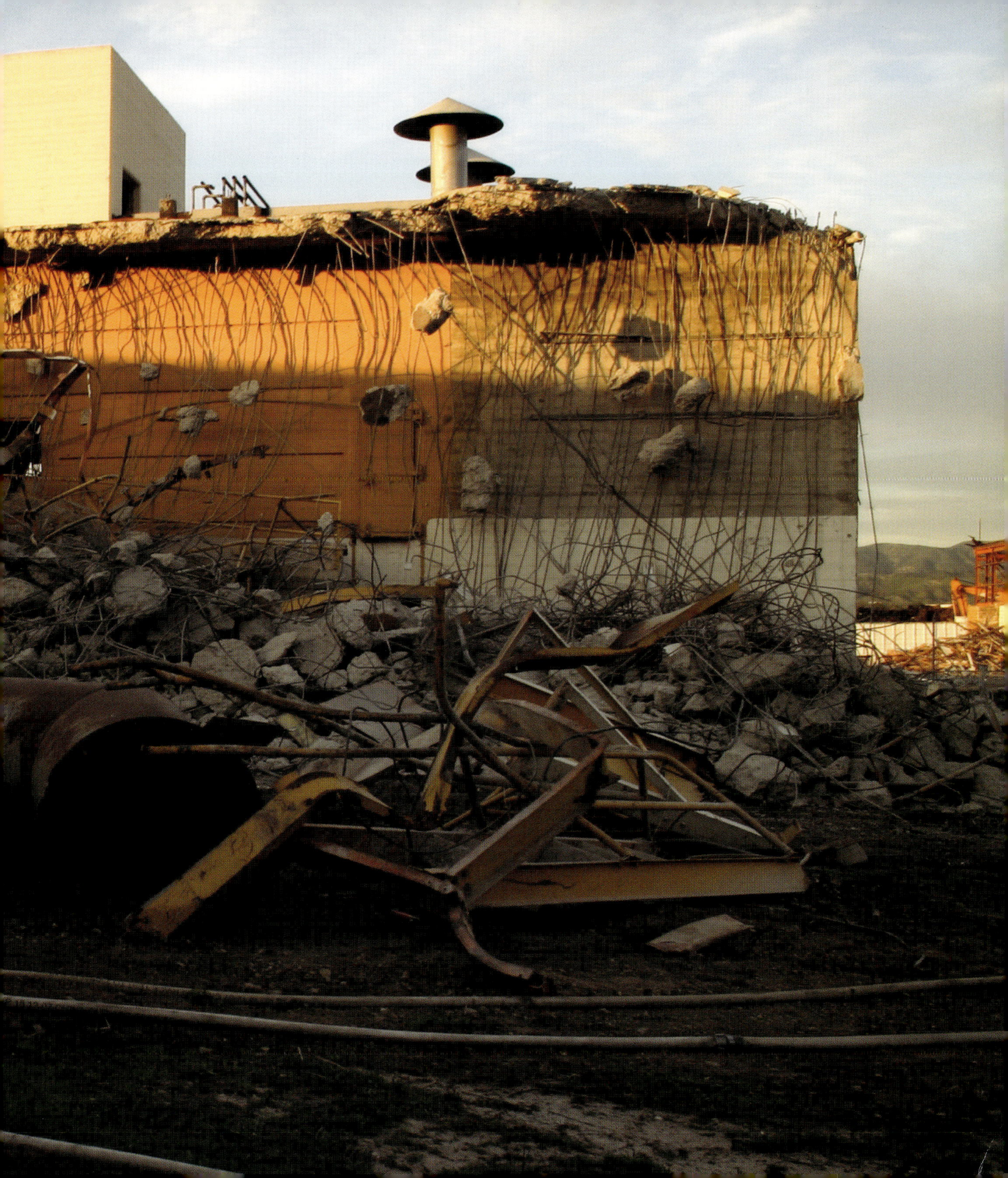

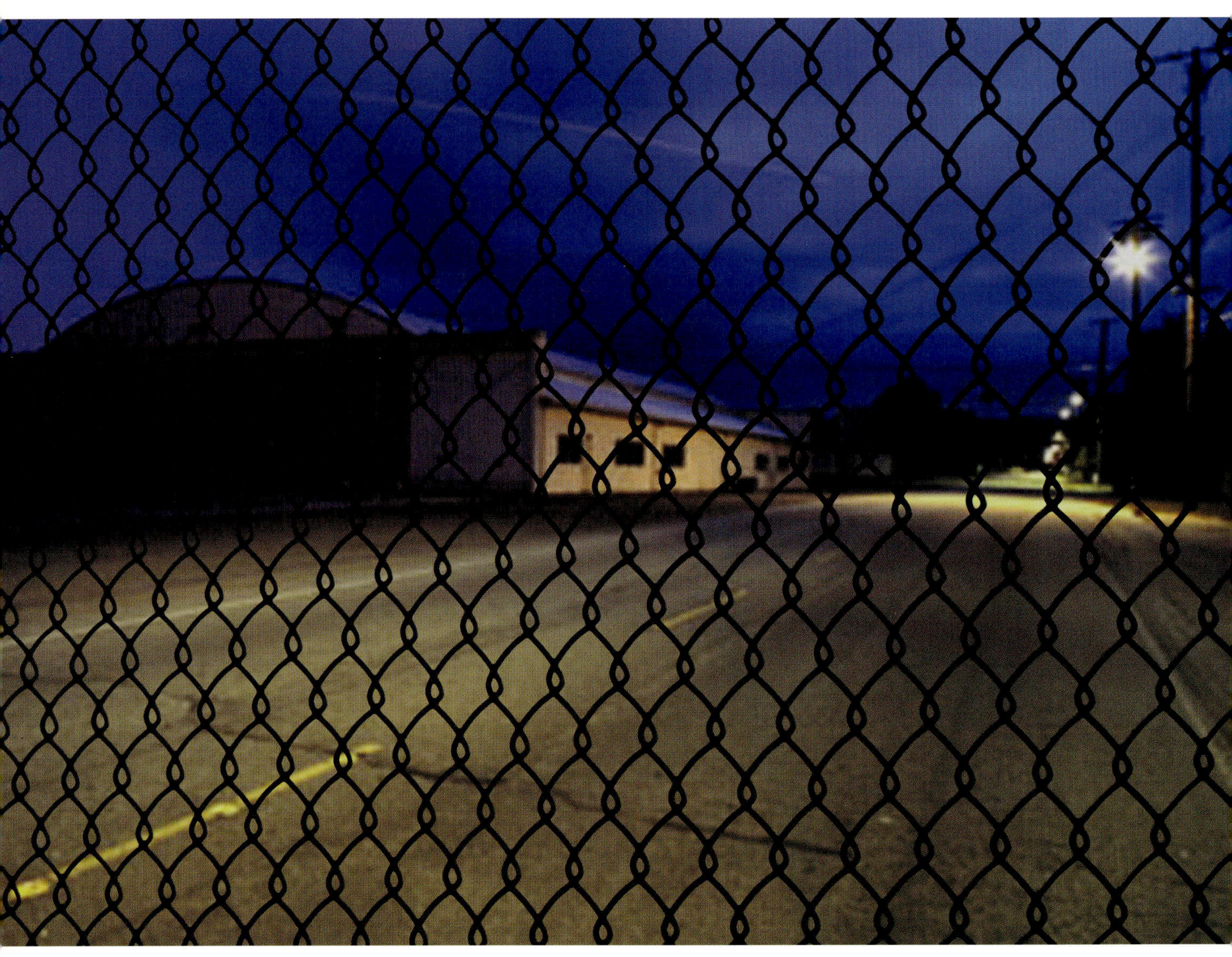

(previous page)
Mark Chamberlain
Coming Down, 2009
Archival lightjet print

Mark Chamberlain
Fenced Night Life on C Street, 2004
Archival lightjet print
Courtesy of the artist

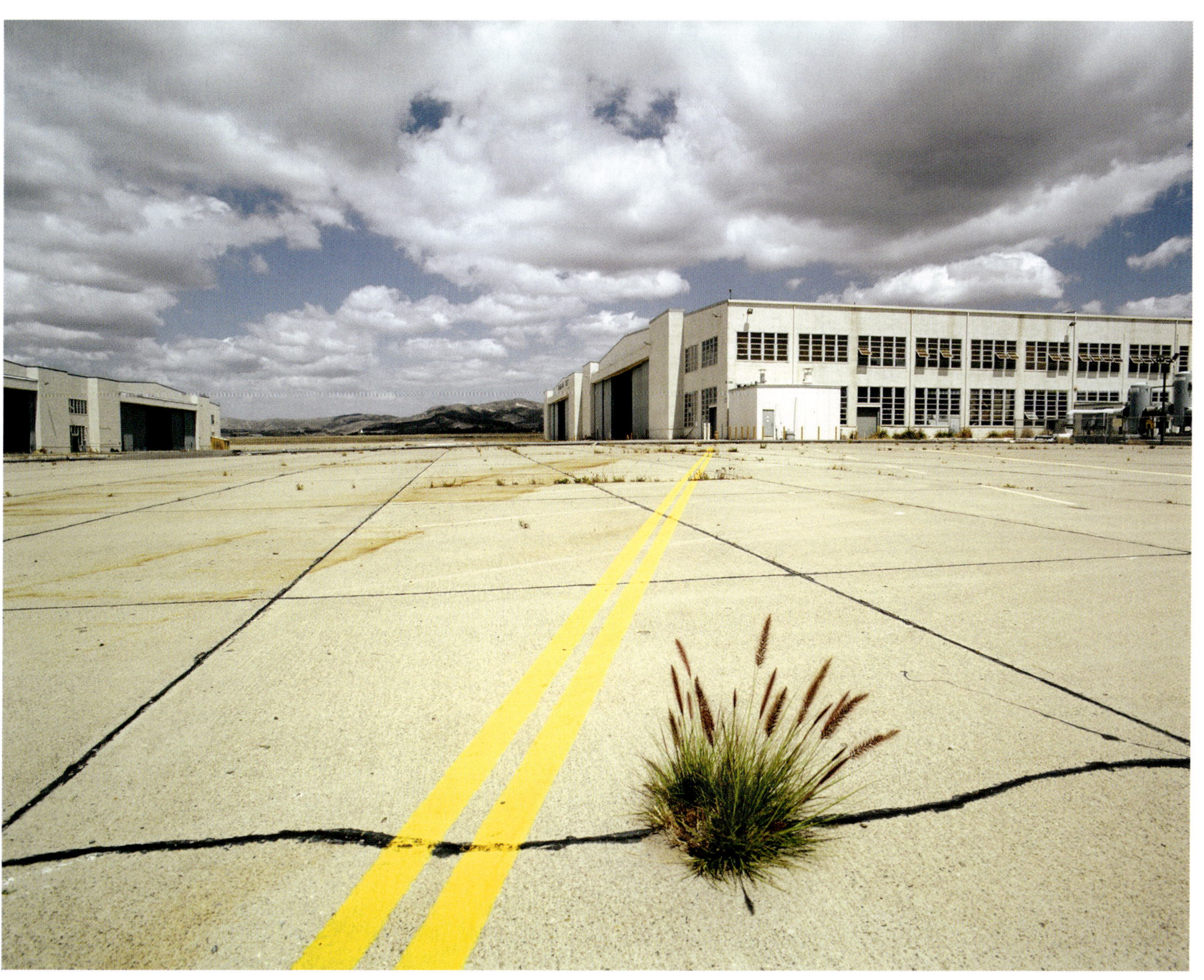

Mark Chamberlain
Nature Prevails, 2002
Archival lightjet print
Courtesy of the artist

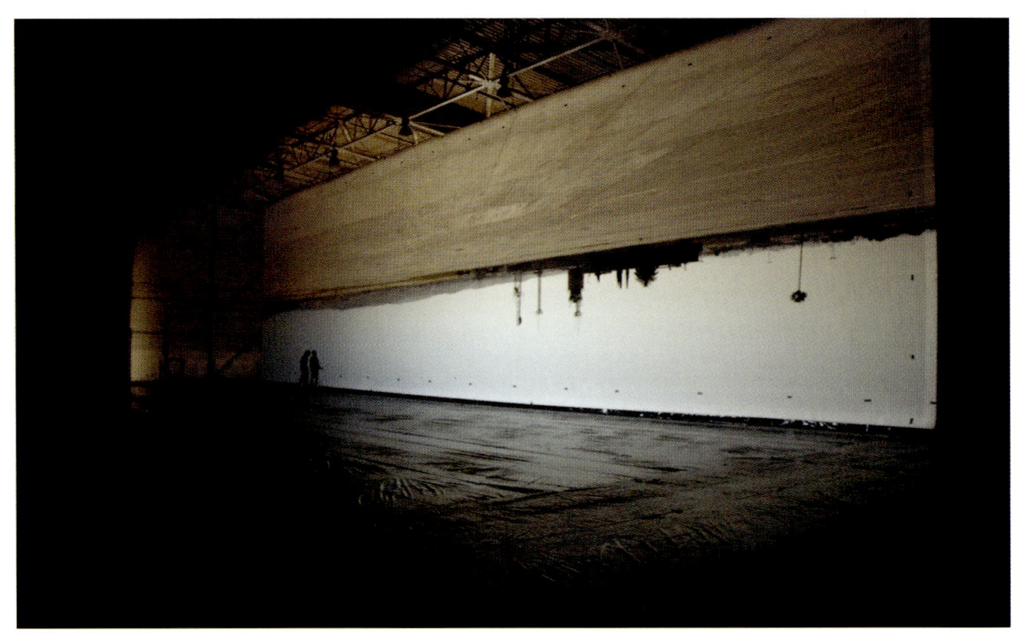

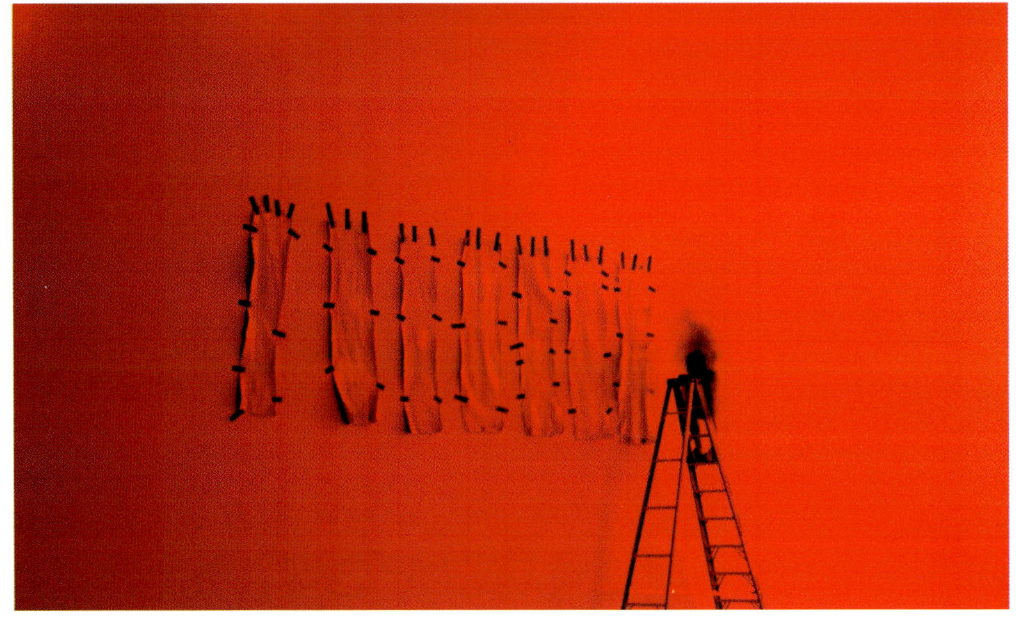

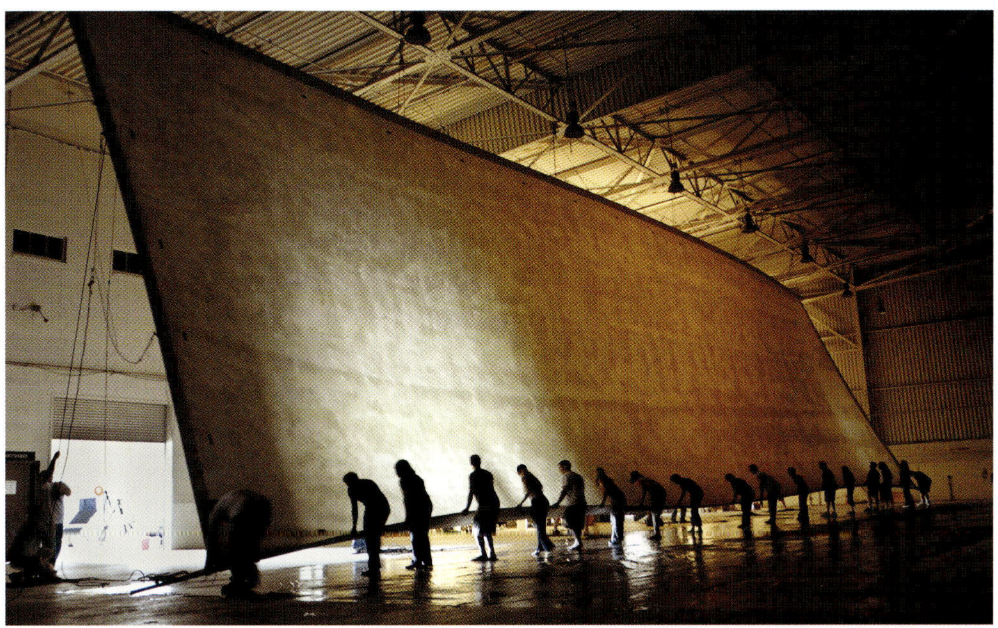

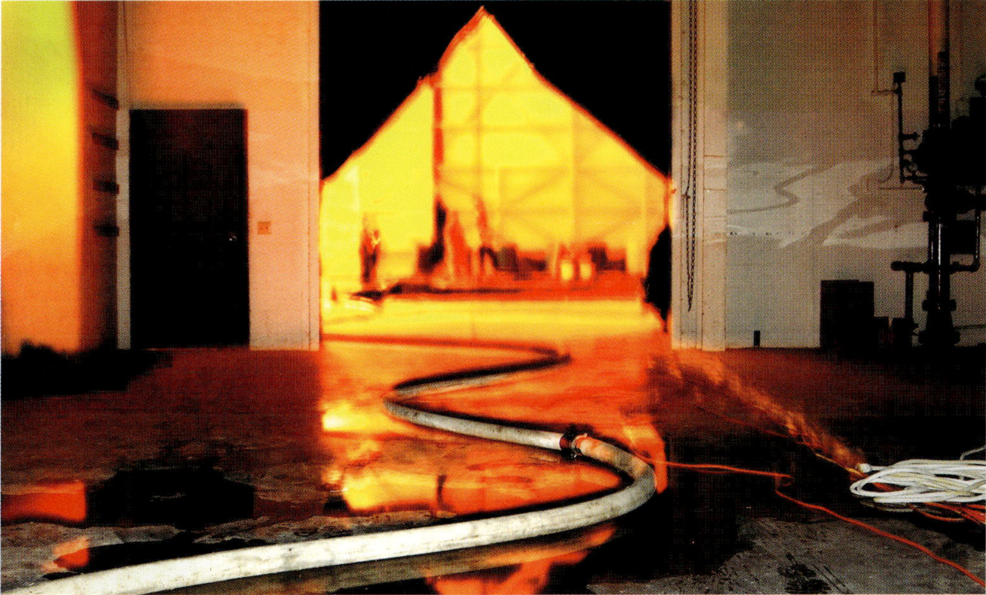

The Great Picture
El Toro Marine Corp Air Station, 2006
Upper Left: Rob Johnson, The Legacy Project
Upper Right: Jacques Garnier, TLP
Lower Left: Rob Johnson, TLP
Lower Right: Jerry Burchfield, TLP

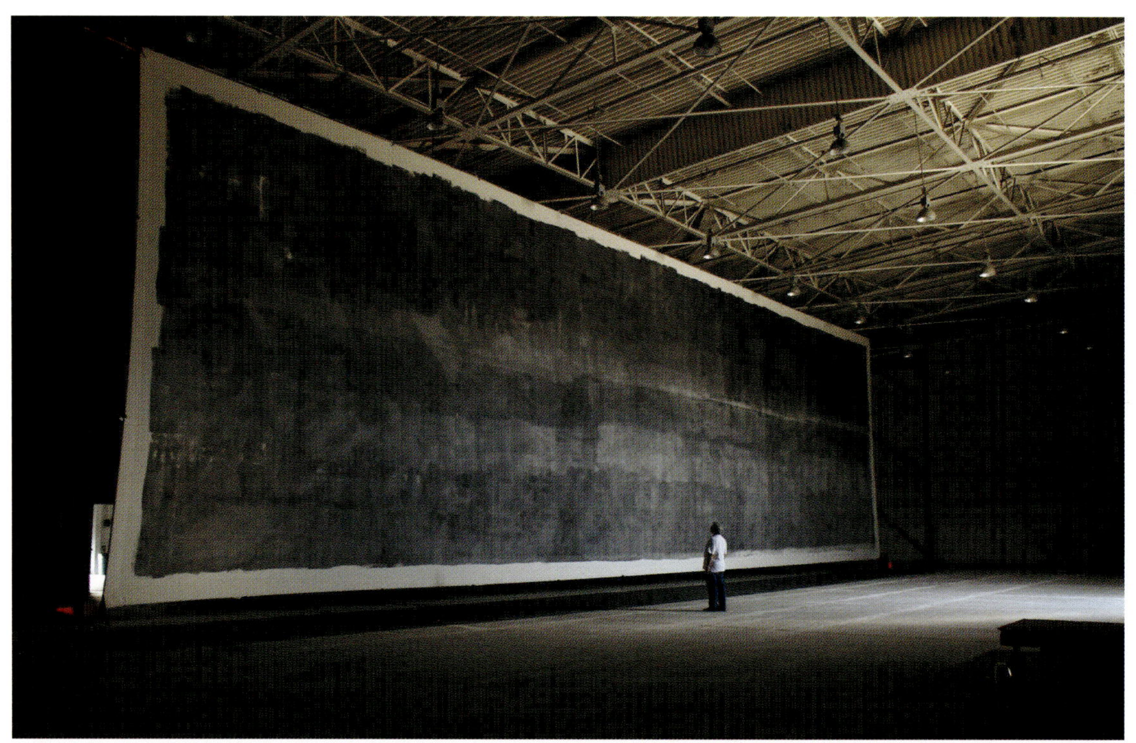

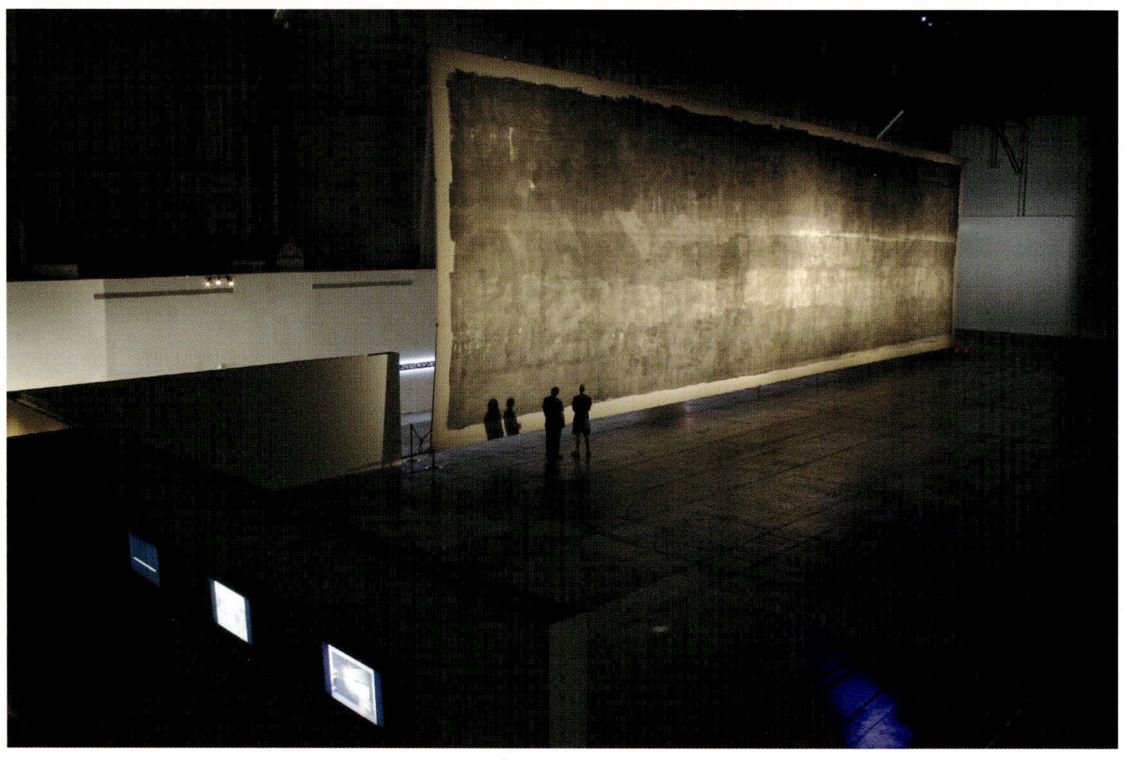

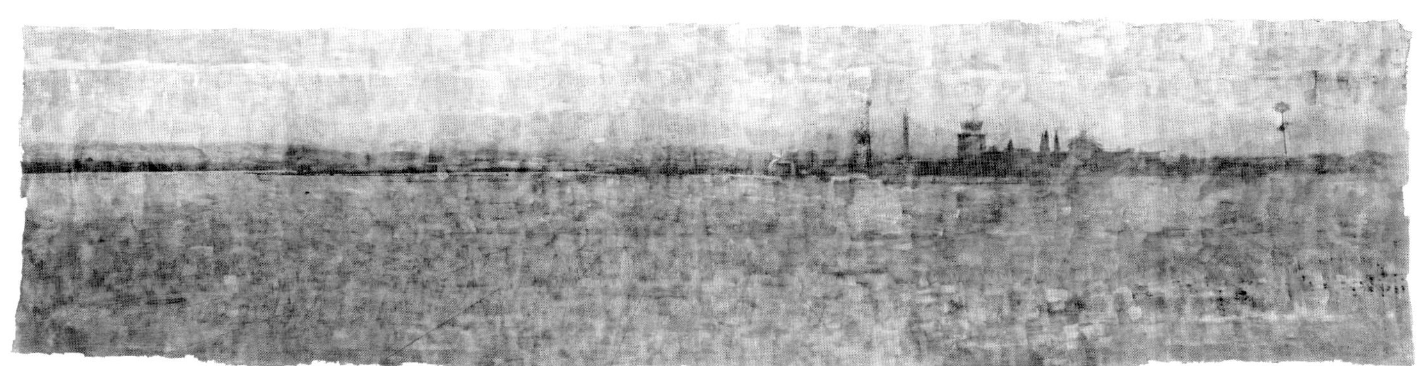

The Legacy Project installations
The Great Picture
El Toro Marine Corp Air Station, 2006
Courtesy of Legacy Project

Wind Tunnel at Pasadena Art Center, 2007
The Great Picture
Courtesy of Mark Chamberlain

Positive Negative Image of The Great Picture, 2006
Courtesy of Legacy Project

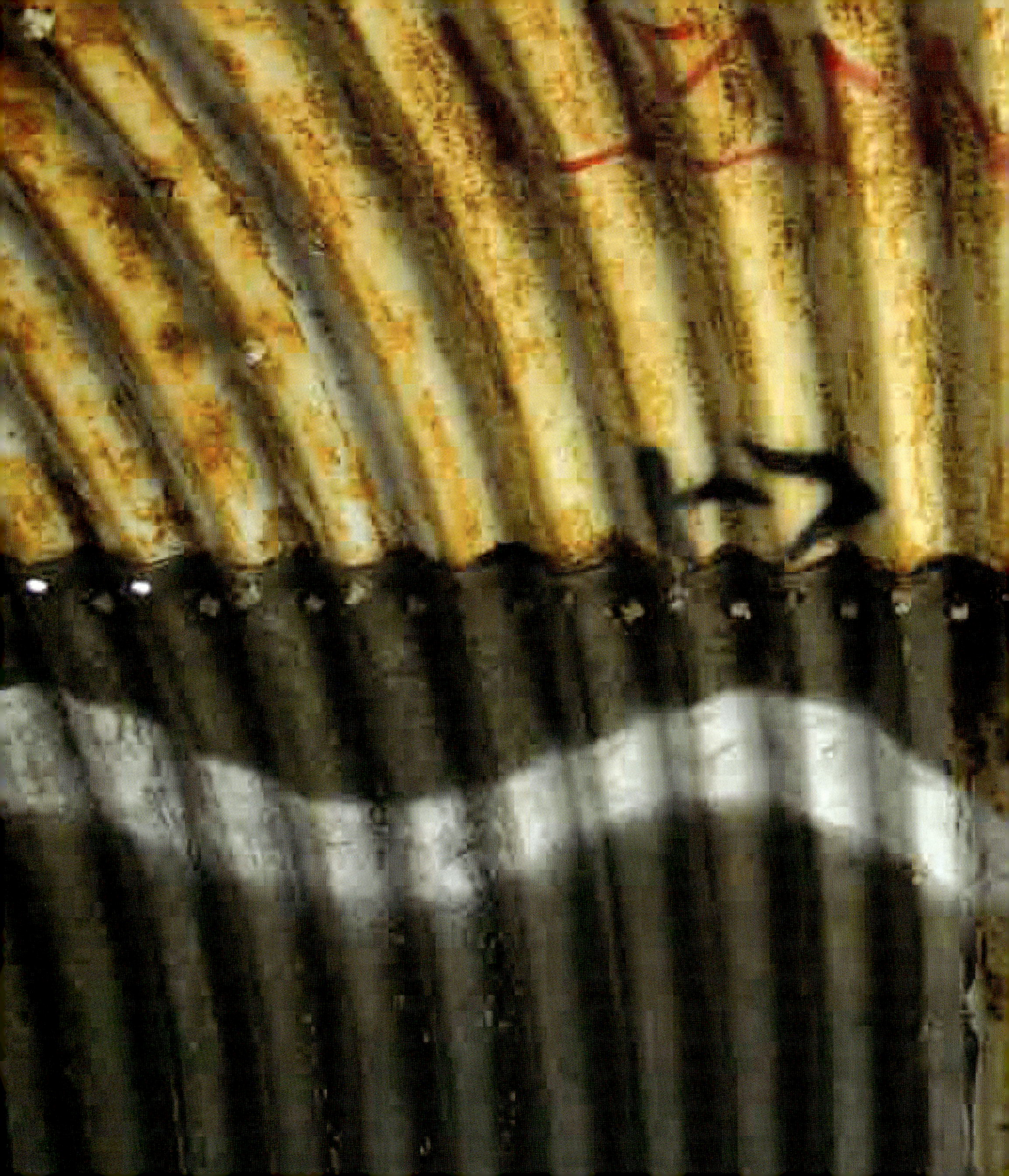

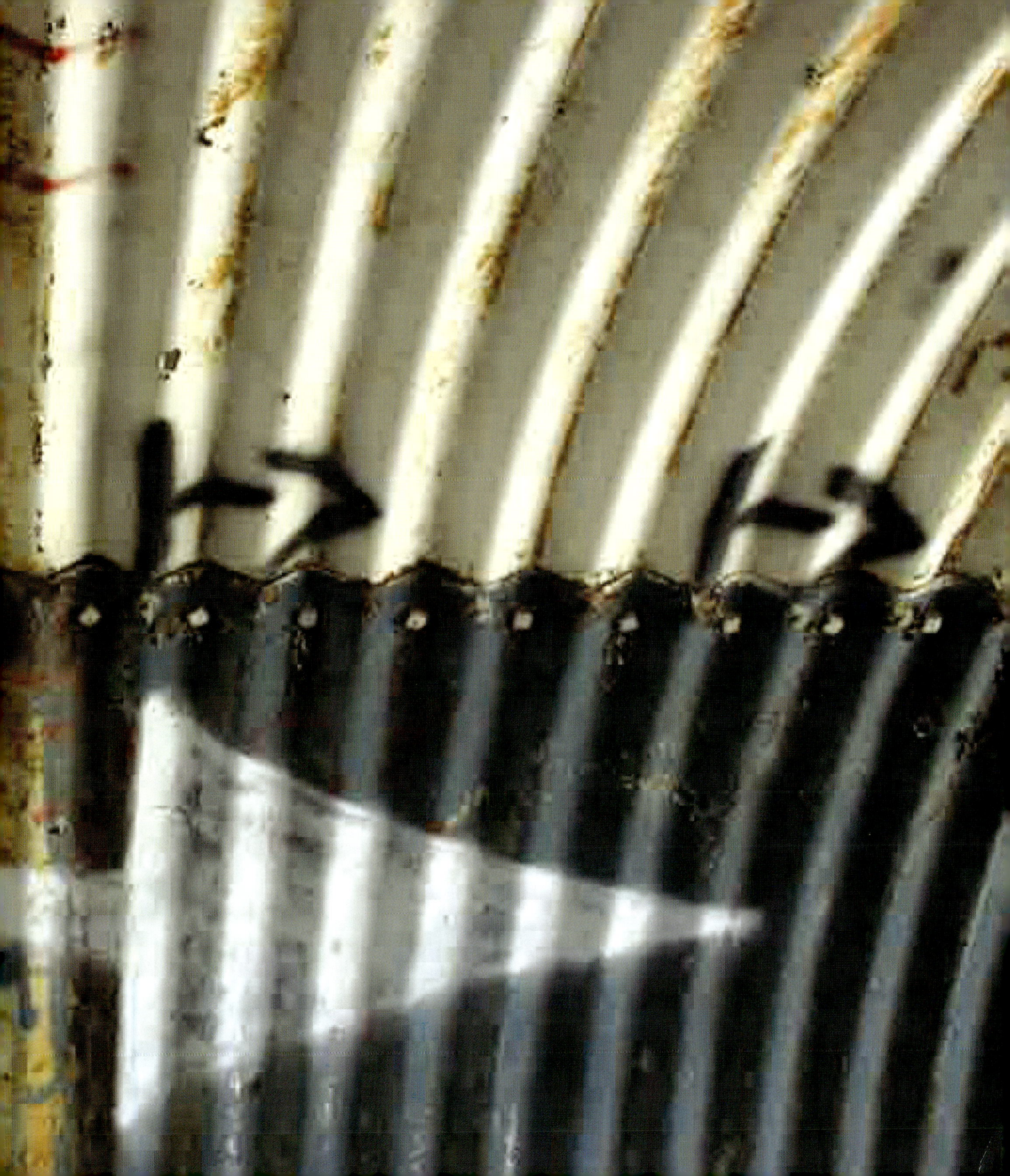

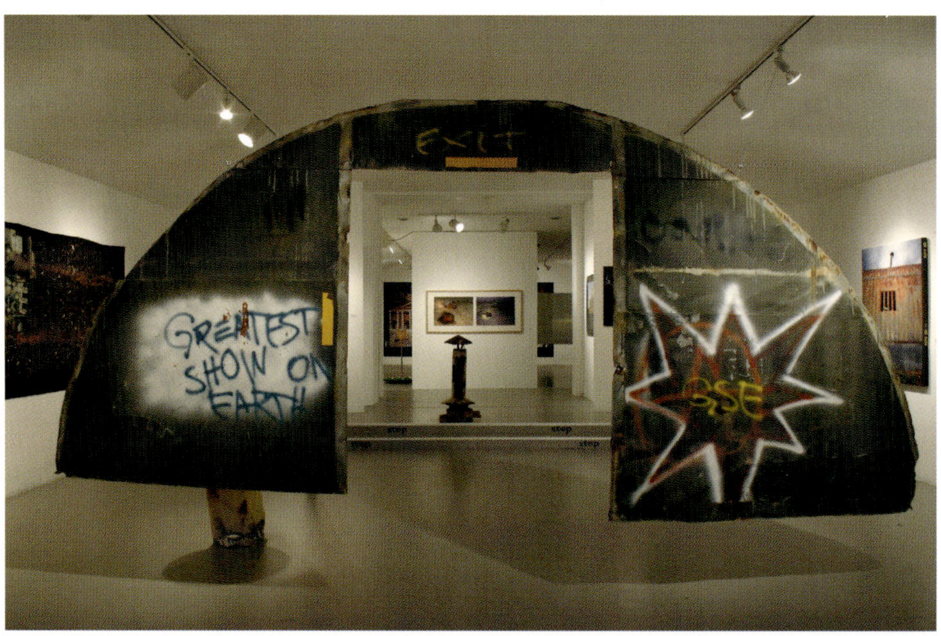

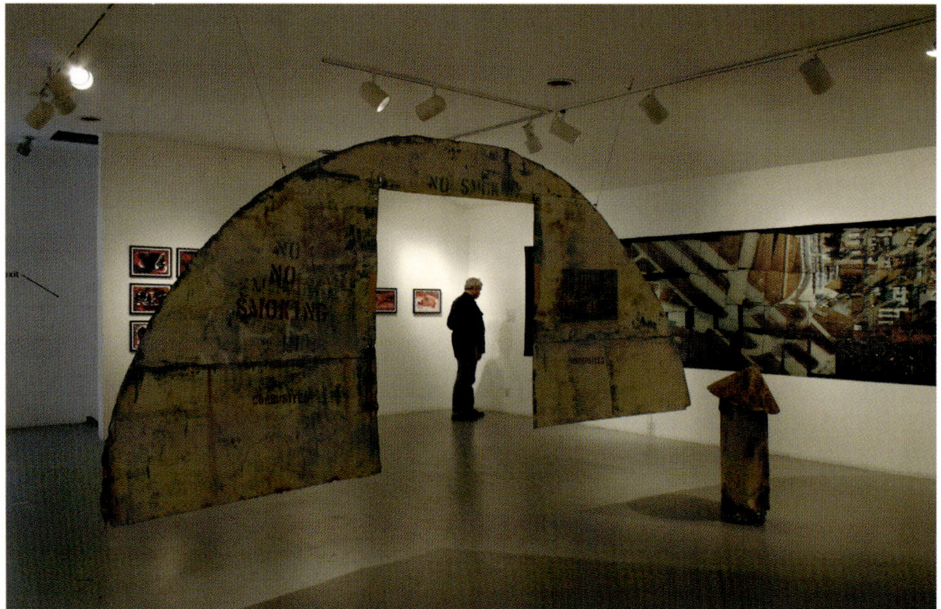

(previous page)
Mark Chamberlain
Direction Q, 2004
Archival lightjet print
Courtesy of the artist

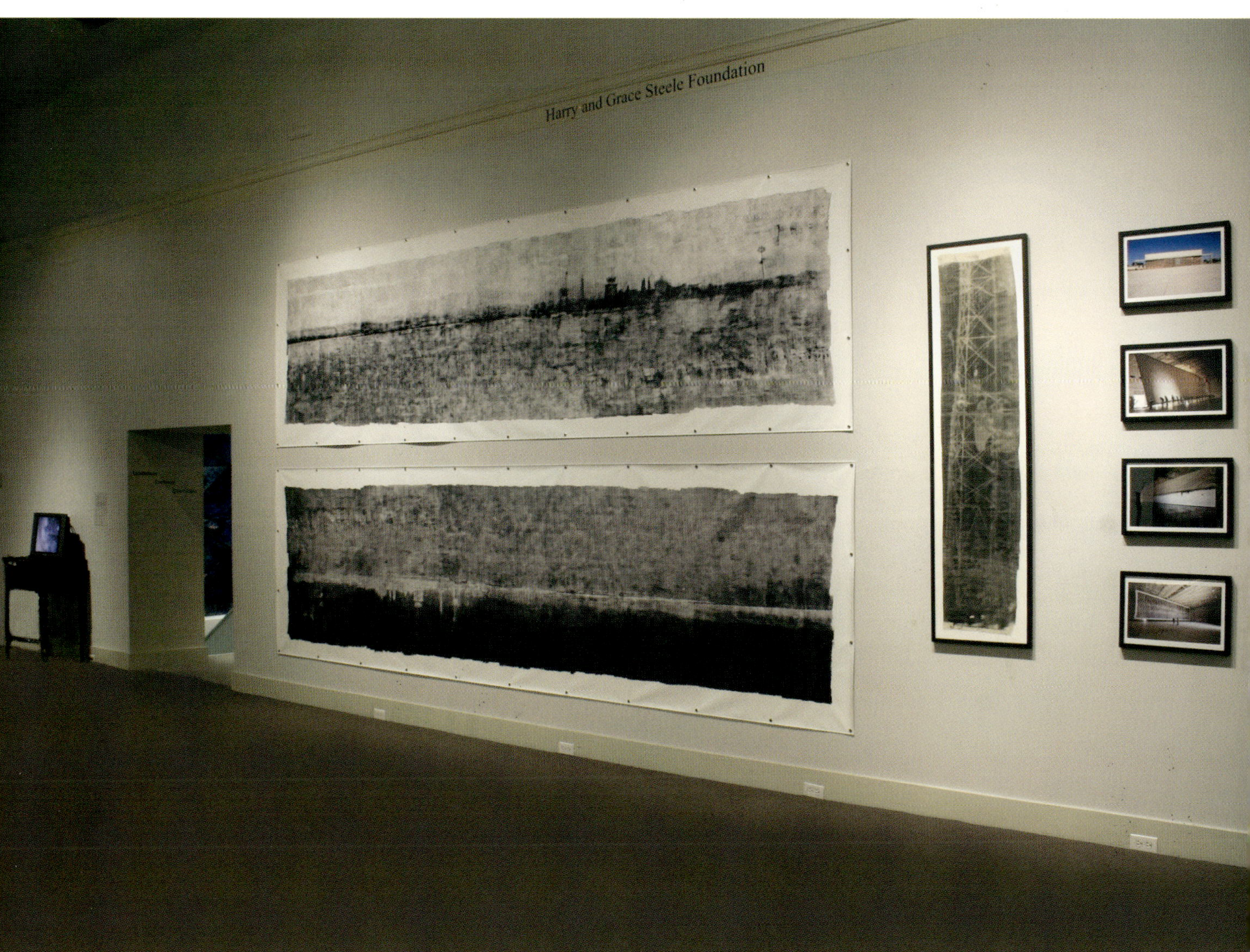

The Legacy Project" Installations
Laguna Art Museum OSCENE, 2007
Laguna Beach, CA
Courtesy of Mark Chamberlain

Angles Gate, 20046
San Pedro, CA
Courtesy of Mark Chamberlain

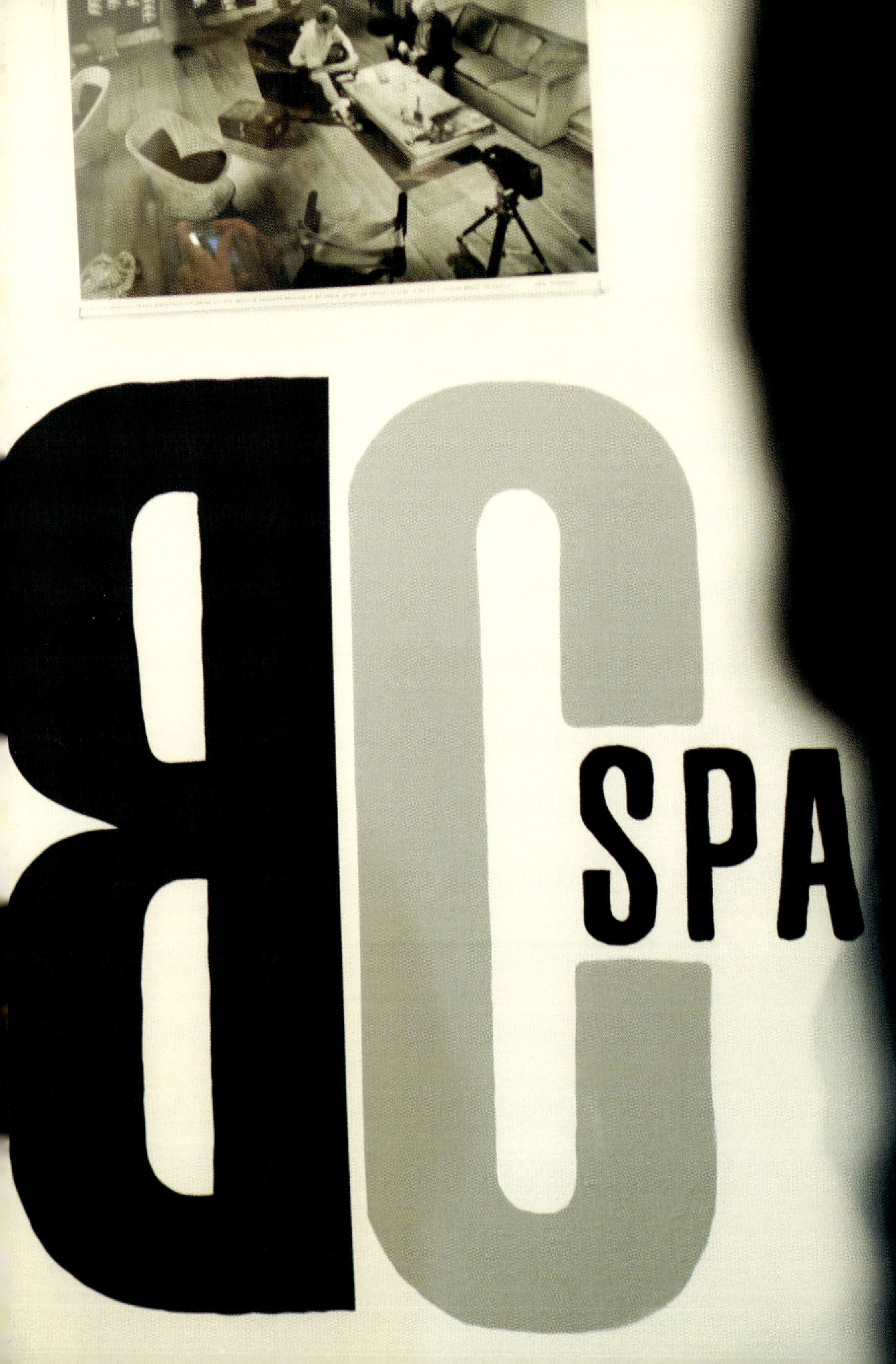

86 SPA

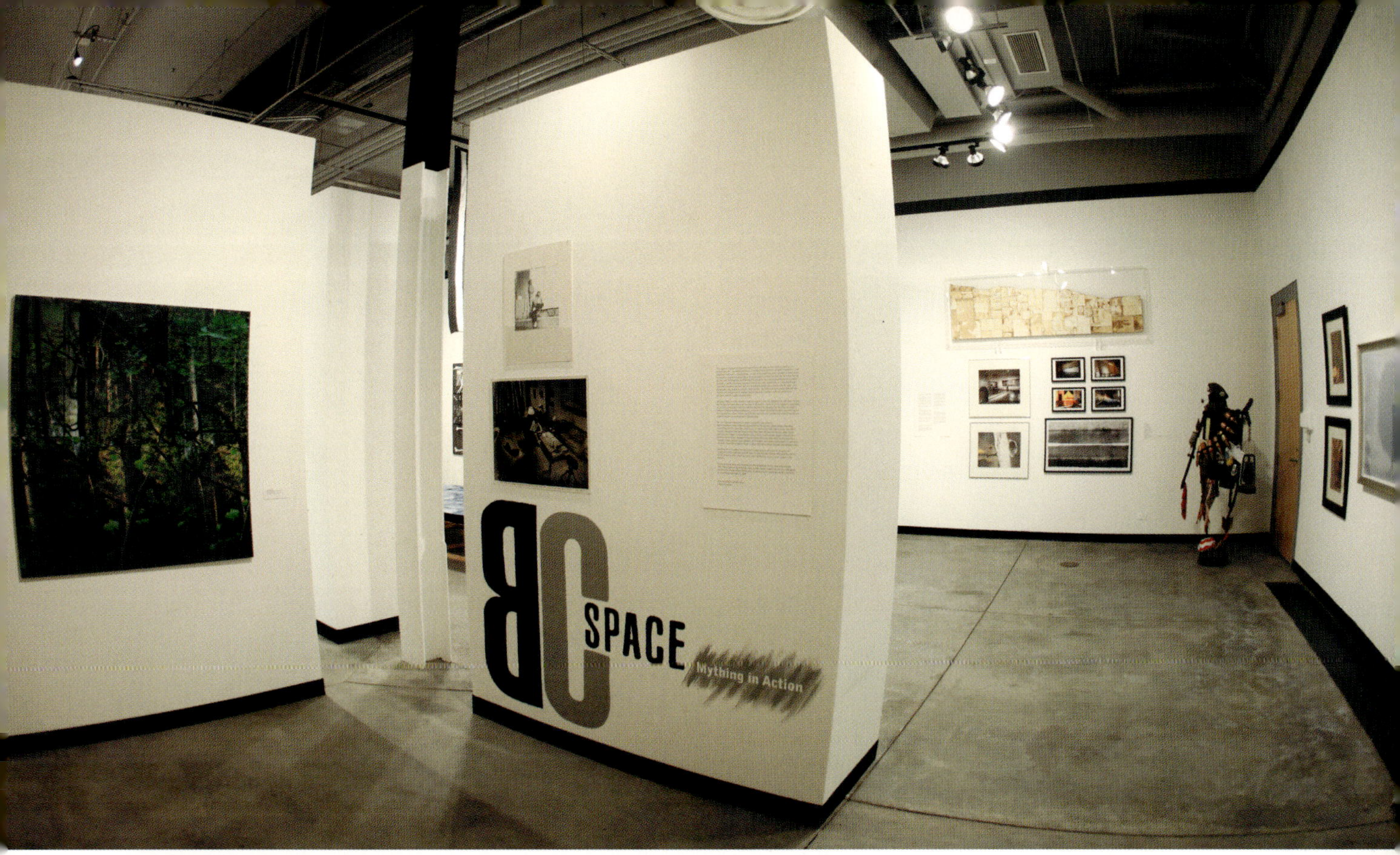

BC SPACE
Mything in Action

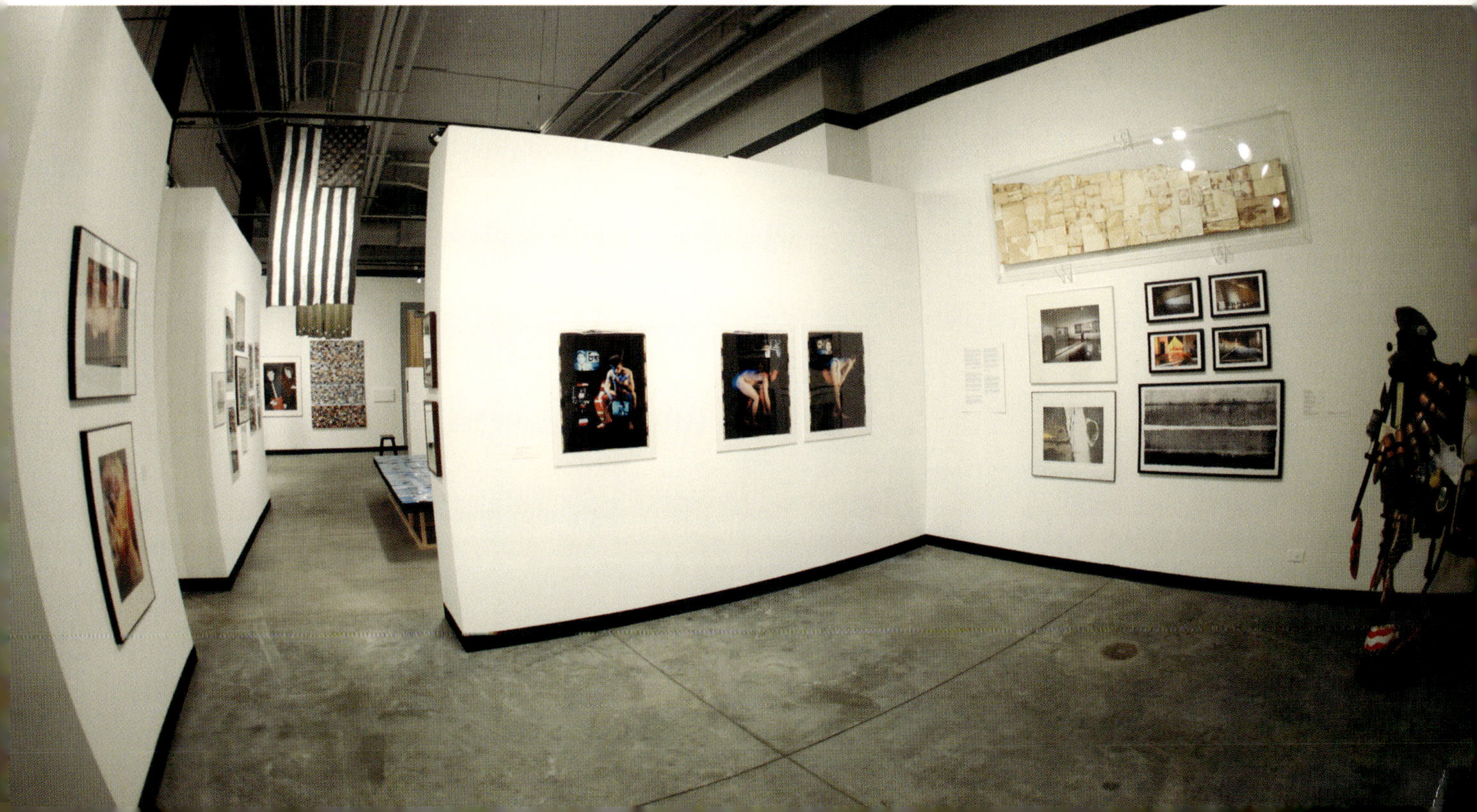

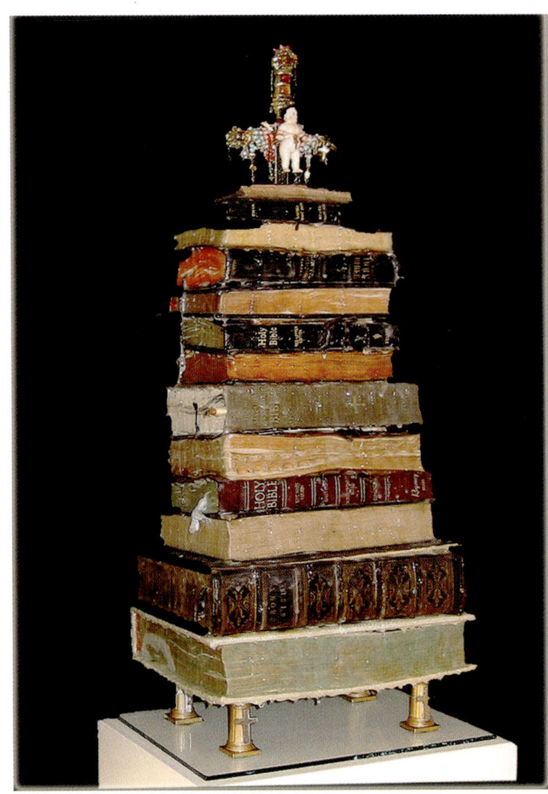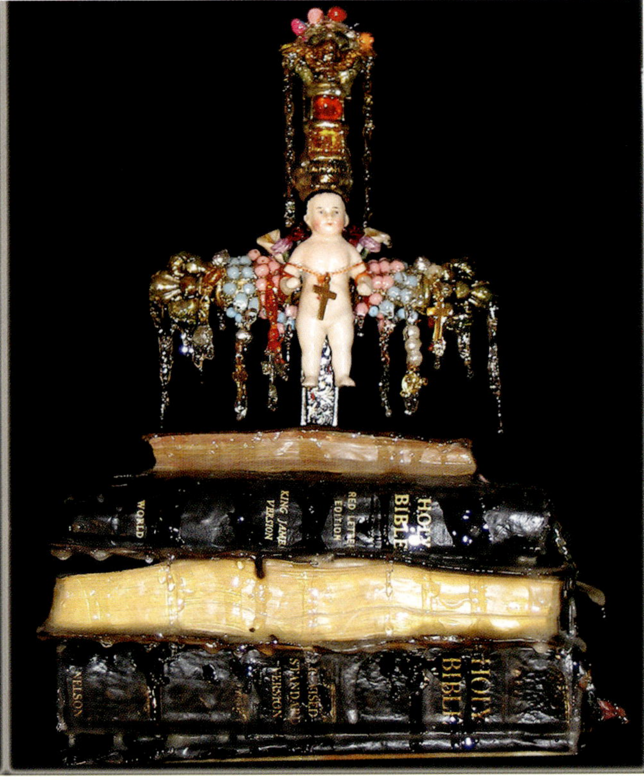

Pat Sparkuhl
Let Us Prey, 2000
Mixed media
Courtesy of the artist

Installation view
Grand Central Art Center, Santa Ana, CA.

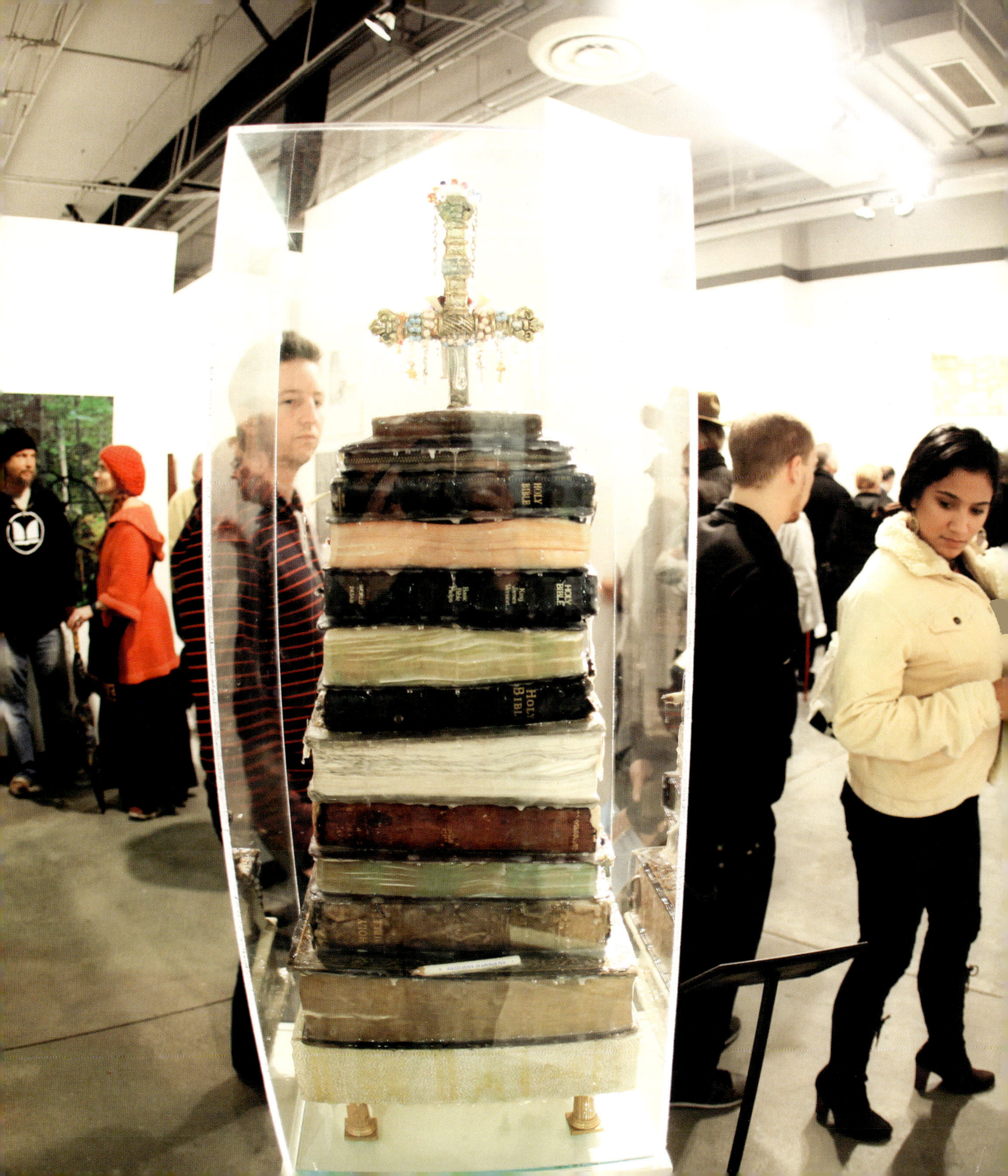

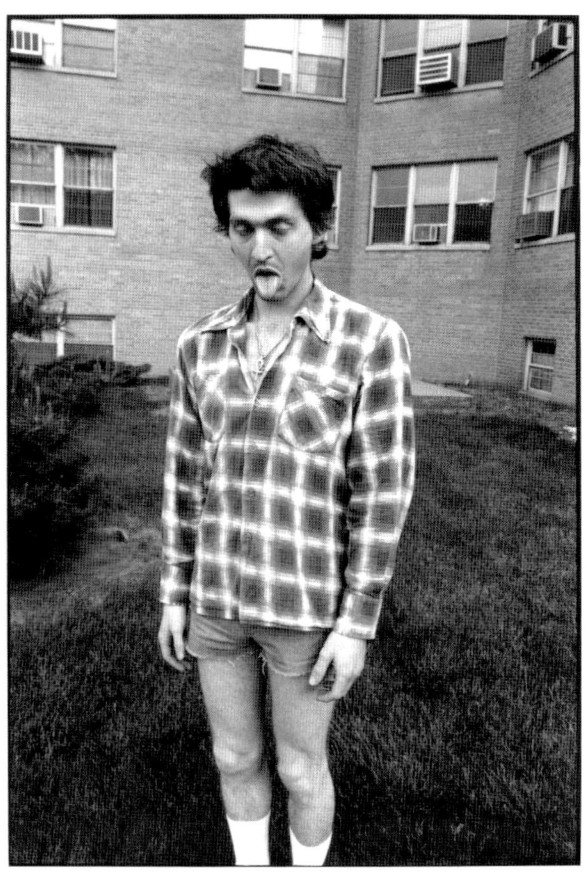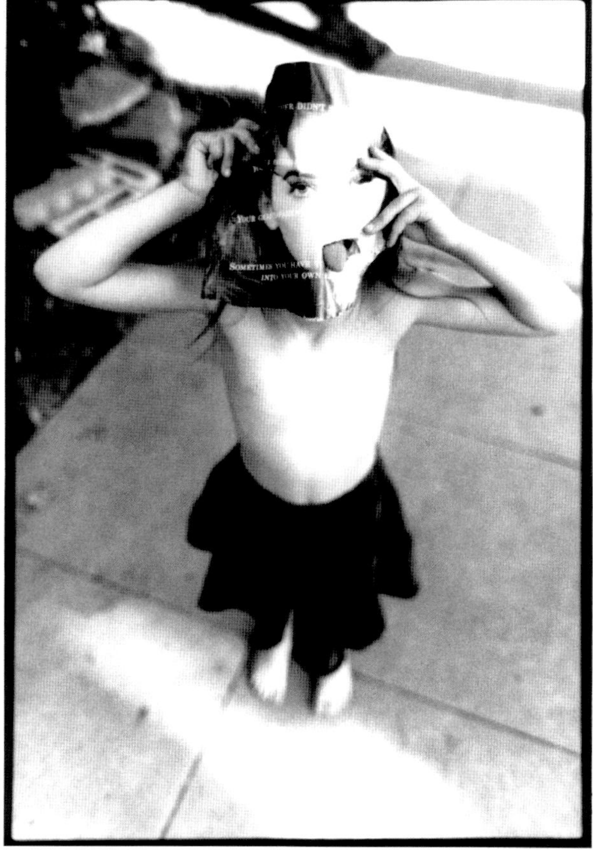

Eadweard r. York
Zoohaus – Omaha, 1989
Archival Silver Gelatin Print

Caitlin with Vogue Magazine - Los Angeles, 1994
Archival Silver Gelatin Print
Courtesy of the artist

Susan Rankaitis
Kuri (Black Line on Green) 2005-2007
Light jet print 2/3
Courtesy of the artist and Robert Mann Gallery

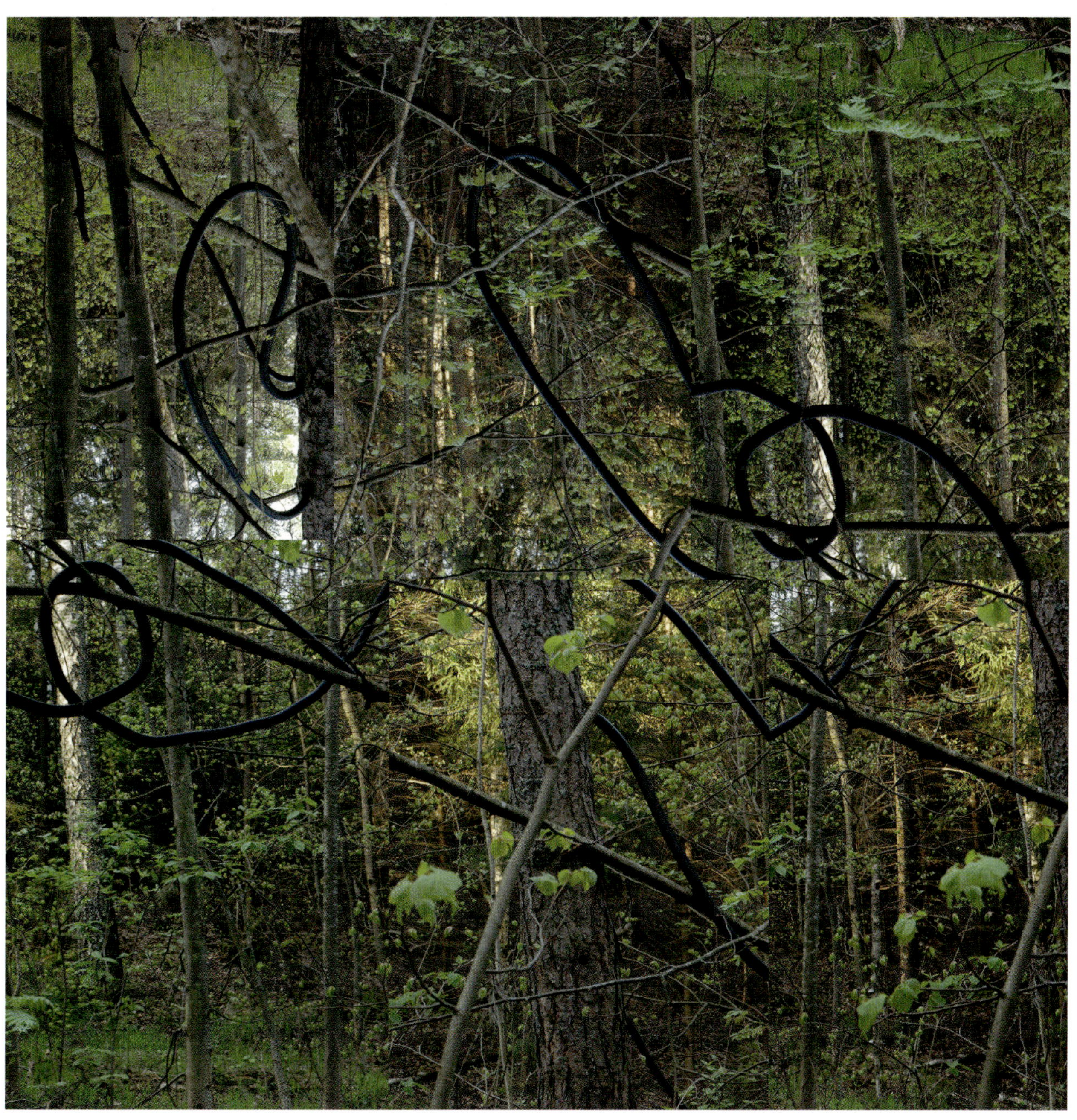

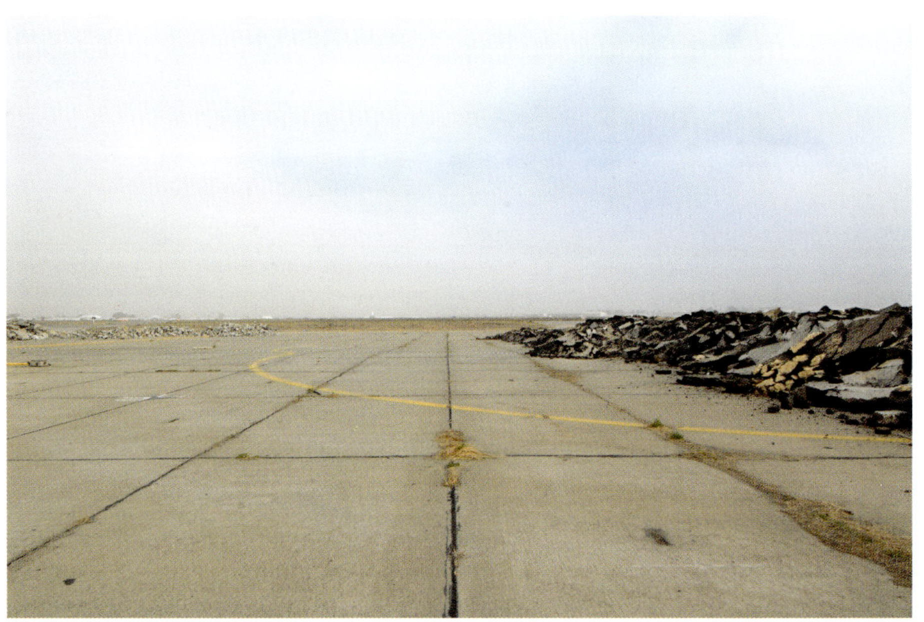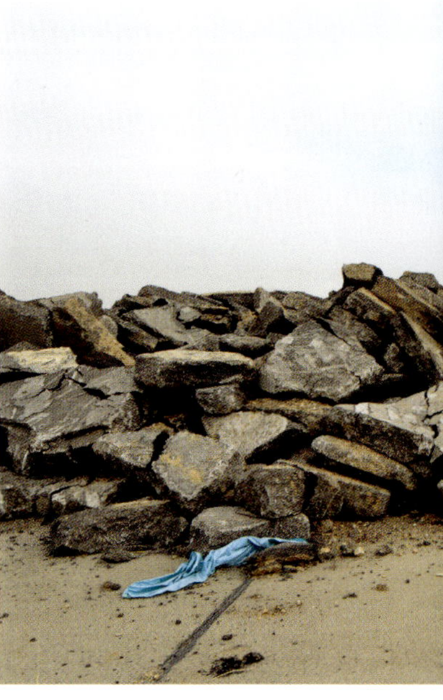

Jacques Garnier
Blue Dress, 2008
Archival pigment on paper
Courtesy of the artist

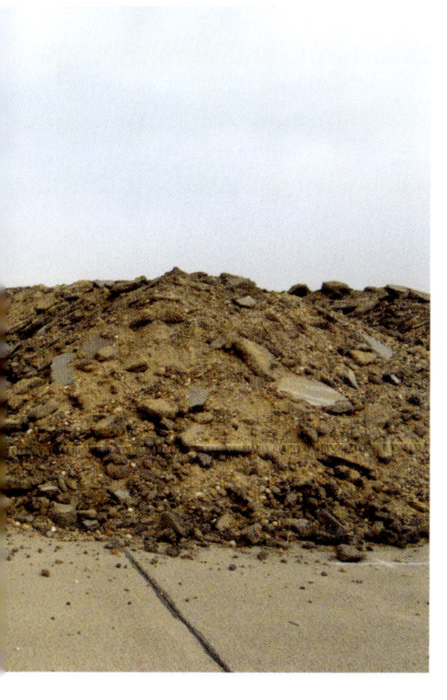
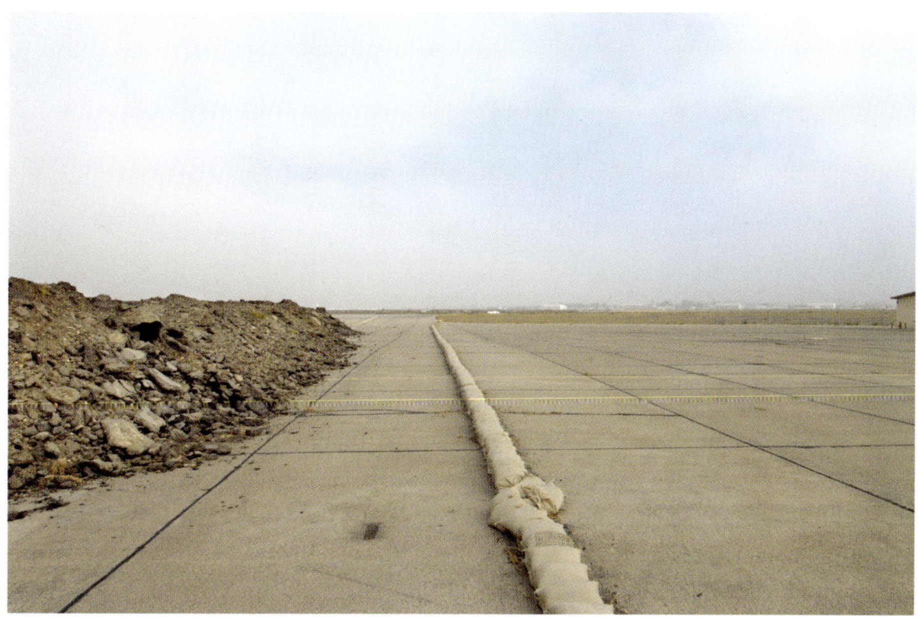
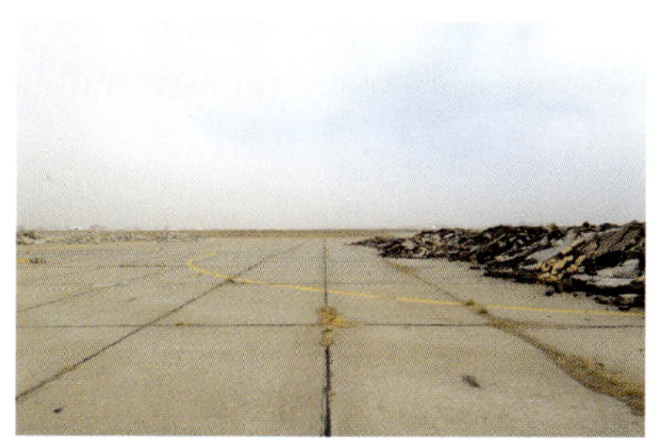
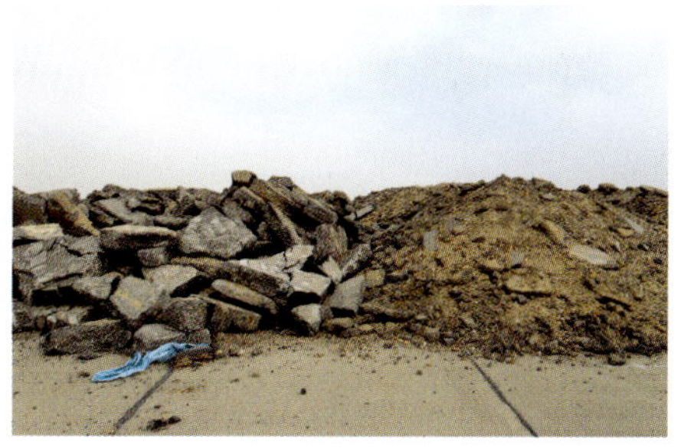
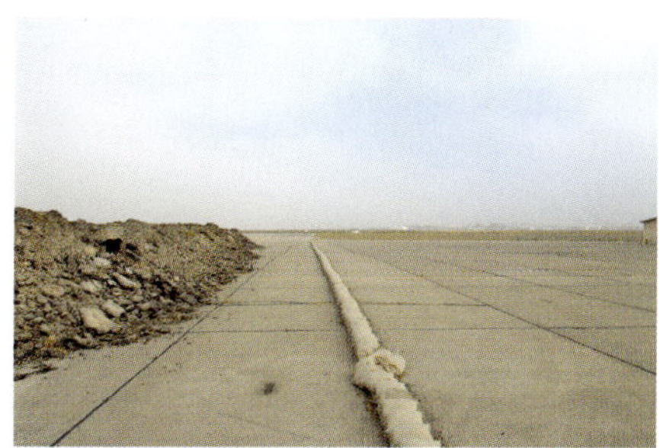

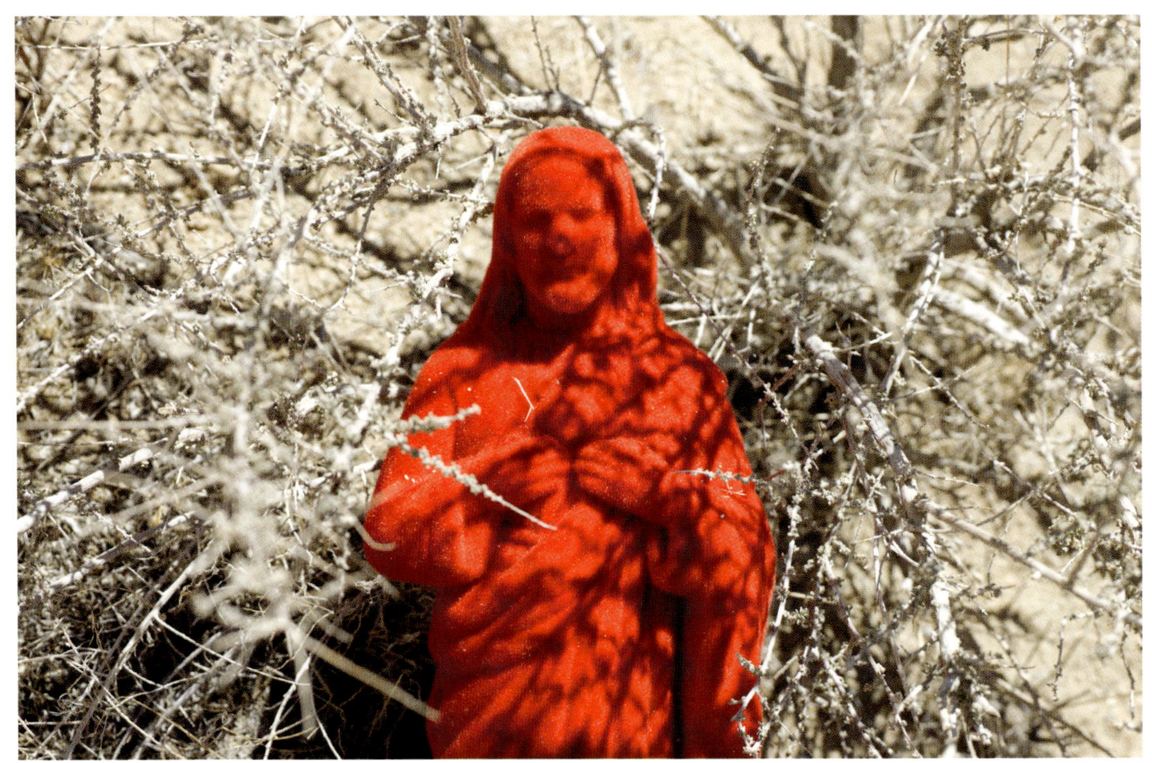

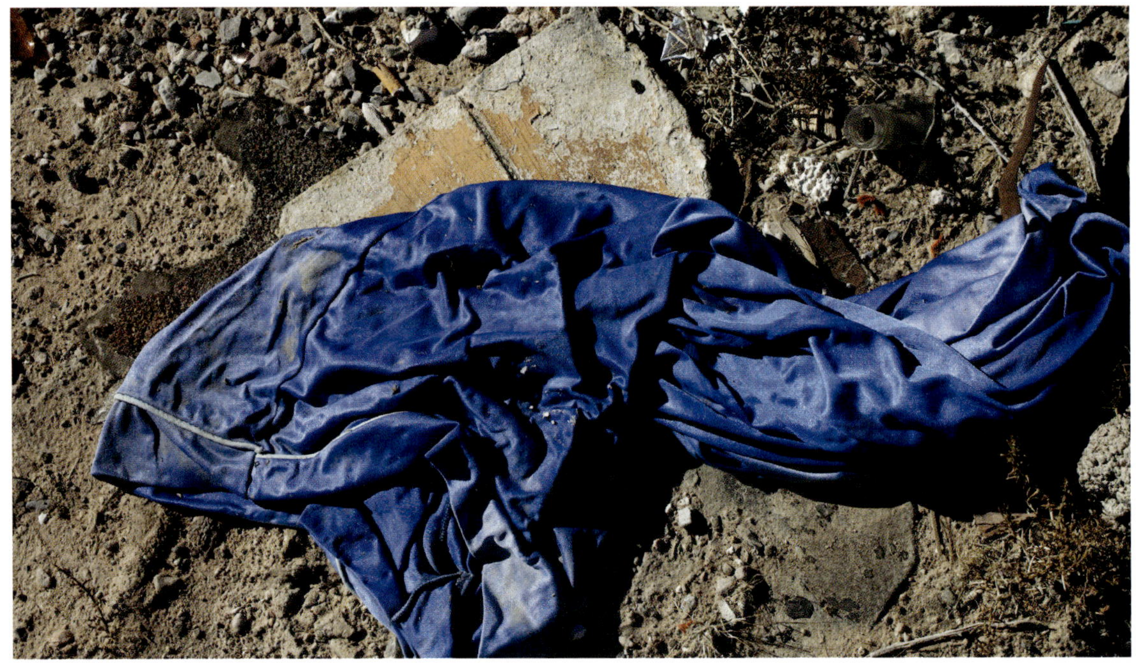

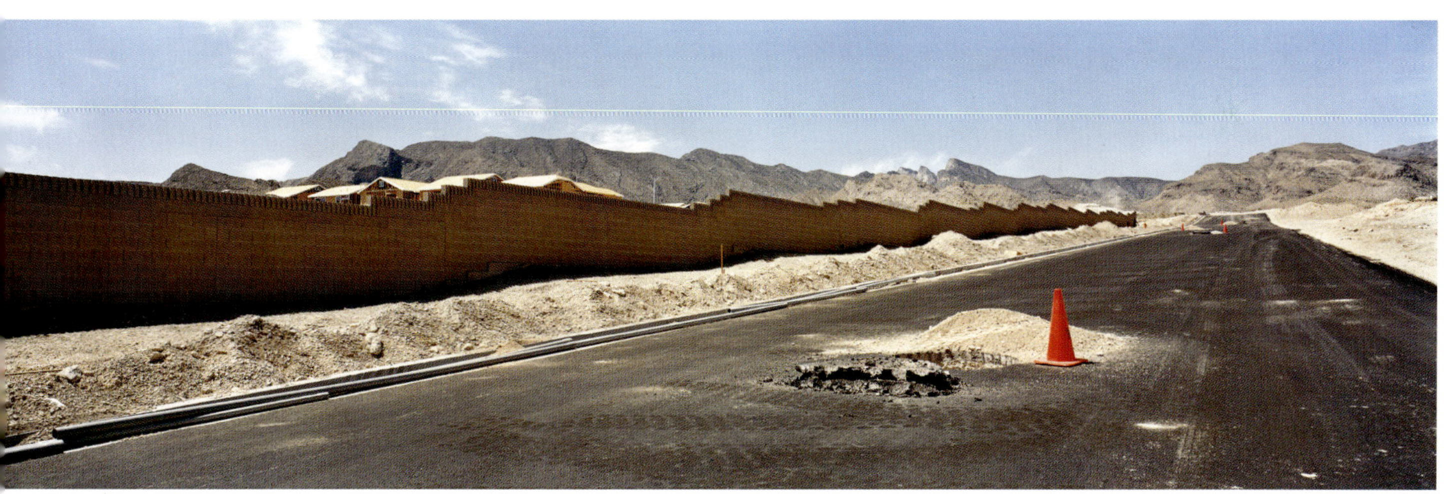

Graham Howe
Red Jesus, 2008
Archive digital ink jet print on Baryta paper

Las Vegas Dump, 2008
Archive digital ink jet print on Baryta paper
Courtesy of the artist

Laurie Brown
Markers at Stoneridge, Southwest Las Vegas, 2006
Archival lightjet print
Courtesy of the artist

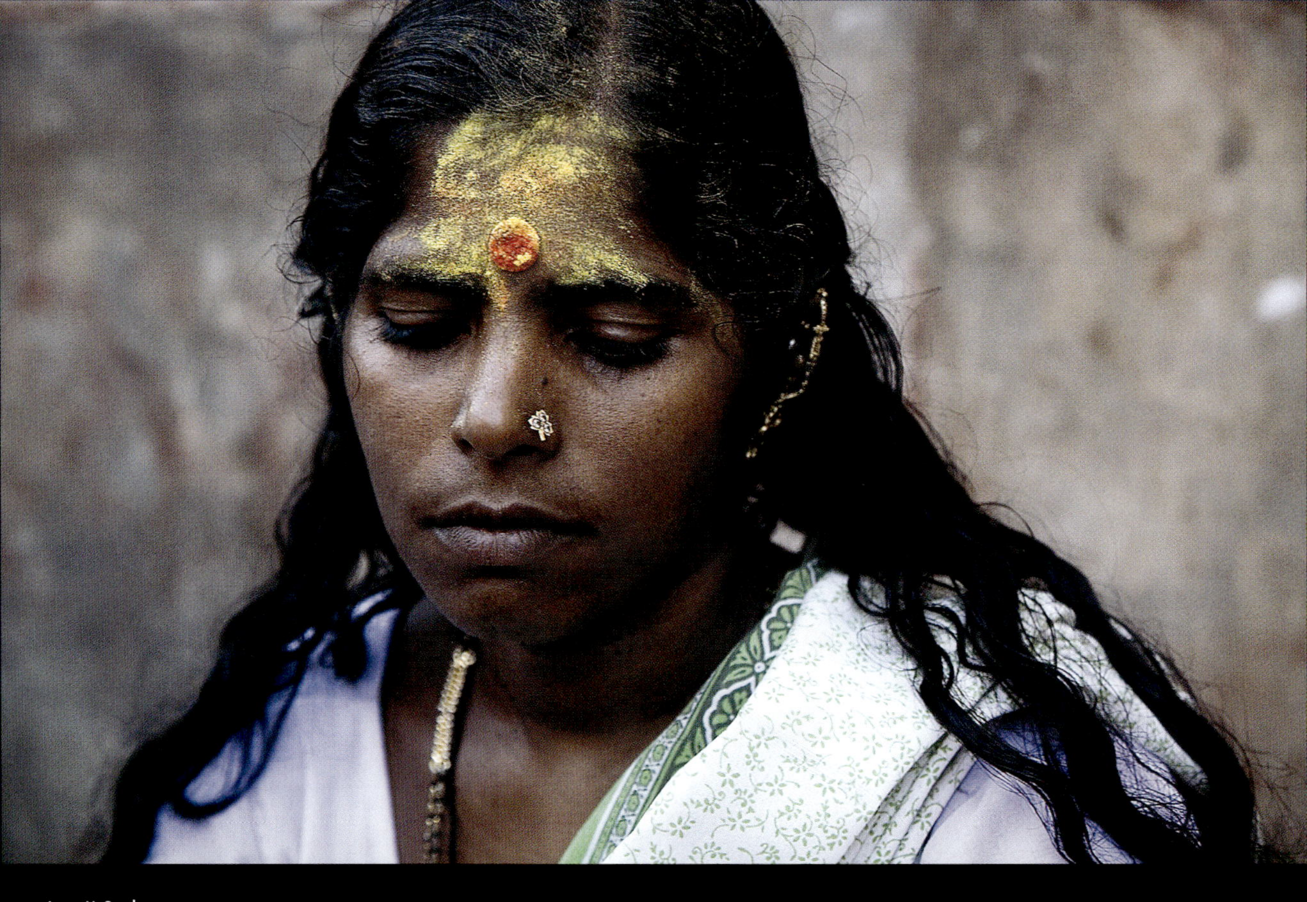

Jerry McGrath
Seventeen Year Old Devadasi Temple Prostitute, Belgaum District, Karnataka State, India, 2006-2009
Color C-print photograph on rag paper

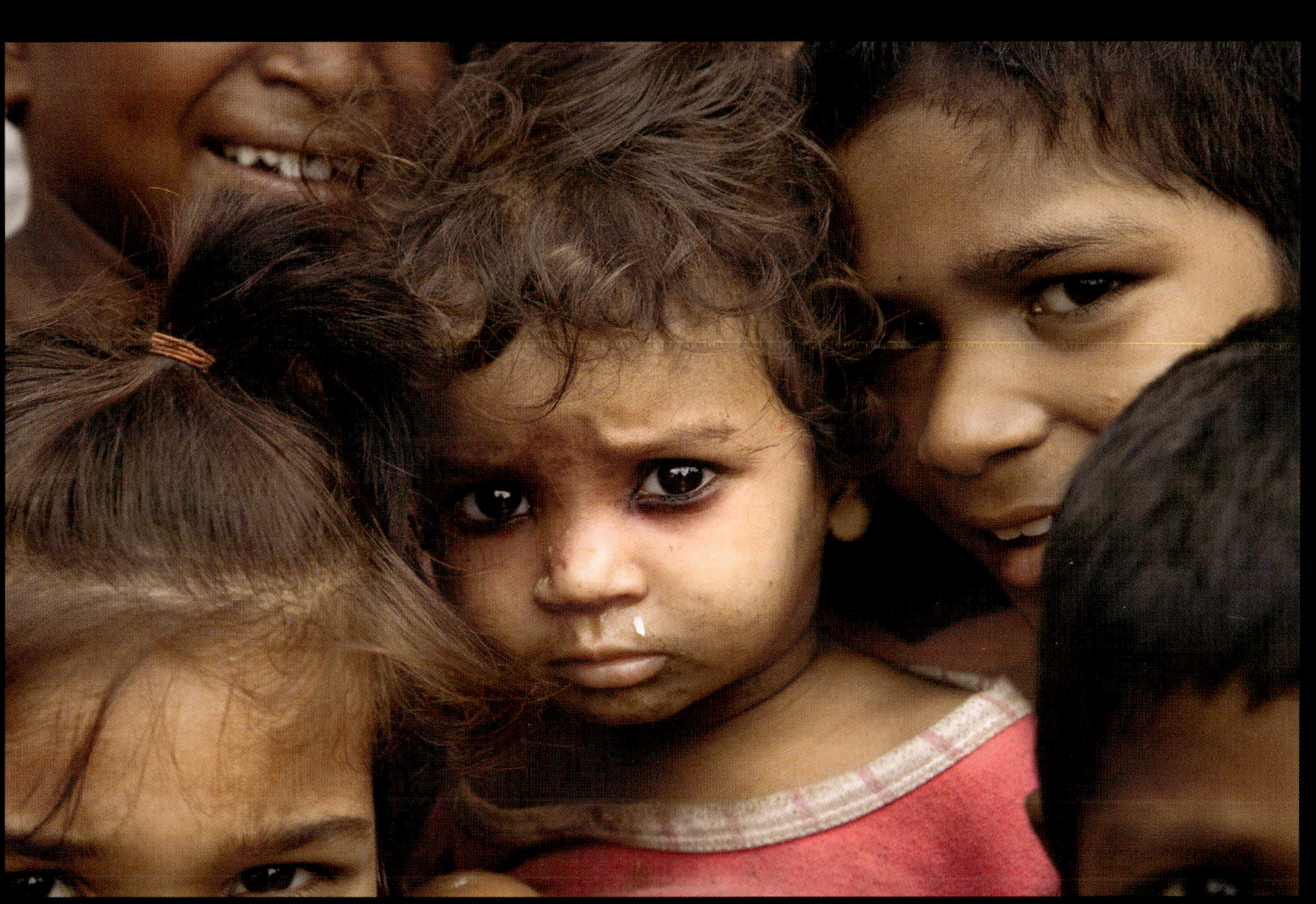

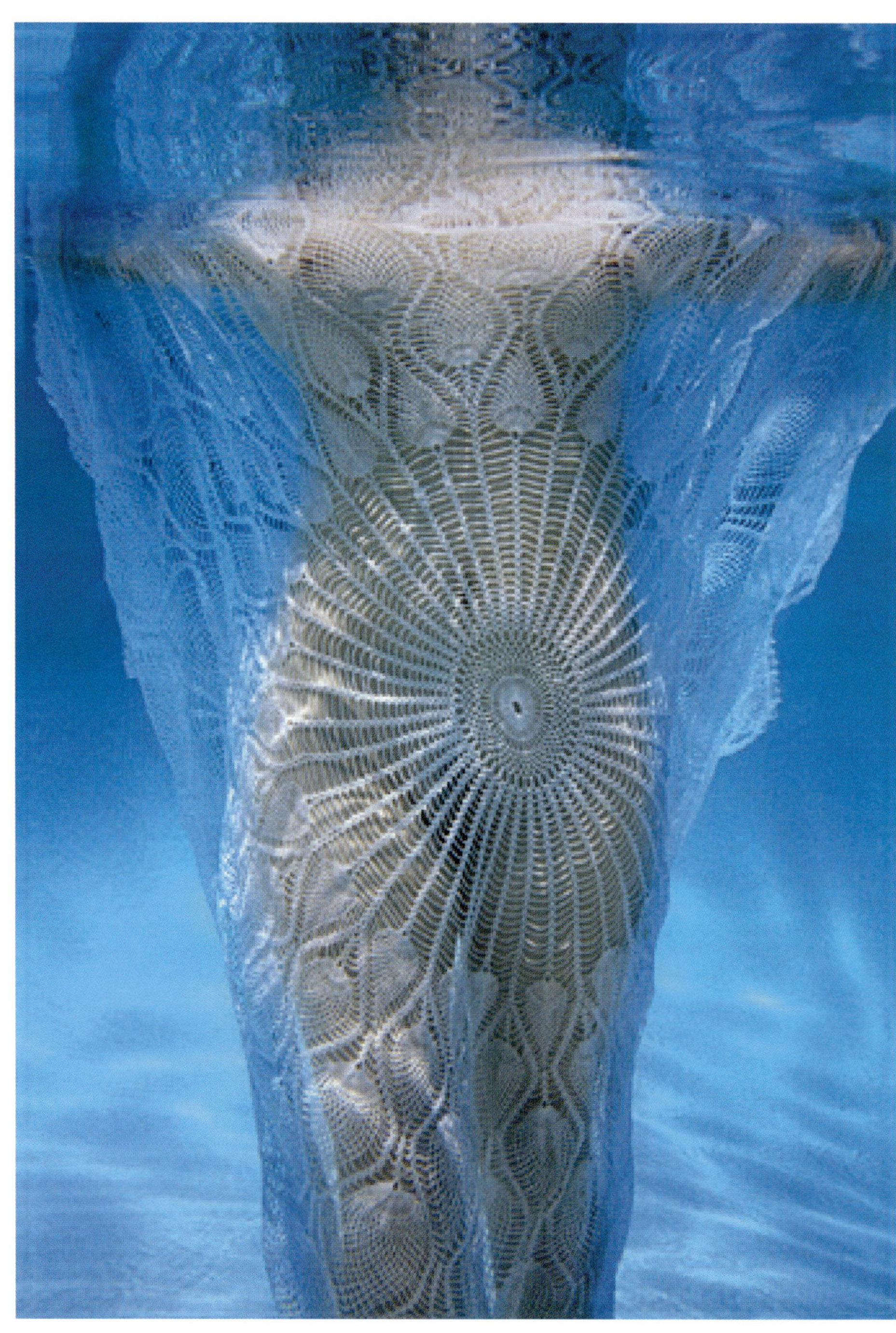

Kenda North
Urban Pools, 2005
Iris giclee print
Courtesy of Susan Spiritus Gallery

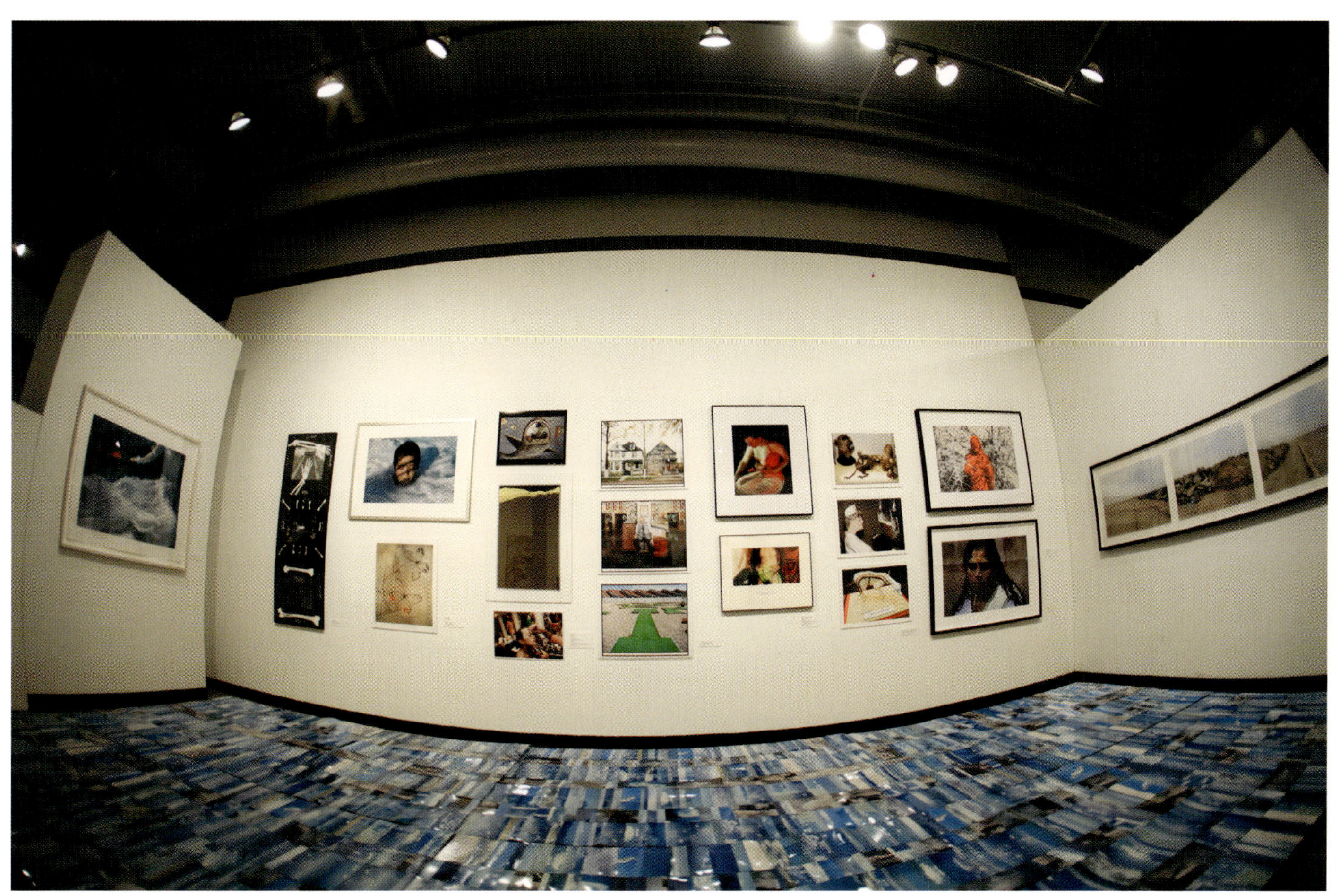

Installation - BC Space Exhibition
CSUF Grand Central Art Center, Santa Ana, CA.

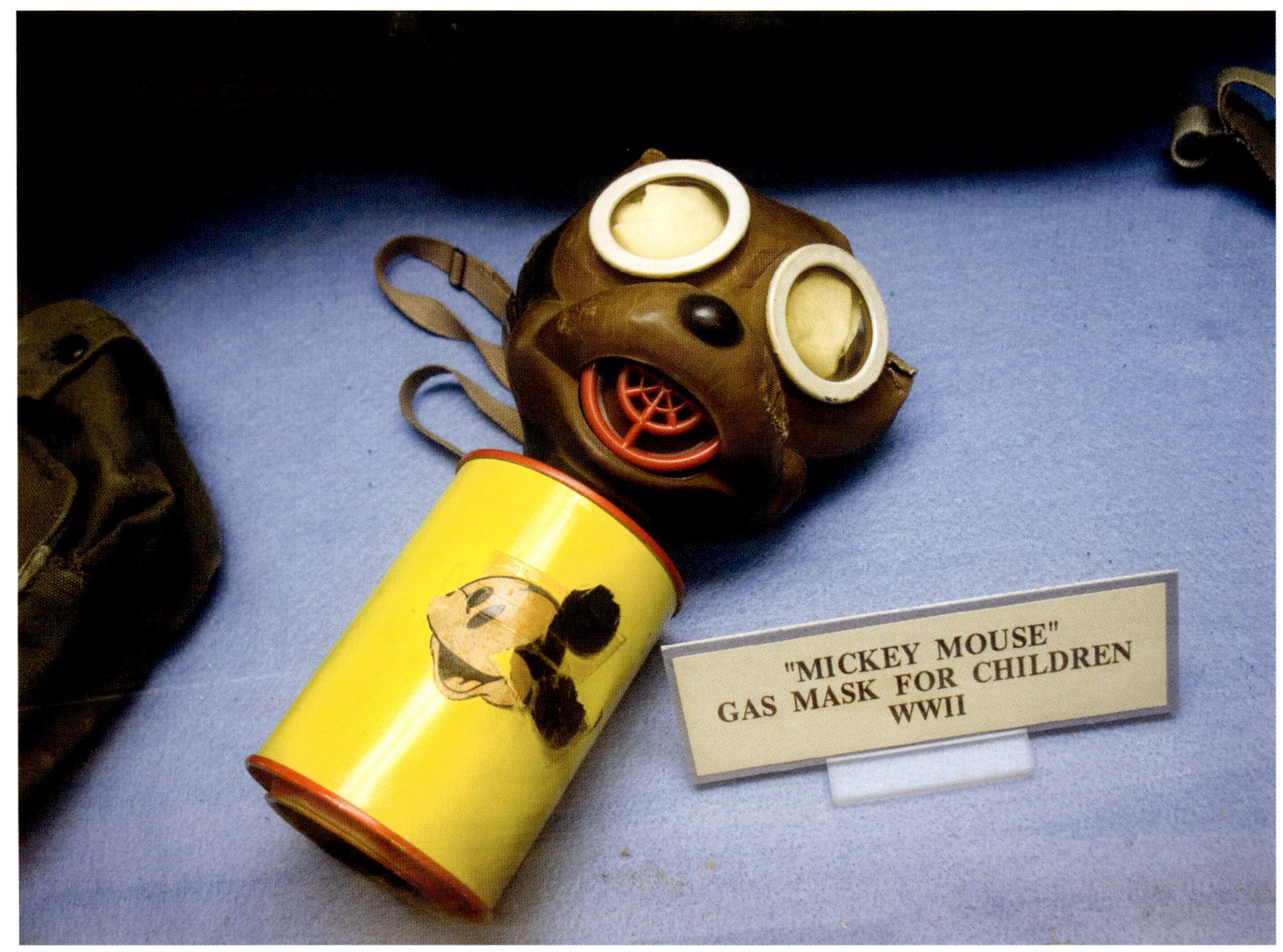

Arthur Taussig
MIckey Mouse Gas Mask for Children WWII, 54th Infantry Division
Museum, Oklahoma City, OK., 1992
Pigmented Archival print

Fiji Mermaid, Buckhorn Saloon and Museum, San Antonio, TX, 2006
Pigmented Archival print

Not Responsible, Dinosaus Land, Front Royal, VA., 2001
Pigmented Archival print
Courtesy of Stephen Cohen Gallery, Los Angeles

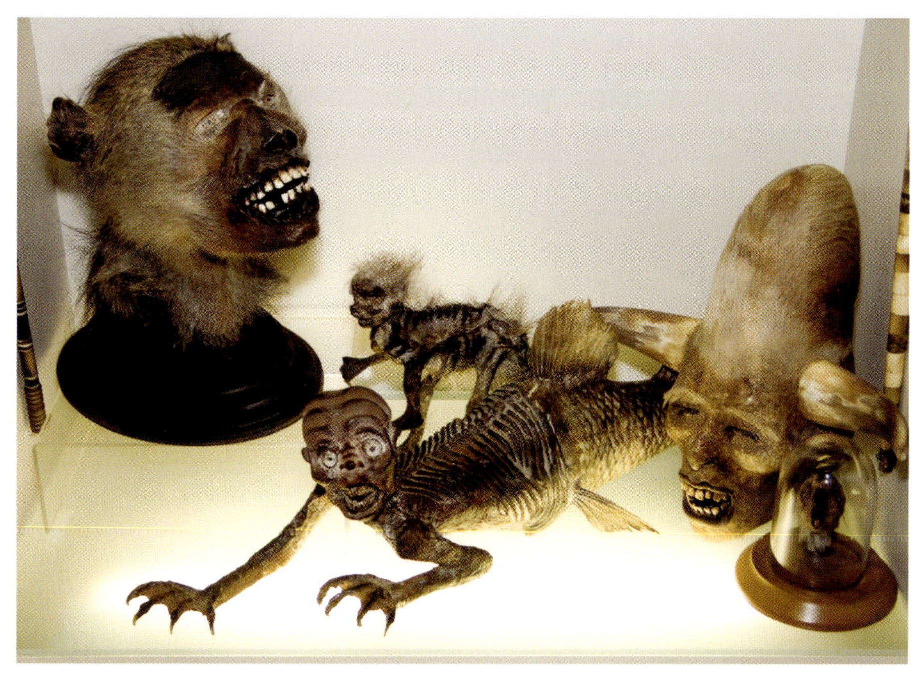

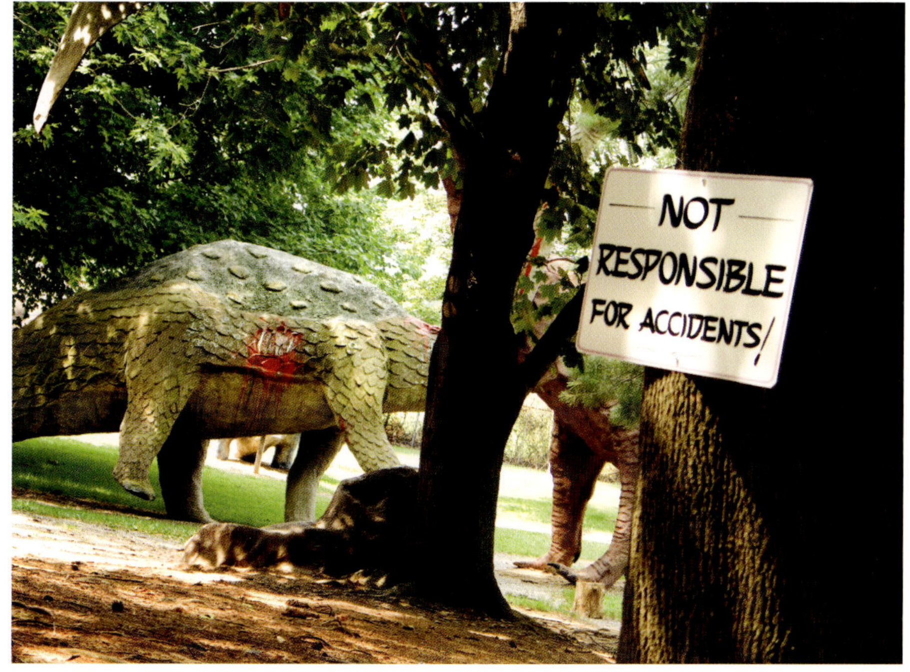
NOT
RESPONSIBLE
FOR ACCIDENTS!

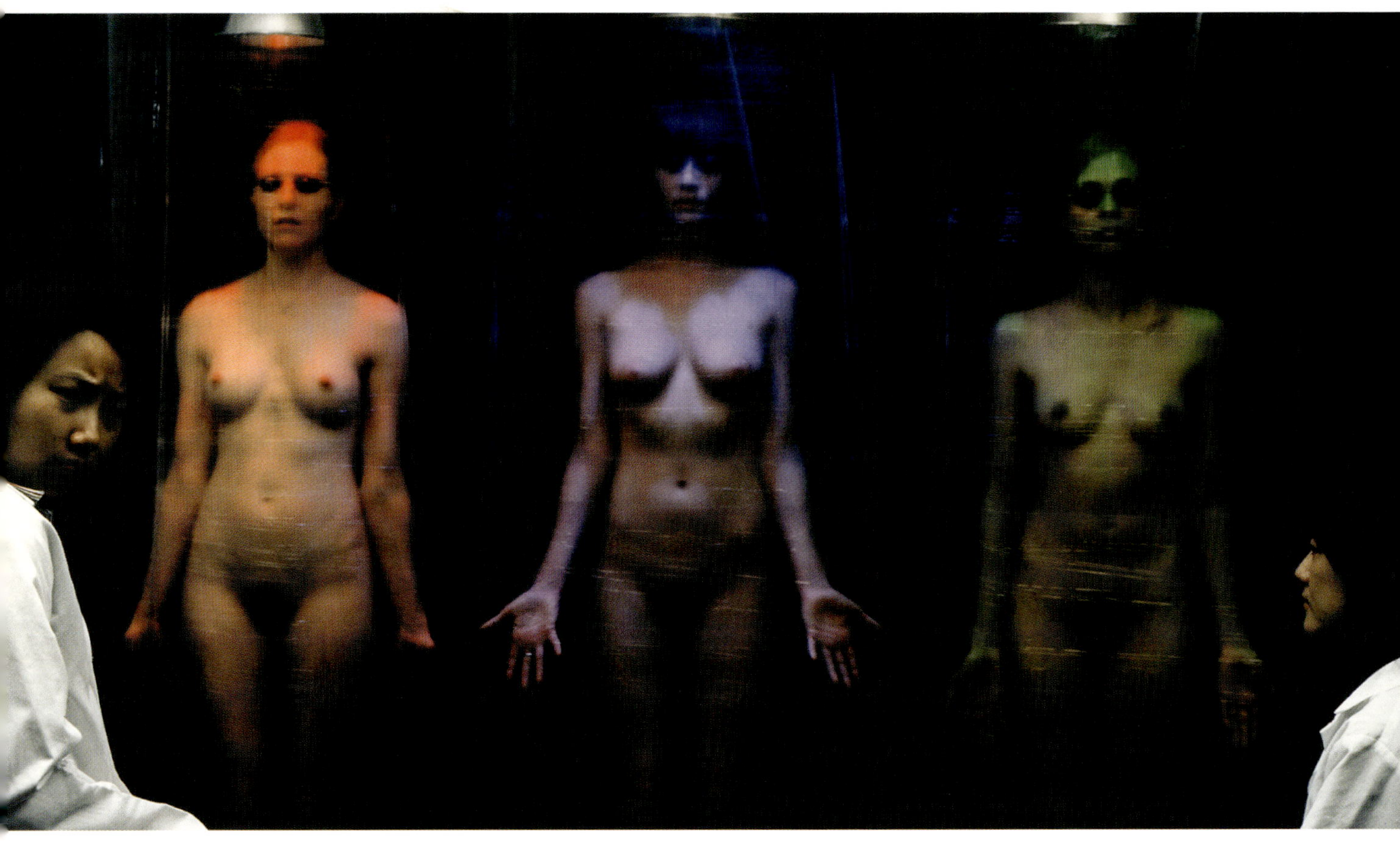

Patrick Ryoichi Nagatani
Chromatherapy Series
Primary Light Test, Beijing Institute Of Scientific Study, China, 2005/2006

Tonation In Color Charged H2O, 2004
Chromogenic Print (Ilfoflex 2000)
Mounted on anodized aluminum

Ryoichi and Sid – Albuquerque, New Mexico, 2005
Chromogenic Print (Ilfoflex 2000)
Mounted on anodized aluminum
Courtesy of the artist

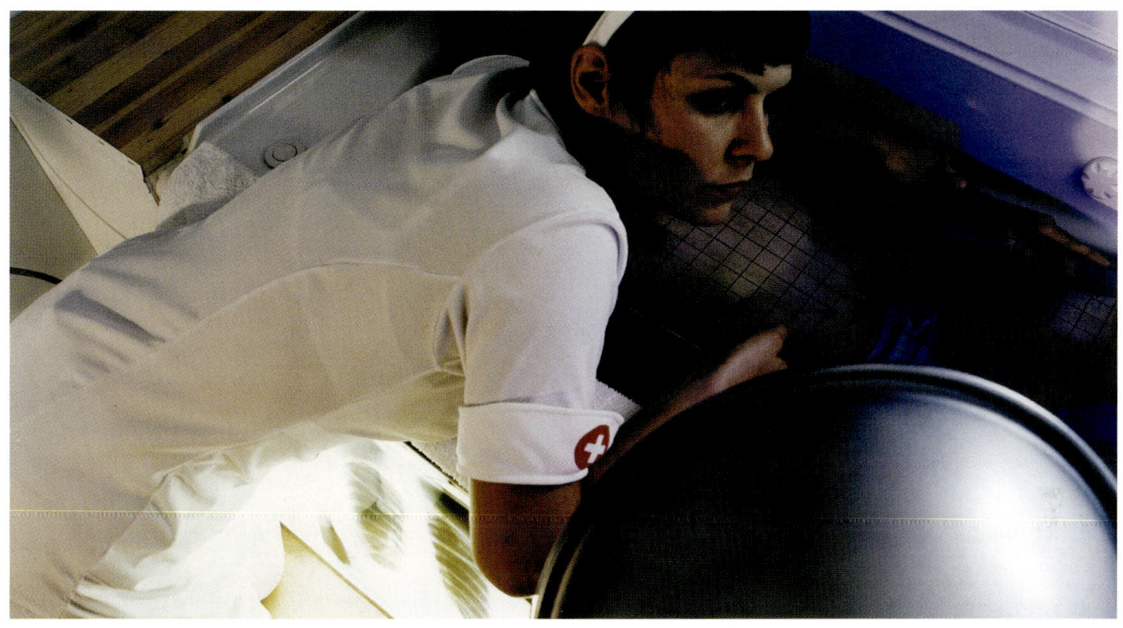

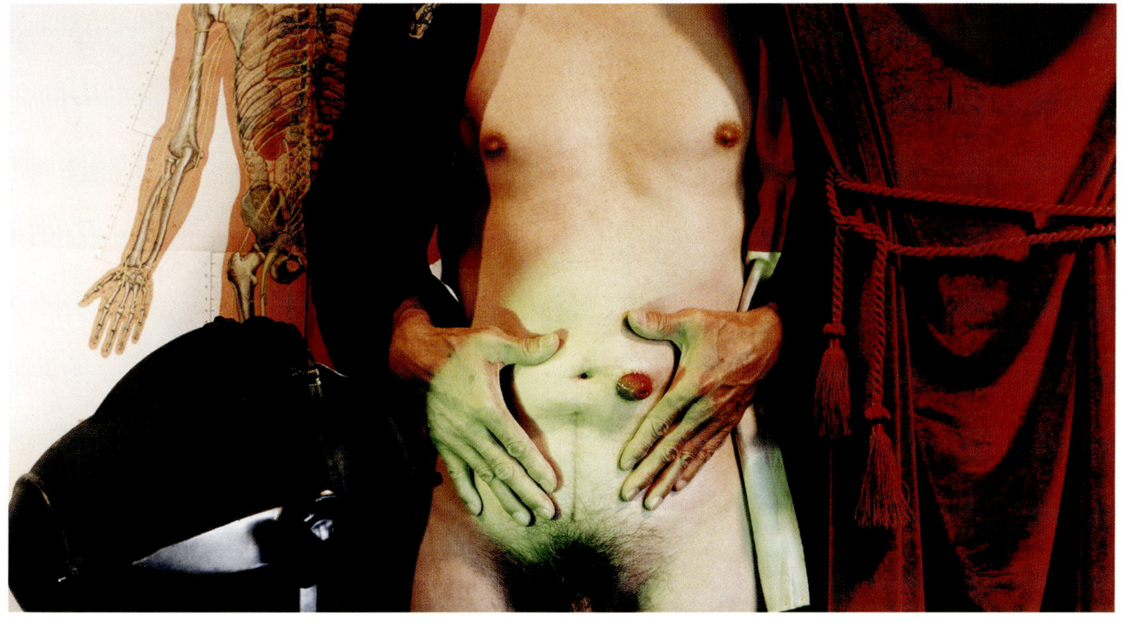

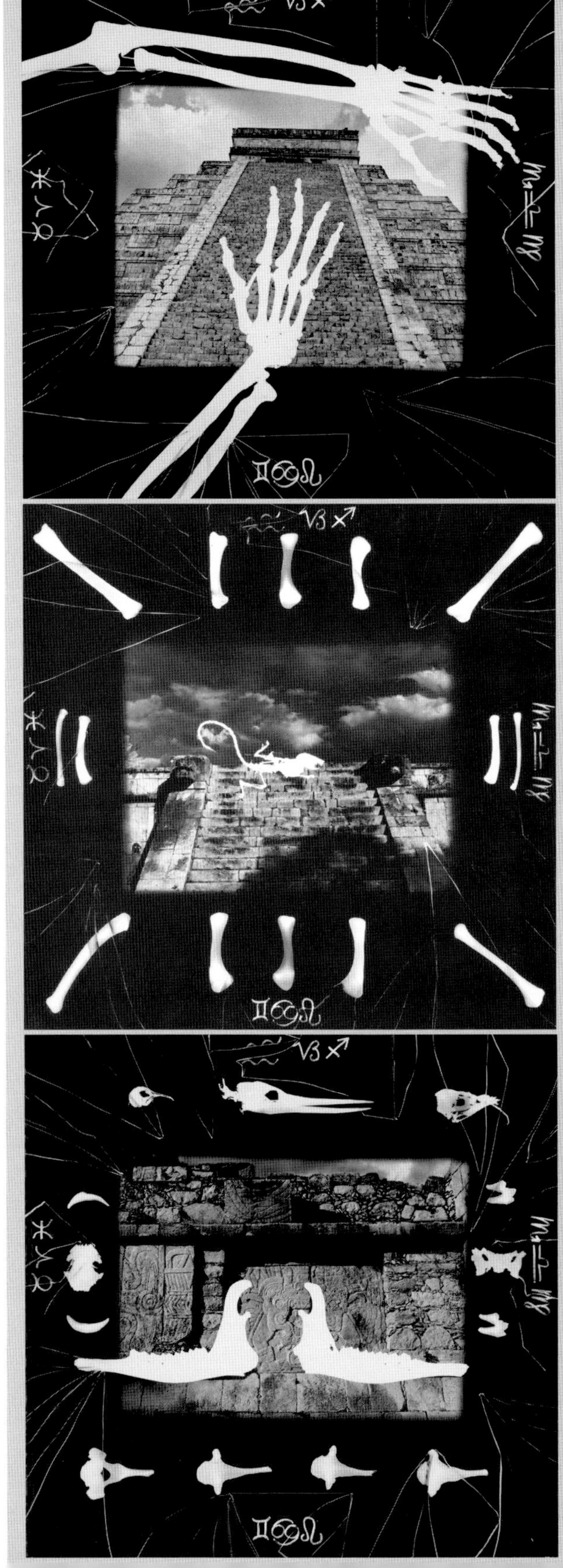

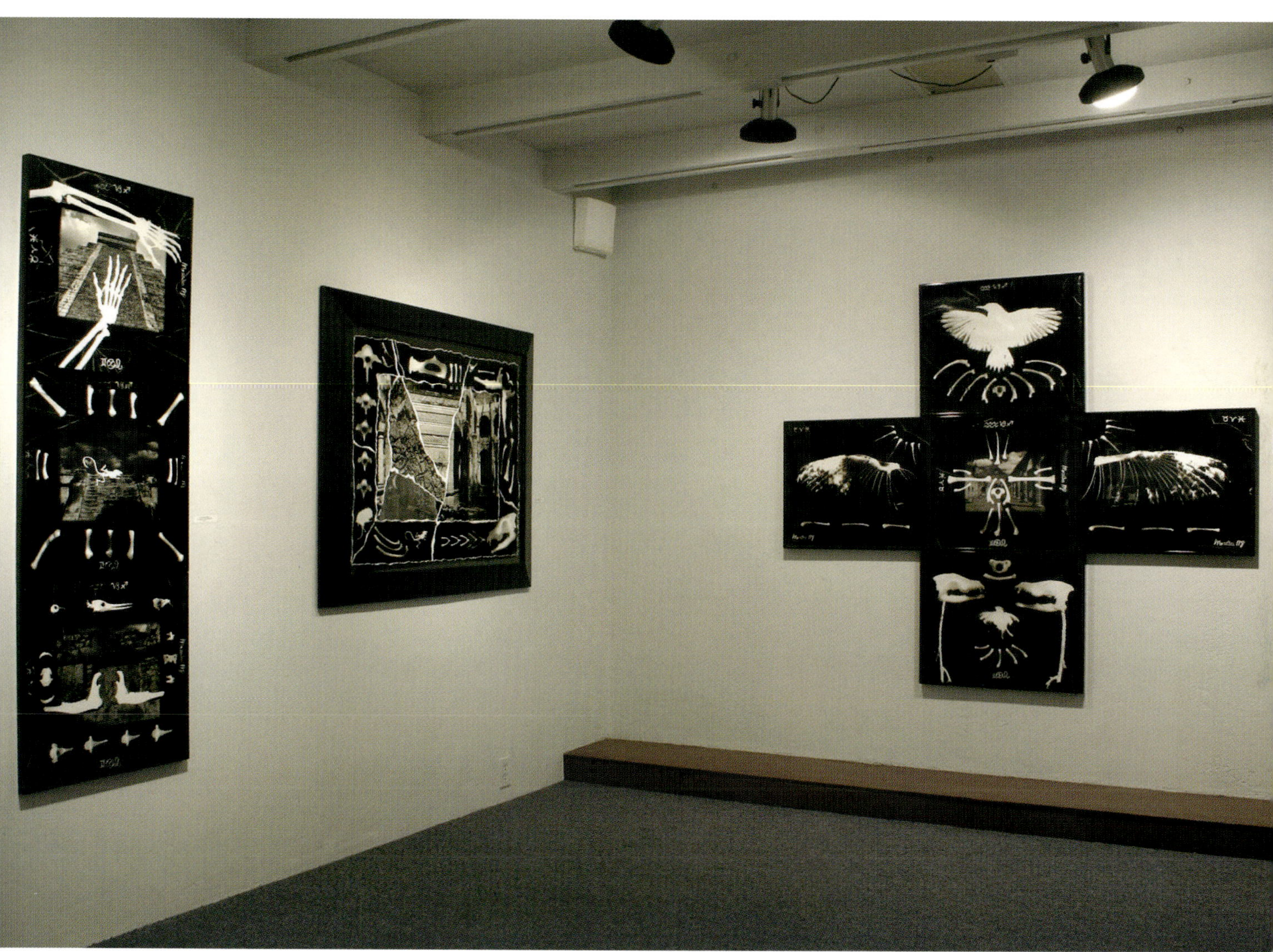

Marsha Red Adams
Chichen Itza' Dream, 1996
Gelatin silver print/photogram and negative image
Courtesy of the artist

Installation BC Space
Laguna Beach , CA.
Image courtesy of BC Space

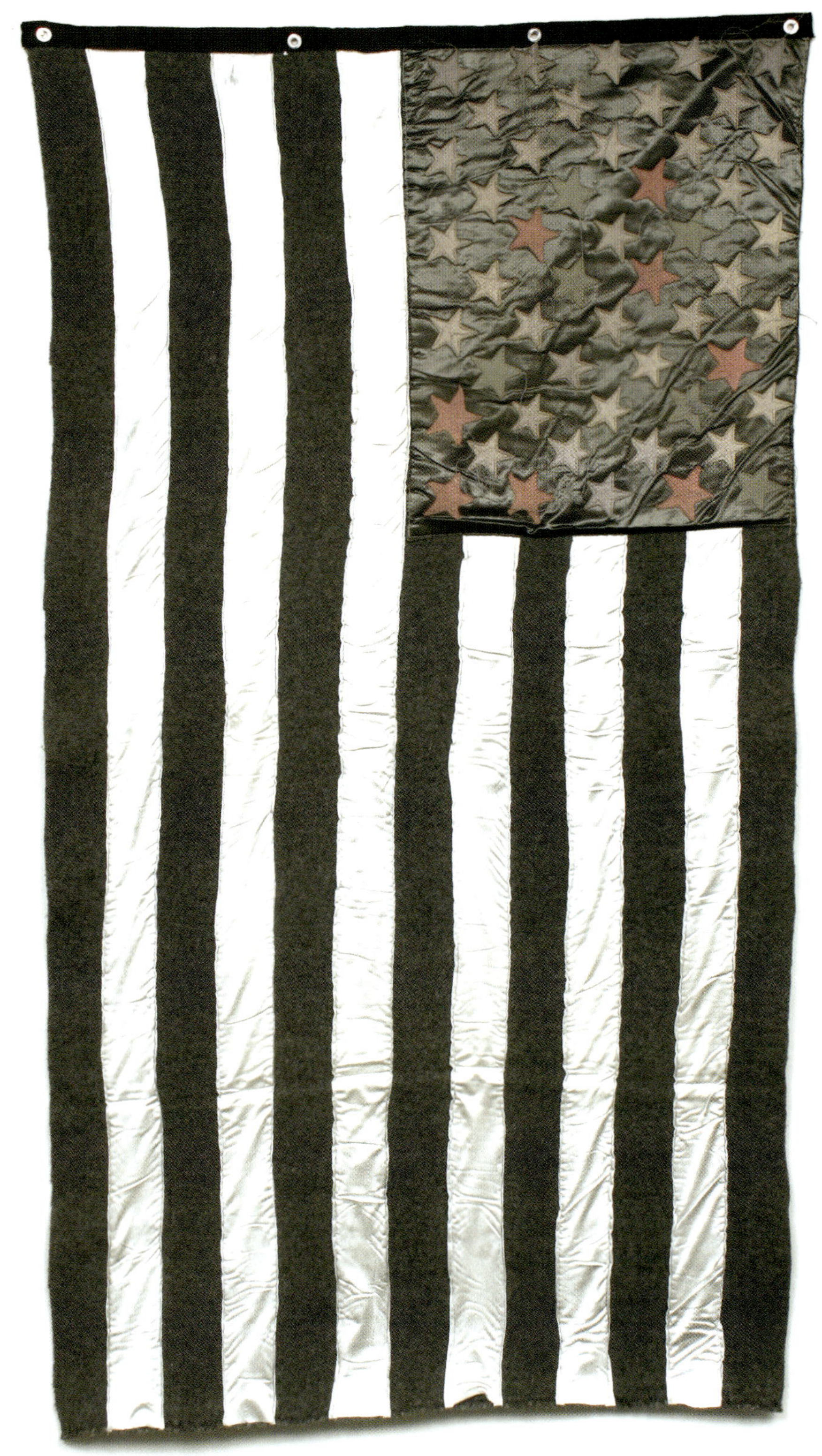

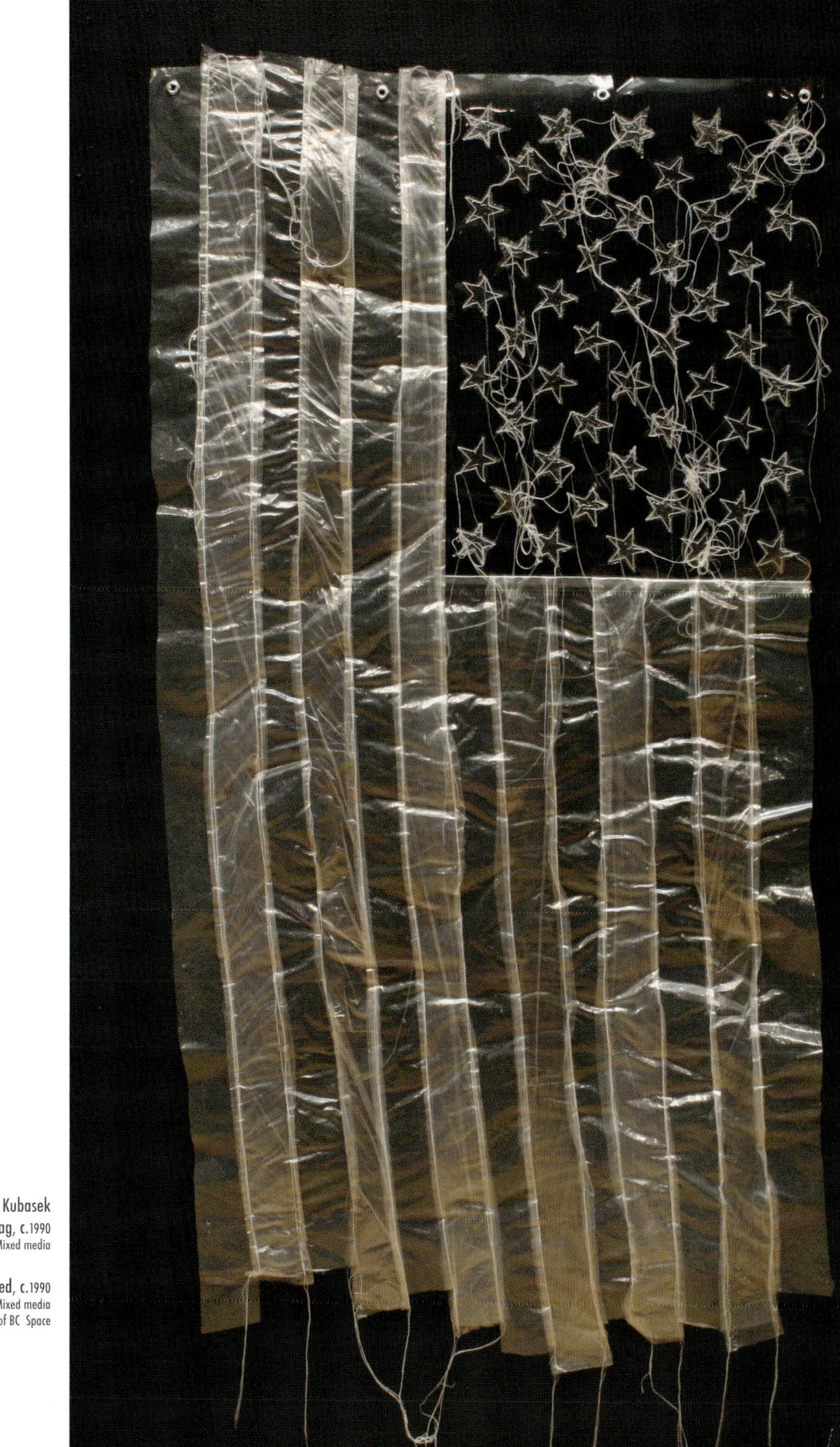

Lynn Kubasek
Space Flag, c.1990
Mixed media

Fatigued, c.1990
Mixed media
Photos courtesy of BC Space

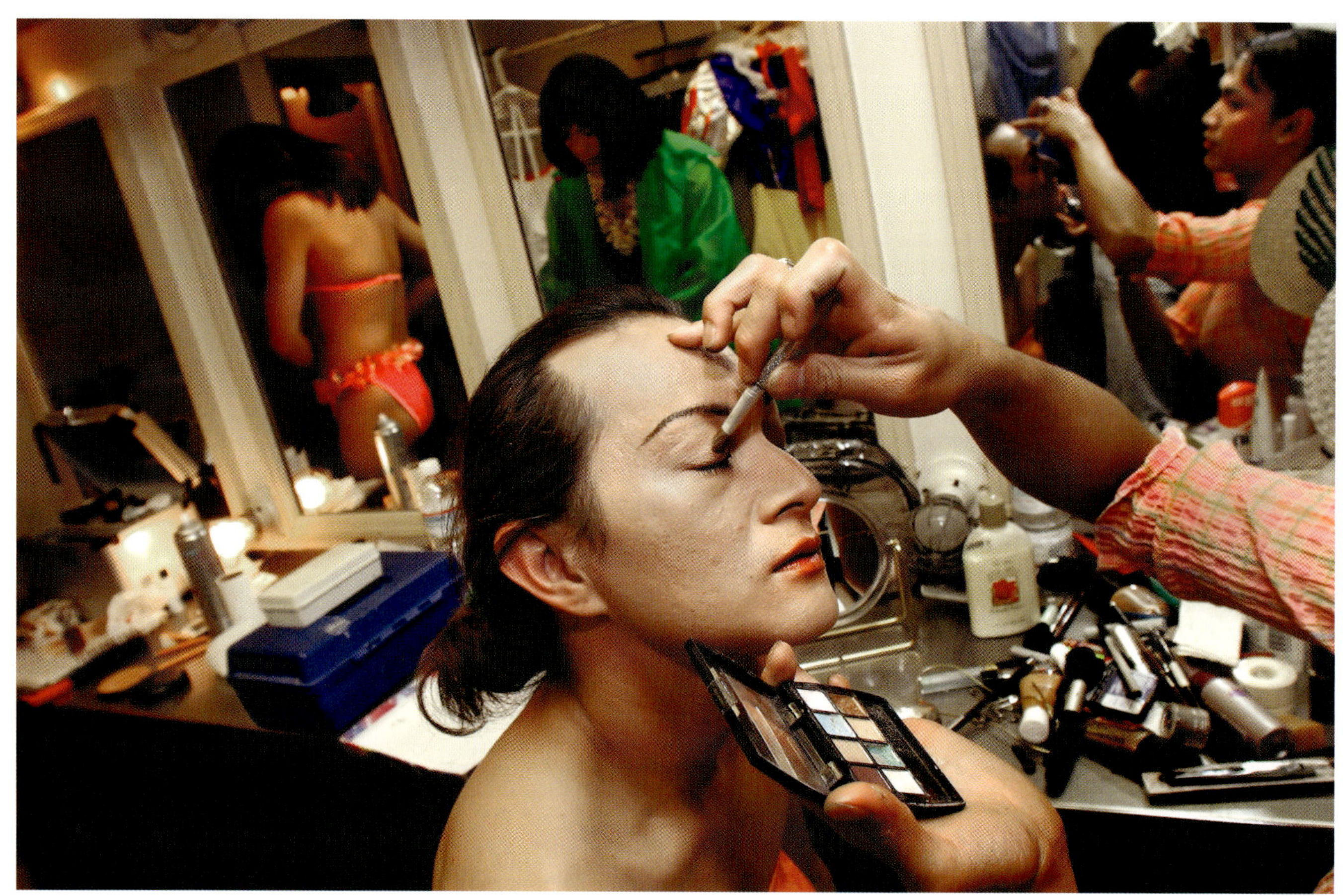

Lonny Shavelson
Gay Asian Pacific Alliance Pageant. San Francisco. July 13, 2002
From the book, "Under the Dragon: California's New Culture."
Digital print
Courtesy of the artist

George Blakely
The Sky is Falling?, 2009
Offset photo collage
Courtesy of the artist

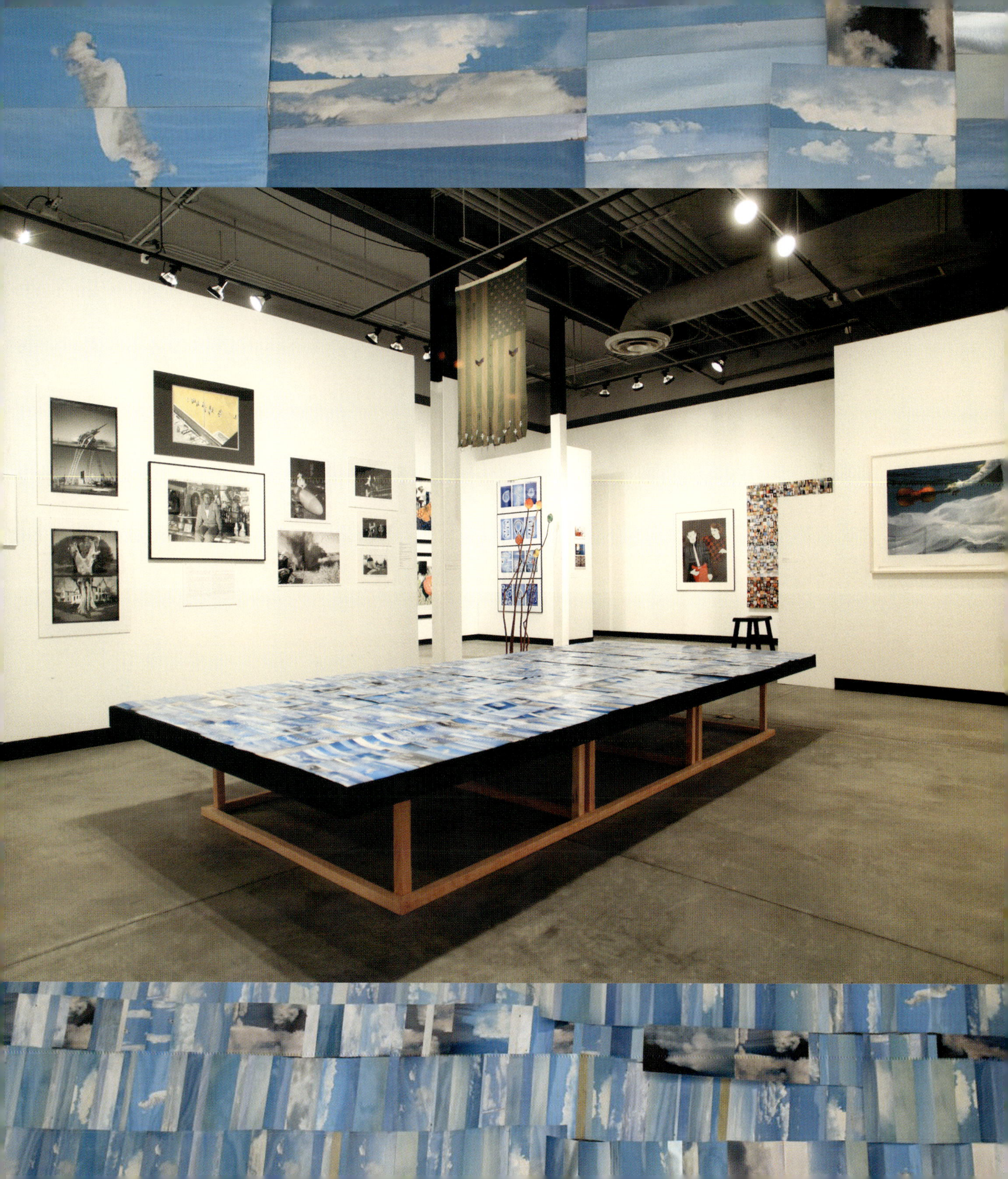

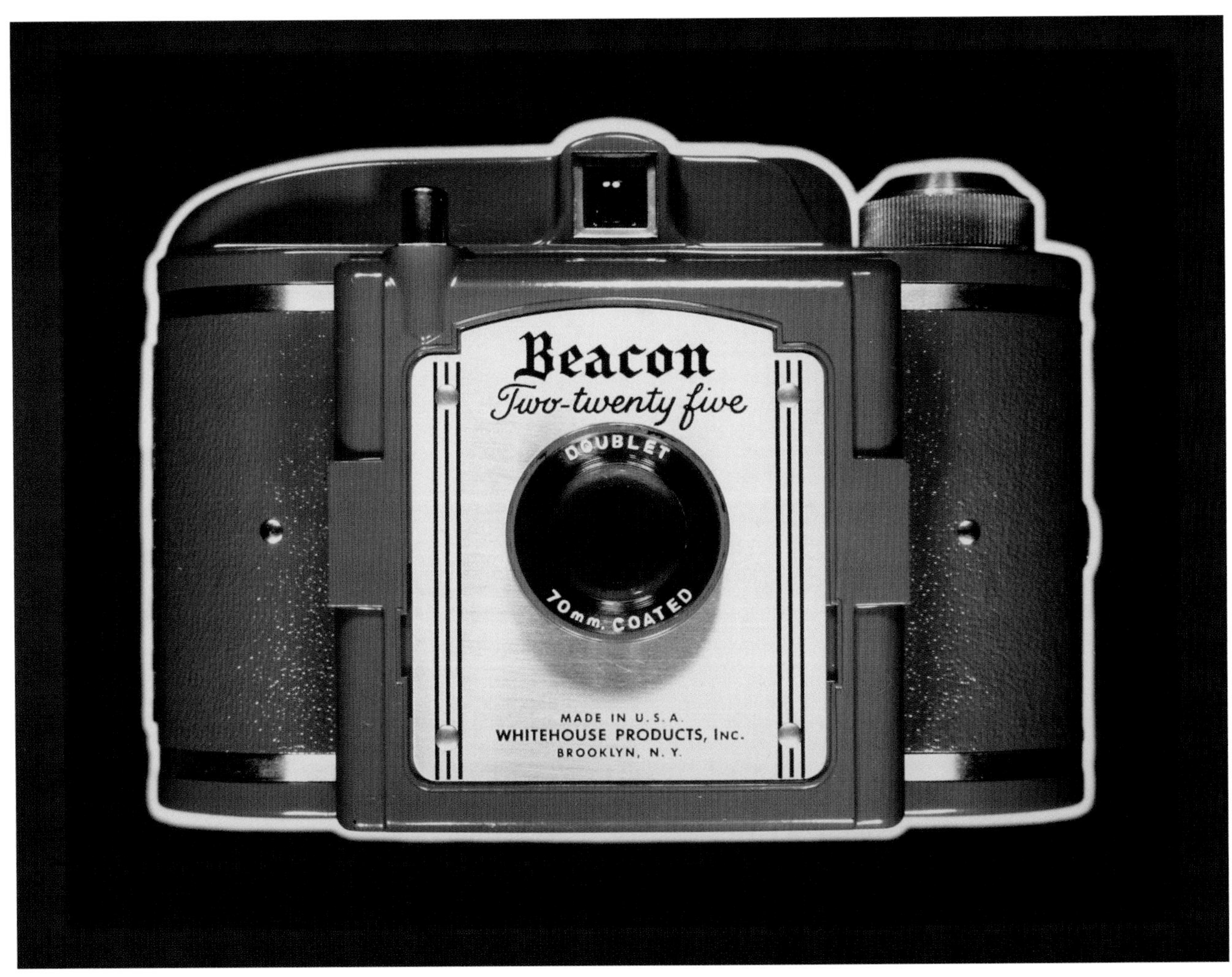

Victor Landweber
Beacon 225, 1988
Cibachrome print
Courtesy of Mark Chamberlain

Jack Butler
Together Series/The Look #10, 1983
Cibachrome with applied color
Courtesy of Sherry Frumkin Gallery

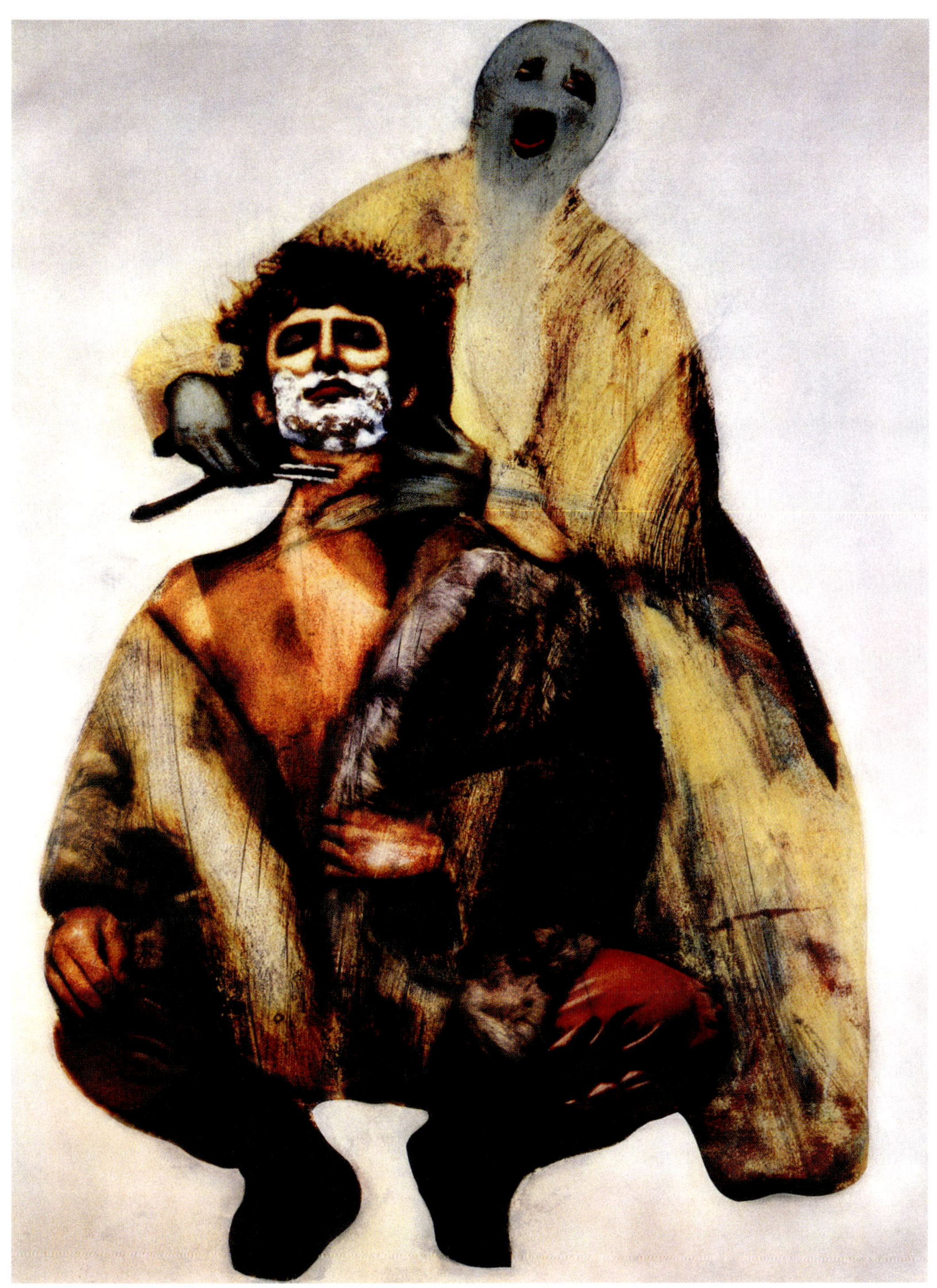

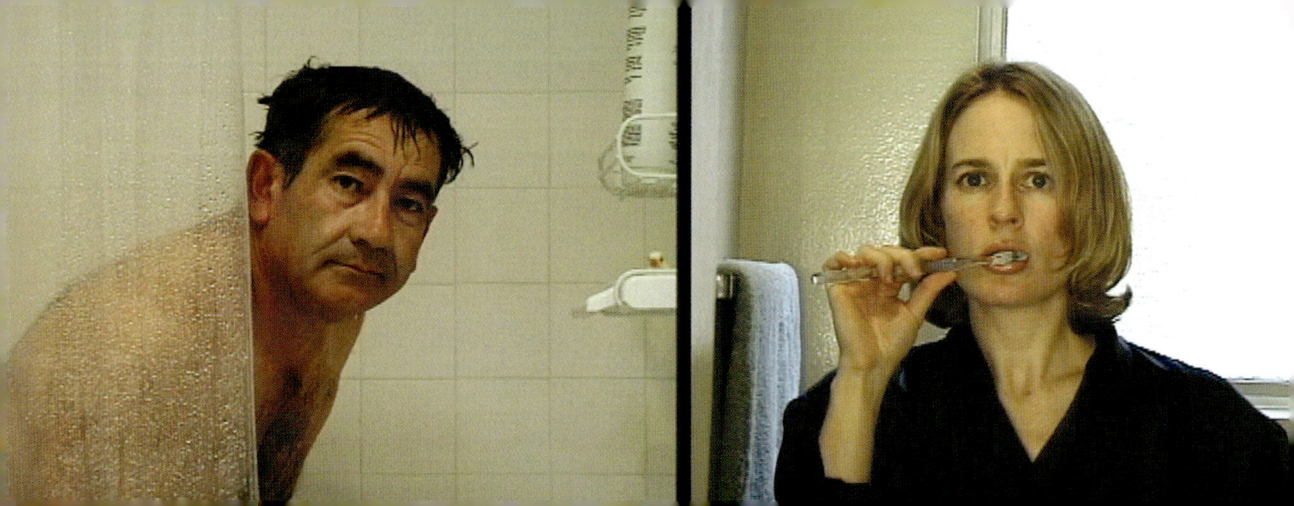

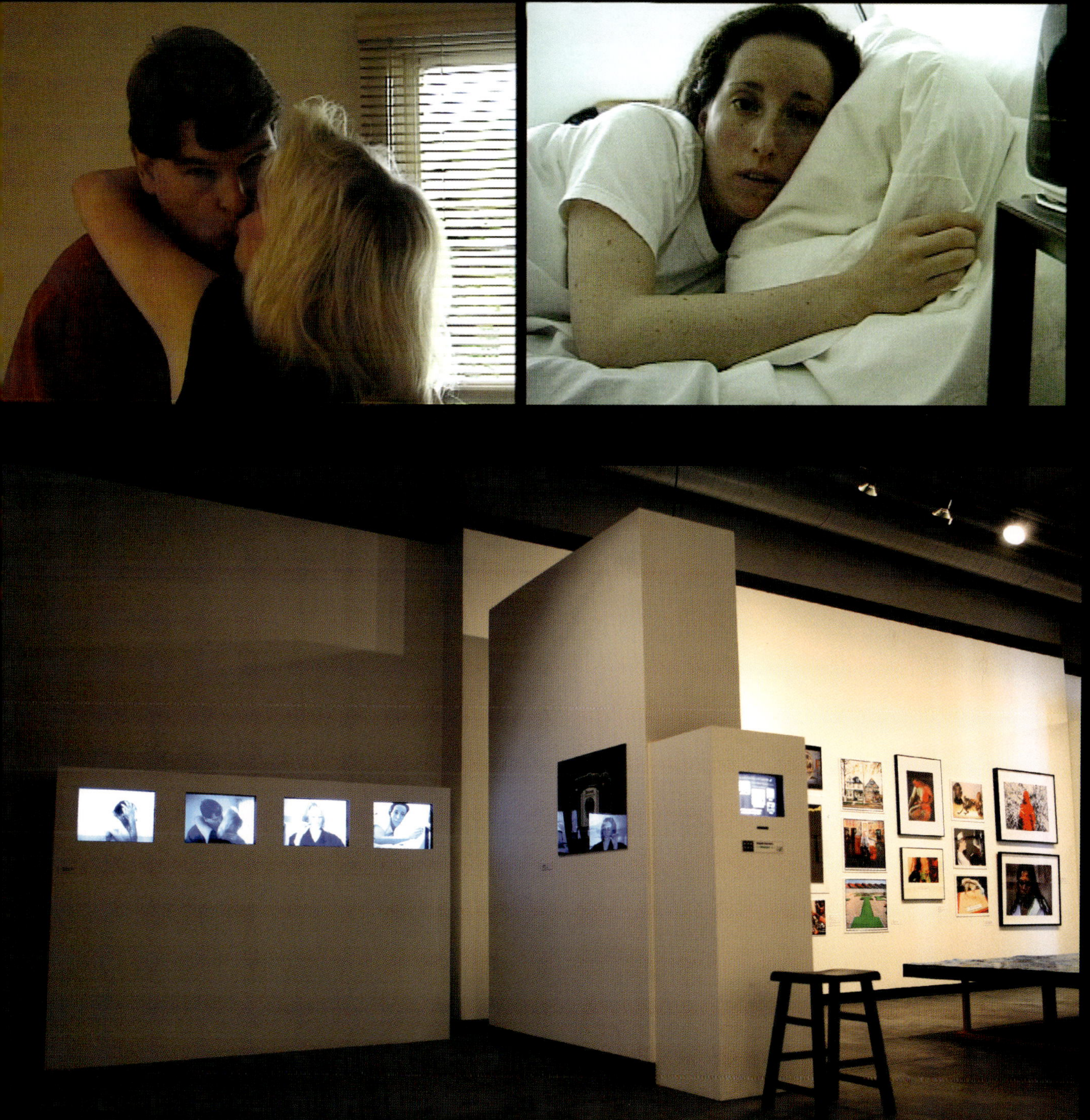

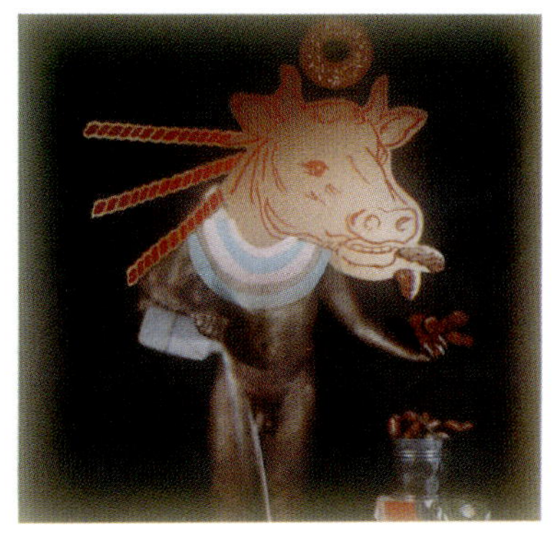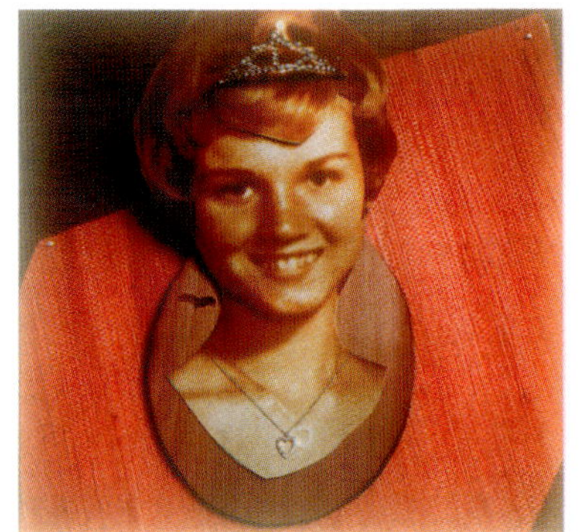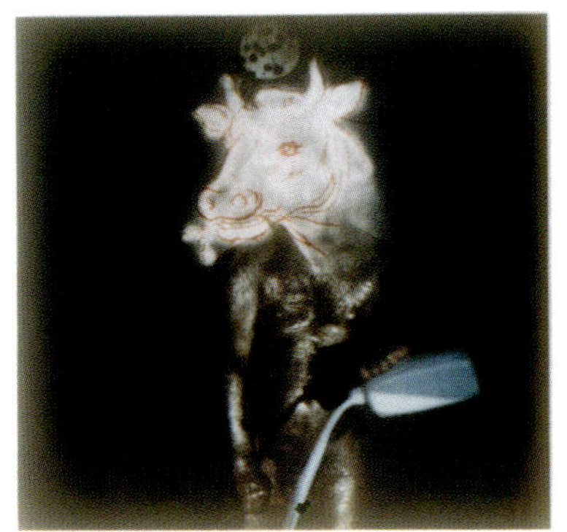

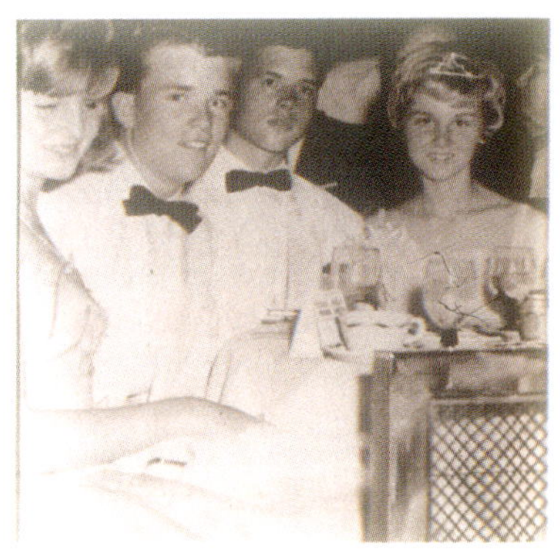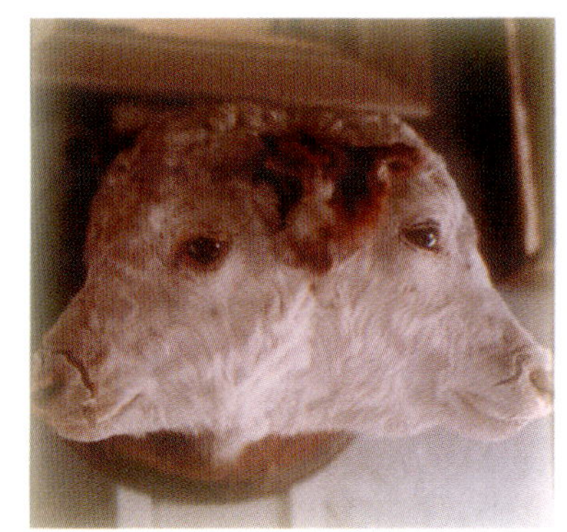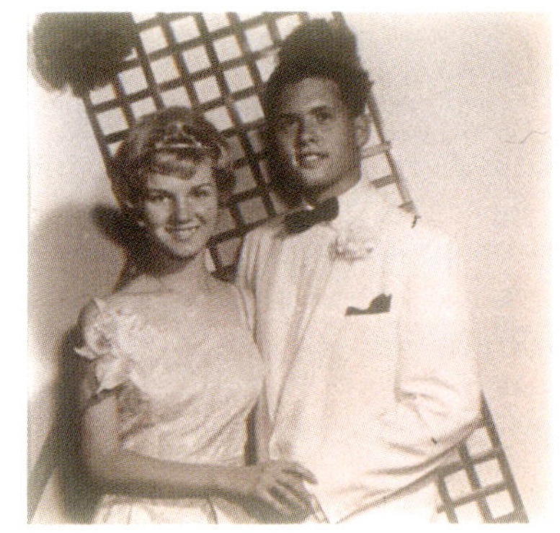

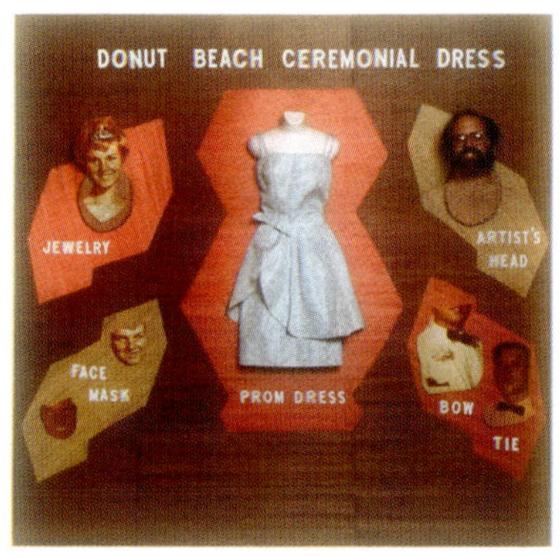
DONUT BEACH CEREMONIAL DRESS
JEWELRY
ARTIST'S HEAD
FACE MASK
PROM DRESS
BOW
TIE

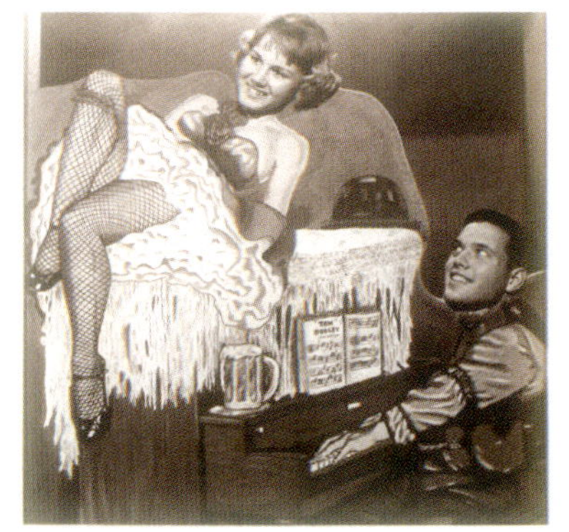

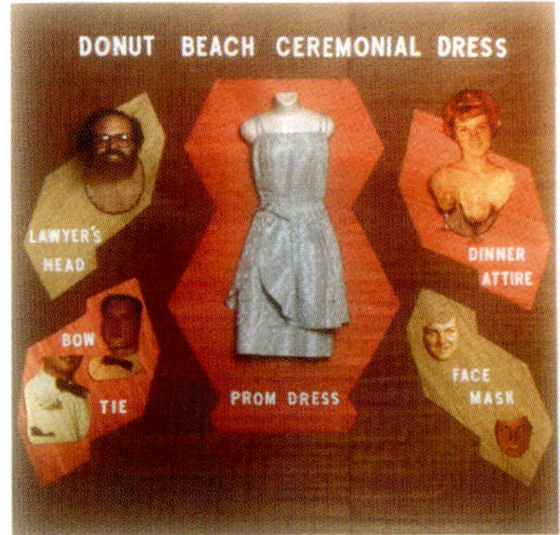
DONUT BEACH CEREMONIAL DRESS
LAWYER'S HEAD
DINNER ATTIRE
BOW
TIE
PROM DRESS
FACE MASK

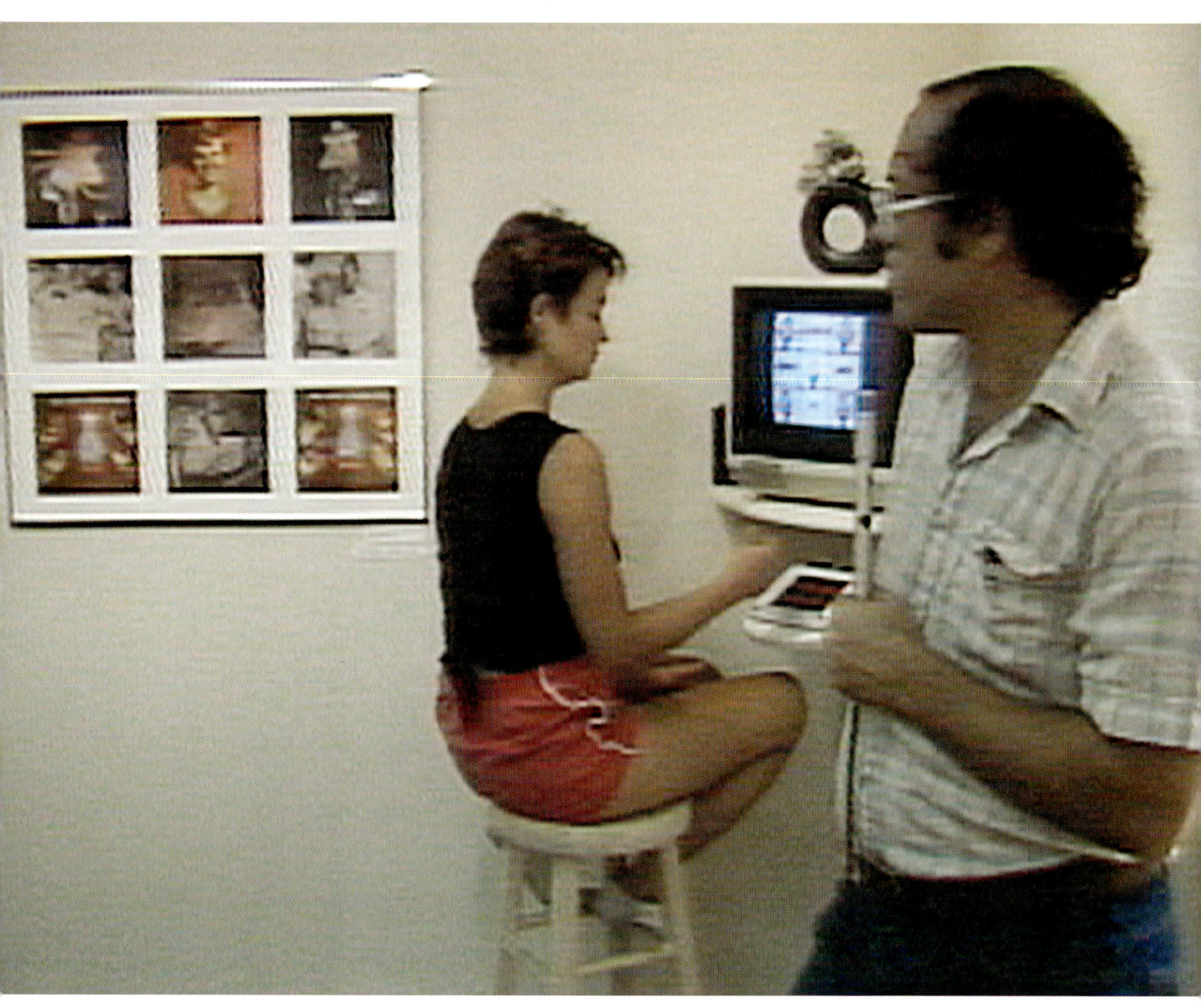

Stephen Axelrad
Donut Beach Research Center: The Documentary, 1984-2010
Interactive Video
Courtesy of the artist

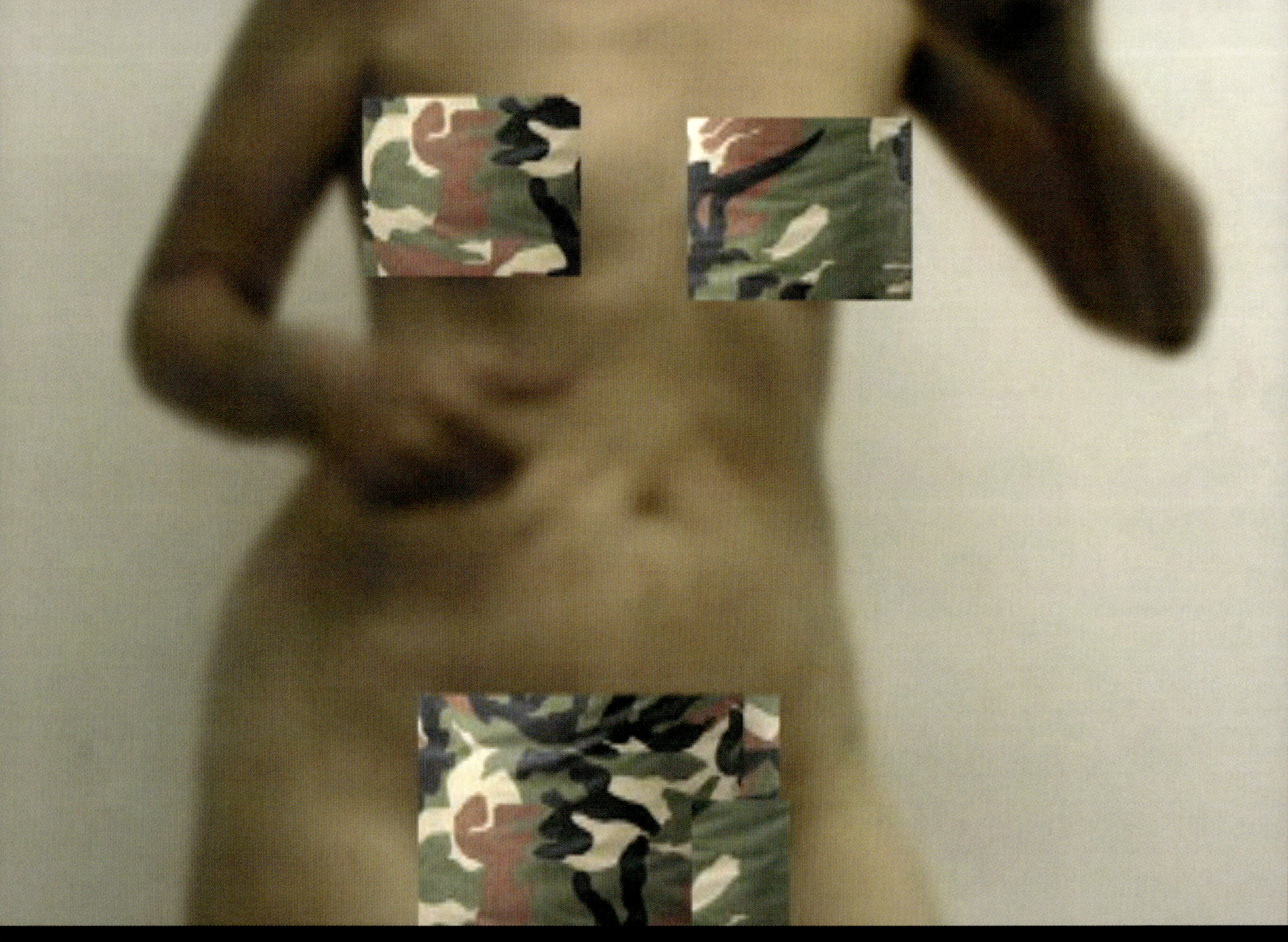

Barbara Berk
hi! hi! hey!, 2005
Video

War and Peace, 2006
Video
Courtesy of the artist

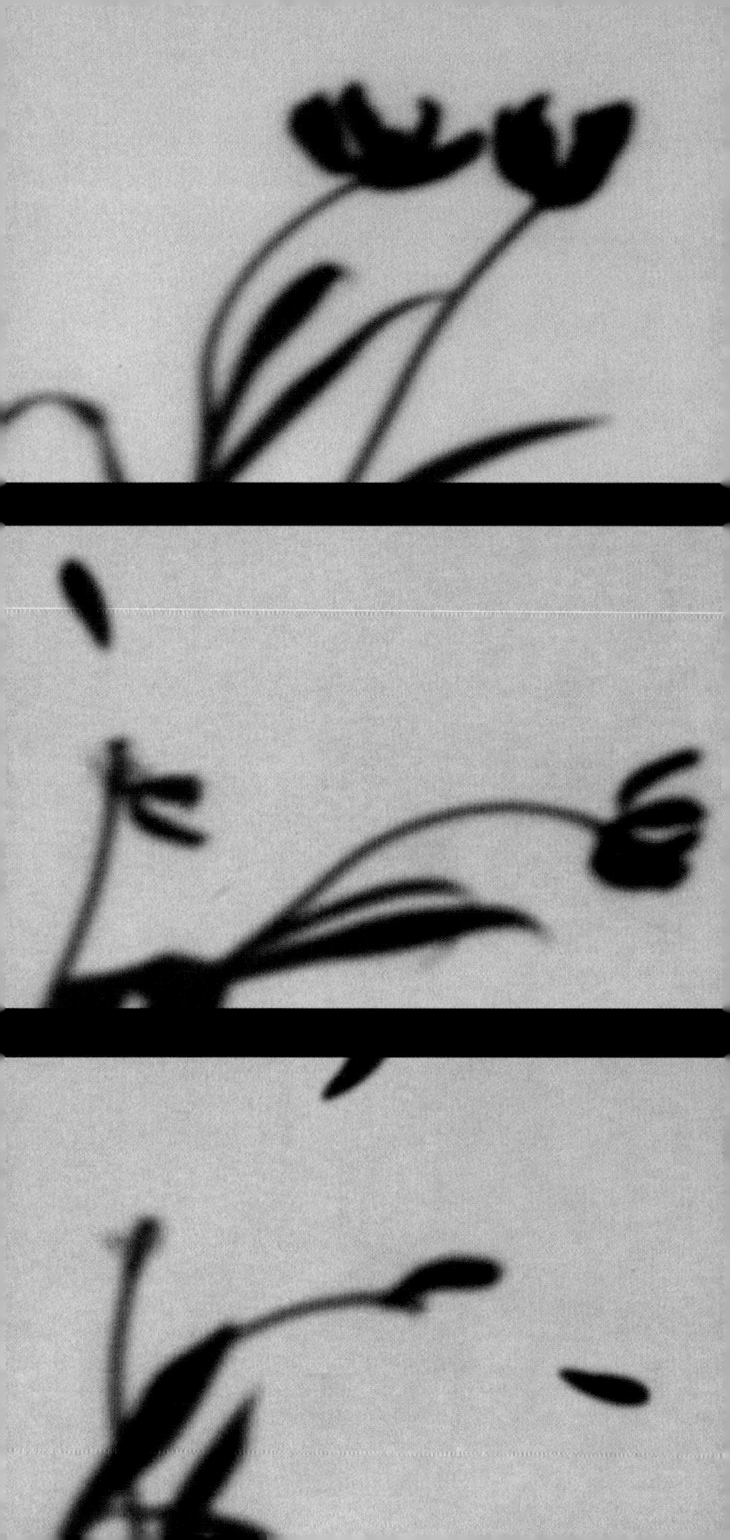

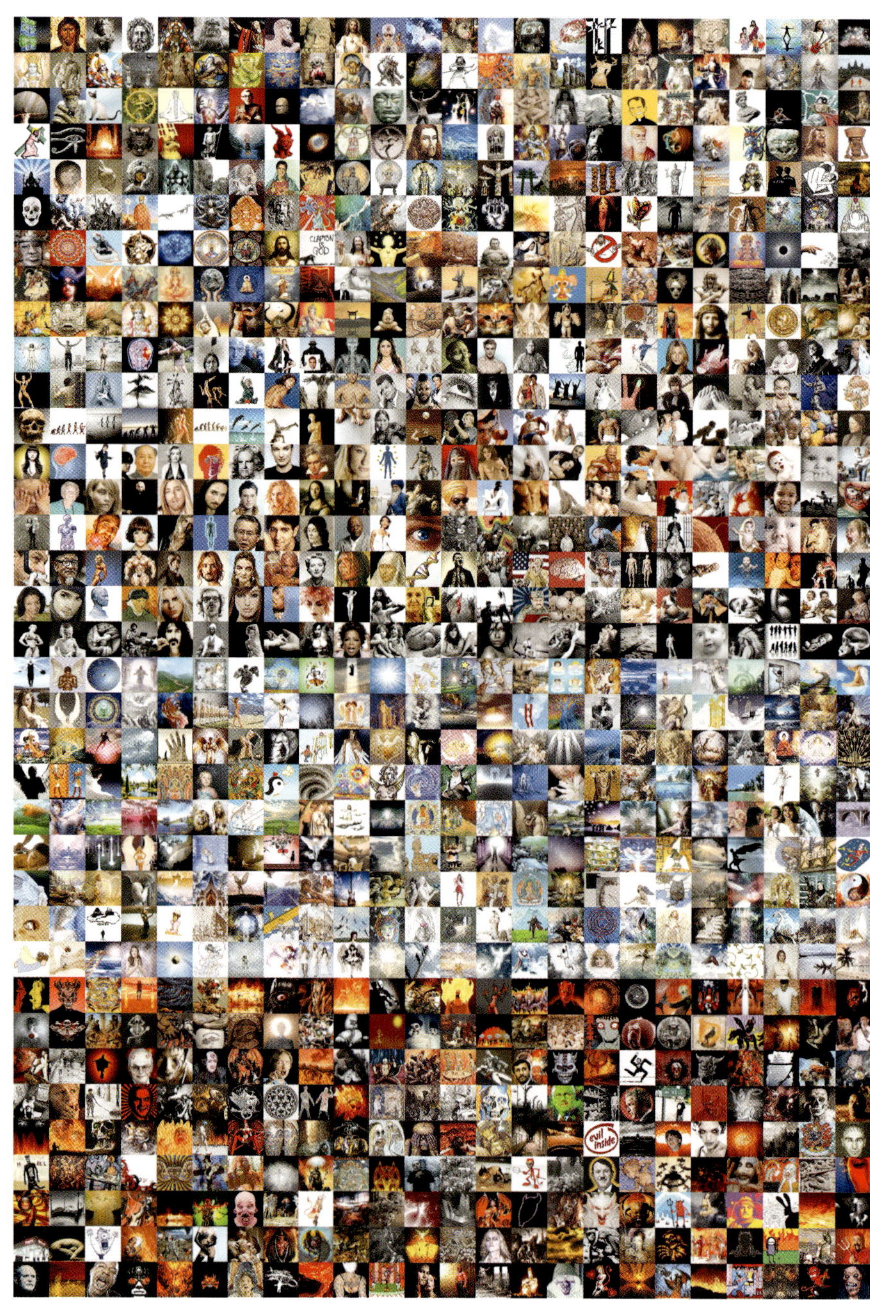

Douglas McCulloh
God/Man/Heaven/Hell, 2008
Archival chromogenic print
Courtesy of the artist

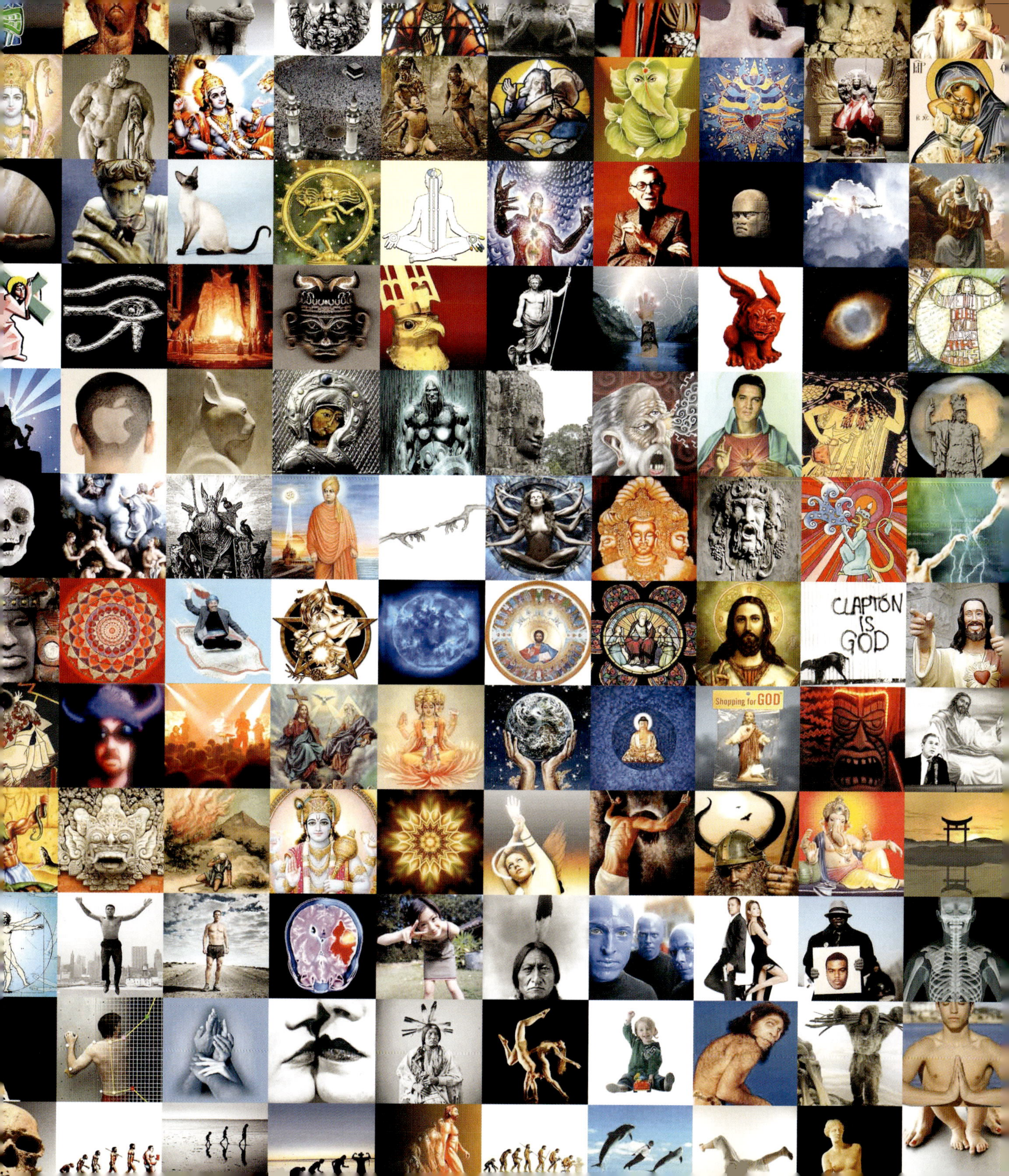

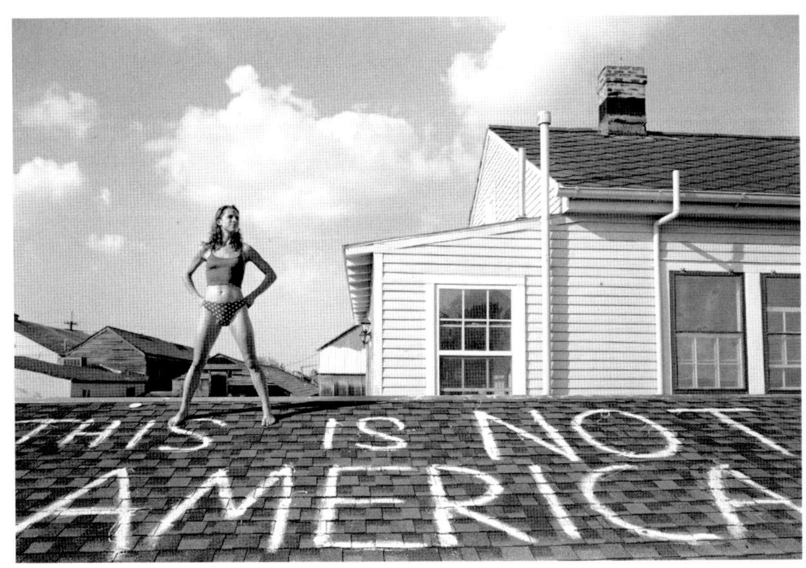

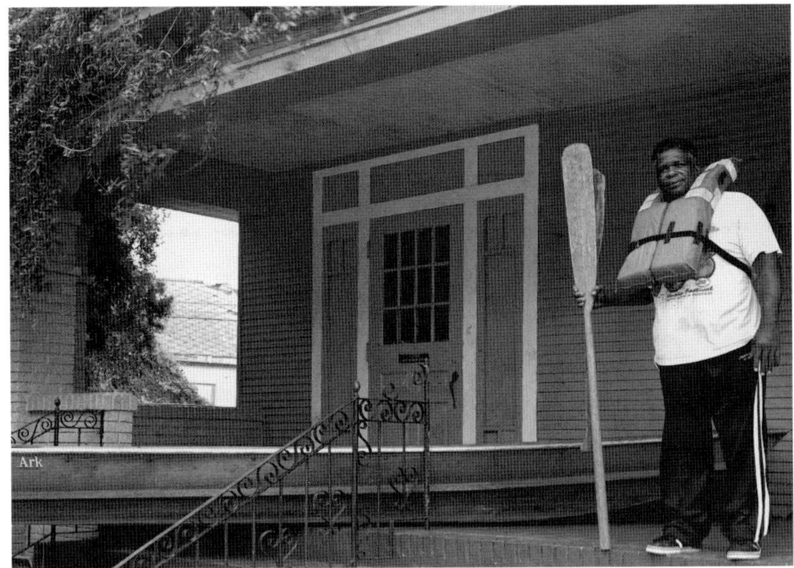

Thomas Neff
Caroline Koch and Melvin Smith, November 2, 2005
Selenium toned silver gelatin prints
Courtesy of the artist

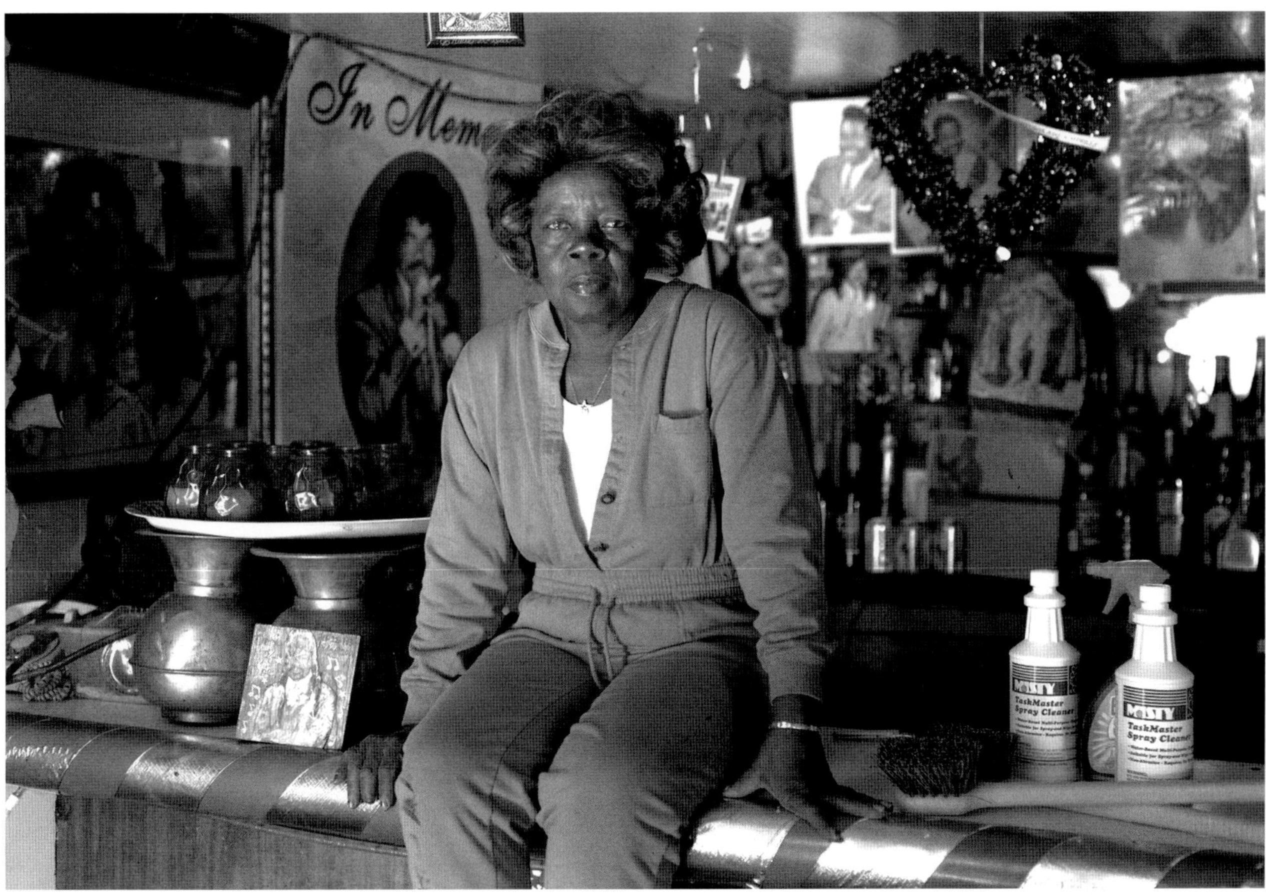

Thomas Neff
Antoinette K-Doe, Mother-In-Law Lounge, November 2, 2005, Selenium toned silver gelatin print
Courtesy of the artist

   Antoinette stayed after the levees broke, determined to protect the lounge and care for her disabled niece, but after seven days isola-tion and of fear of the unknown, she'd had enough. After flagging down a National Guard boat from an upstairs window, she and her niece were taken to an I-10 on-ramp, bussed to the airport, and flown out of state.

   When two of her dear friends, Savannah-Rose I and Savannah-Rose II, DJs by trade, discovered that Antoinette had been taken to parts unknown, they launched a frantic search. It took them a month to find her, living in a Boy Scout camp near Atlanta. By that time Antoinette was more than ready to leave, even to return to a devastated New Orleans.

   She had been gone only five weeks, but in that time, the mold and bacteria populations had multiplied so that the entire city was permeated by their rankness. When she returned to the lounge, saw the dam-age, and smelled that odor, she totally lost it, and the thought of even trying to rebuild seemed incomprehensible.

   As she reflected to me on her life with Ernie K-Doe, who wrote the classic R&B hit Mother-in-Law for which the lounge was named, and recalled her part in resurrecting his career before he died—helping him to regain his self proclaimed title,

   "Emperor of the World"—she began to feel renewed hope. Together they had made the lounge, with its brightly painted murals, into a New Orleans cultural treasure, as evidenced by a bronze plaque from the city, which was mounted near the entrance.   She realized that she could save the lounge, even if she had to do it alone. With renewed strength and confidence she began the arduous task of gutting the ruined interior.

   Antoinette's efforts gained force when rebuilding the lounge be-came the first project undertaken by the Hands On network (a group of sixty national and international volunteer organizations whose role focuses on entrepreneurial civic action). When the project was less than half complete, Hands On partner and hip-hop superstar Usher visited the site one Sunday in May and asked the team leader to finish the project, including the second-floor apartment, at his expense. Antoinette was overwhelmed by the outpouring of support and reverence for Ernie's legacy and his music.

   On August 30, 2006, three thousand people attended a gala celebrating the reopening of the newly restored Mother-in-Law Lounge. In typical New Orleans style, an open casket was on hand into which guests could deposit a written memory of Hurricane Ka-trina. Once filled with memento-mori, it was buried right next to the lounge, on a site previously occupied by Ernie's Pink Cadillac Limo, which had been ruined in the great flood.

   In February of 2008, early Mardi Gras morning, Antoinette suf-fered a mild heart attack, from which she recovered in due course. As fate would have it, another coronary event took her life on the same morn-ing a year later, on Fat Tuesday, 2009.

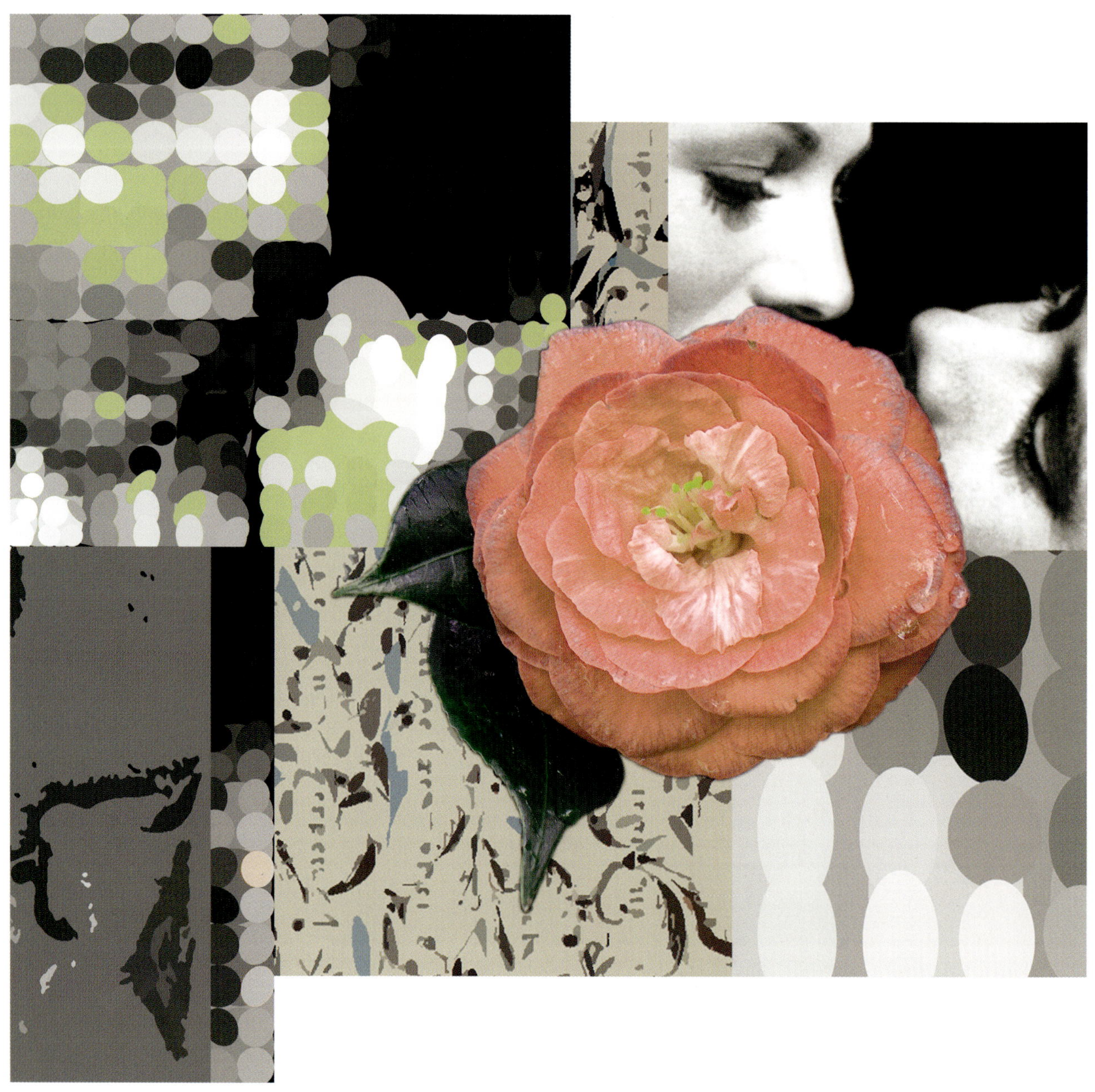

Ilene Segalove
Kiss Me Still Life Butterfly, 2006
Digital photograph

Kiss Me Still Life Camellia, 2006
Digital photograph
Courtesy of the artist

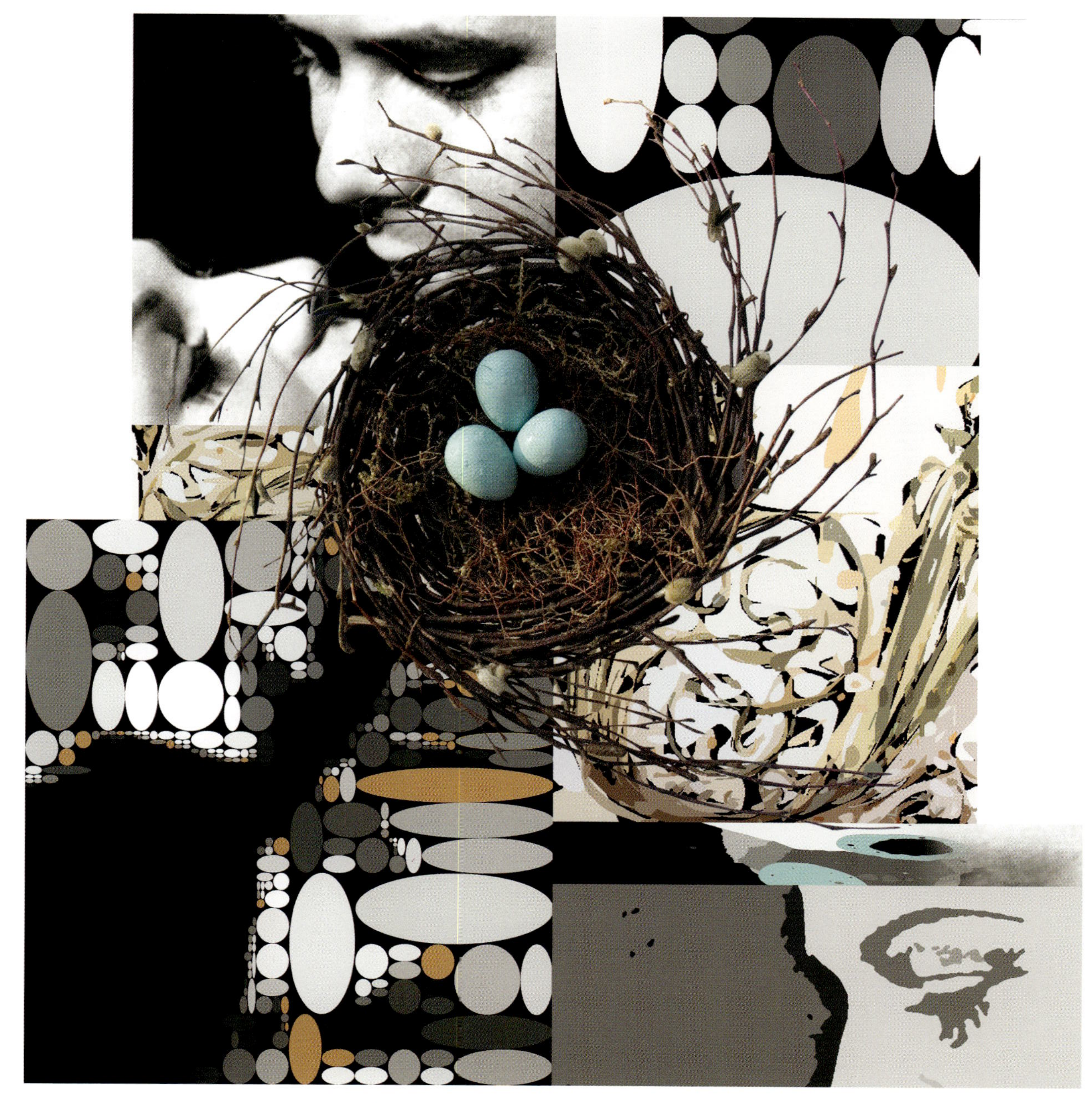

93

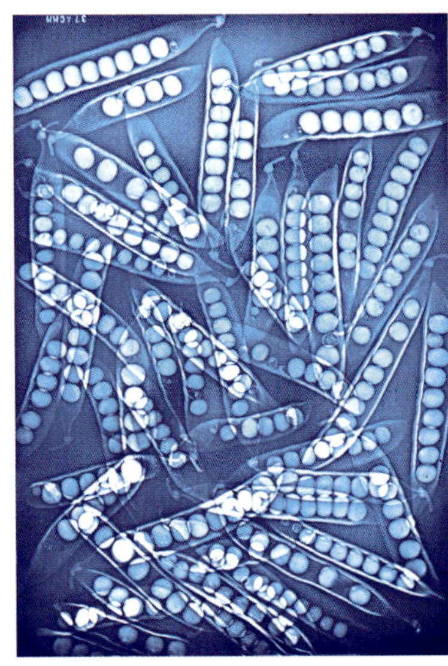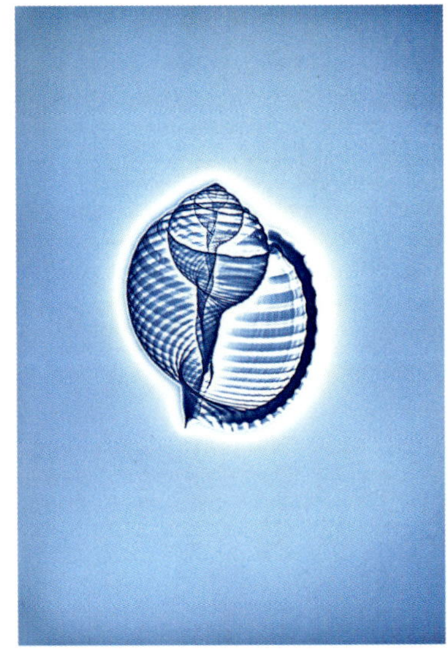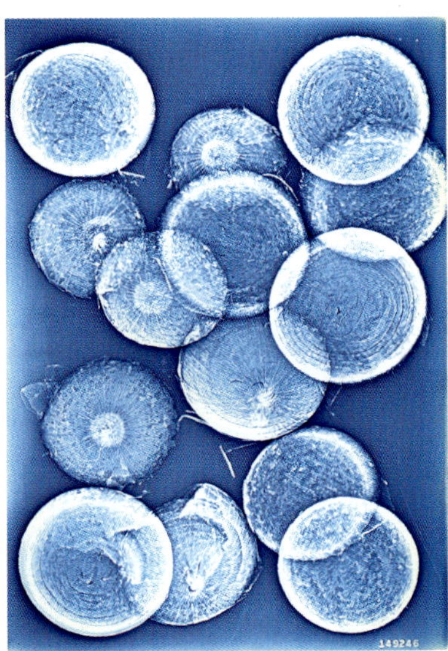

Who owns nature?

Sheila Pinkel
Who Owns Nature, 1977-1983
Archival lightjet print edition 2/3
Courtesy of the artist and Robert Mann Gallery

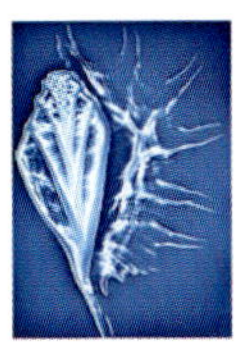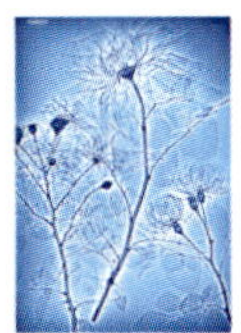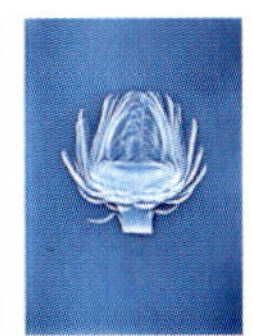

How old are roses?

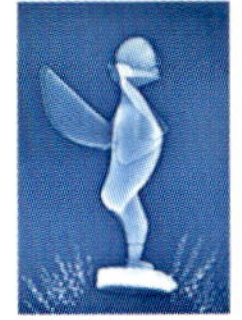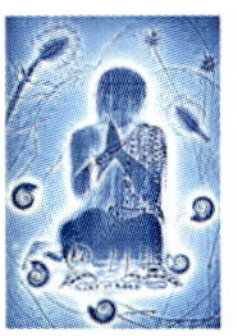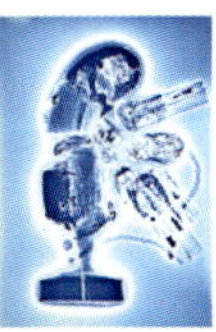

How old are human eyes?

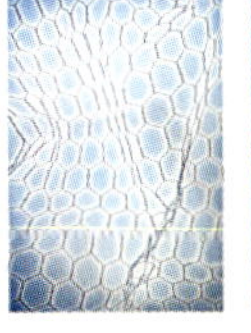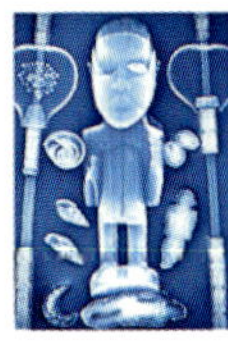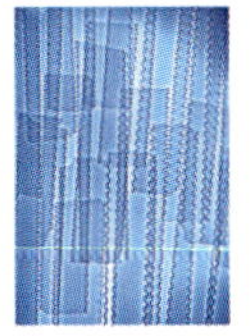

How old are ideas?

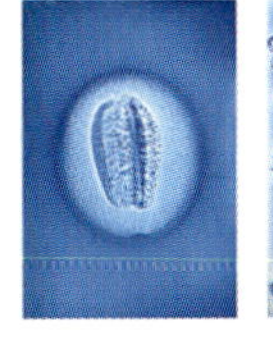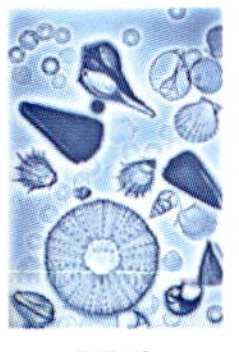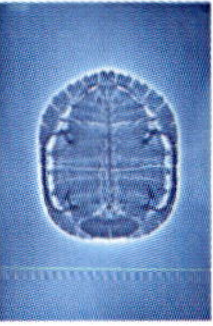

How old is rain?

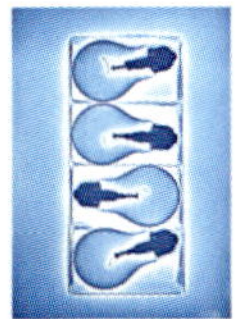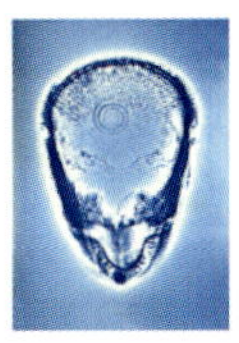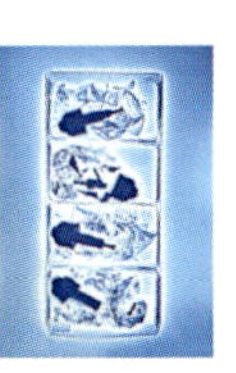

How old are hopes and dreams?

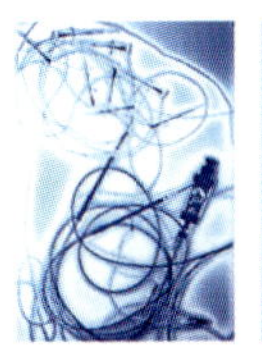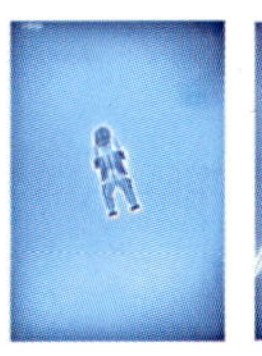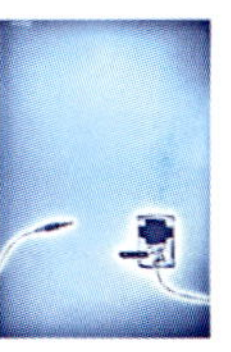

How old is toxic waste?

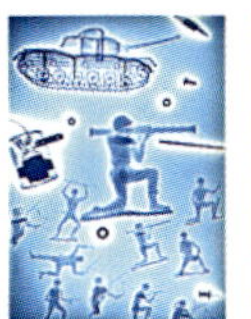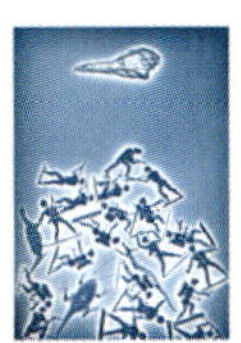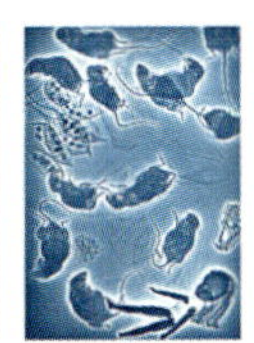

How old are mushroom clouds?

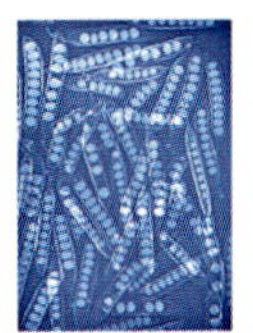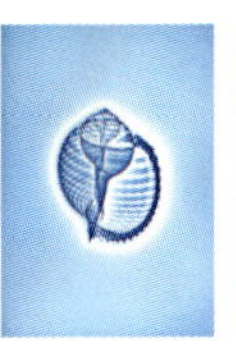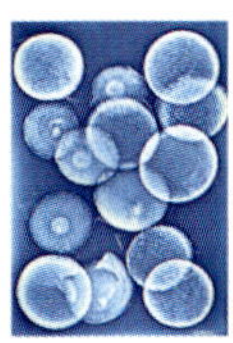

Who owns nature?

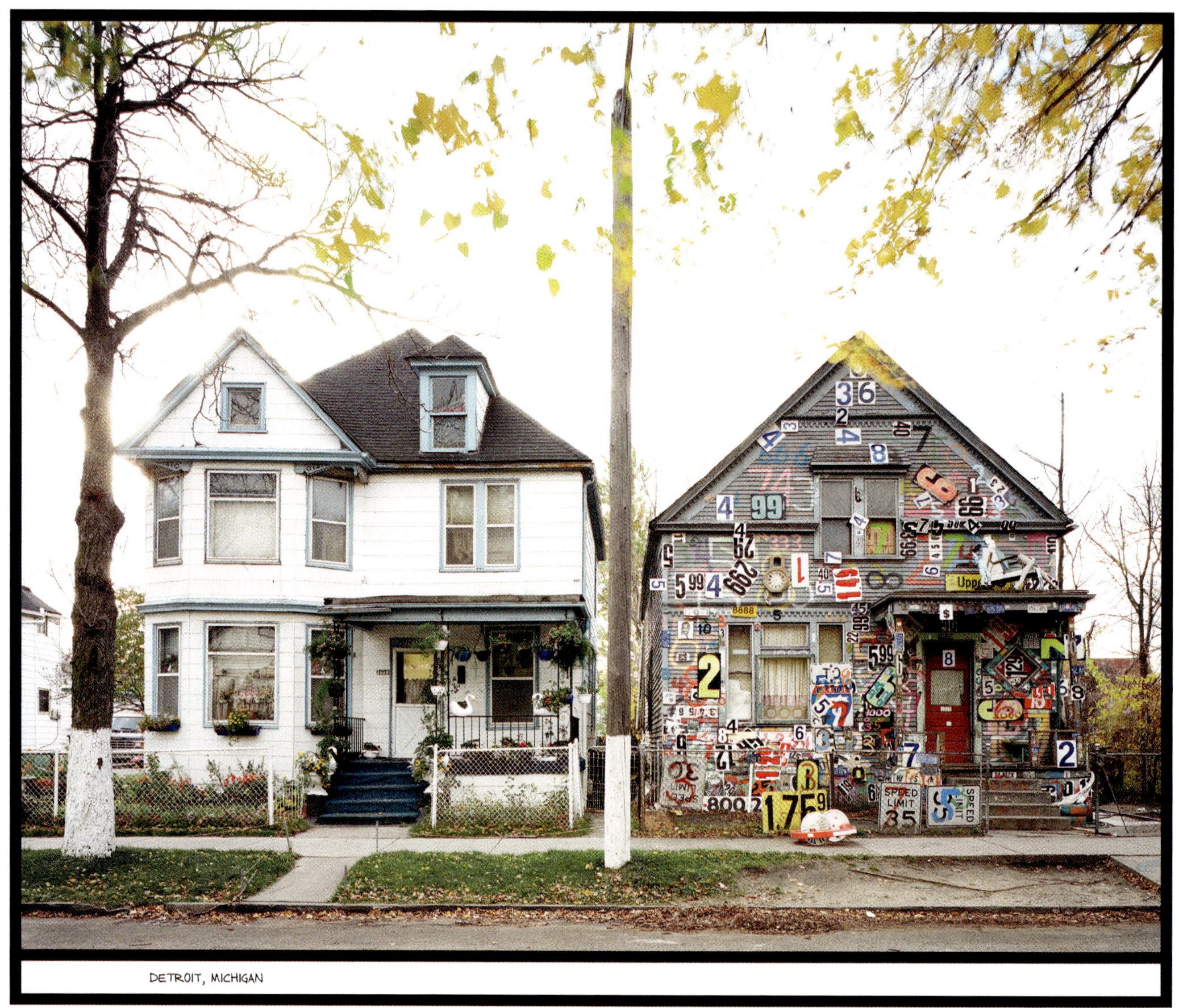

Jim Stone
Detroit Michigan - The Two Houses, 1996
Pigment ink jet print

Ada McGregor and her Squash, La Crosse, Wisconsin, 1984
Pigment ink jet print

Heidi Guarding the Beauty Rings, Old Town, Florida, 1984
Pigment ink jet print
Courtesy of the artist

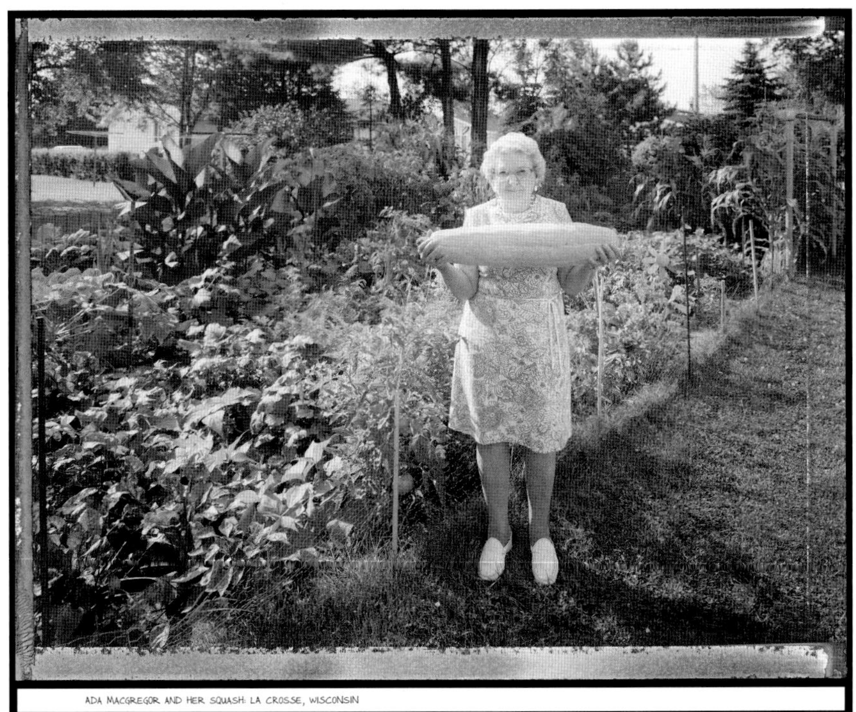

ADA MACGREGOR AND HER SQUASH: LA CROSSE, WISCONSIN

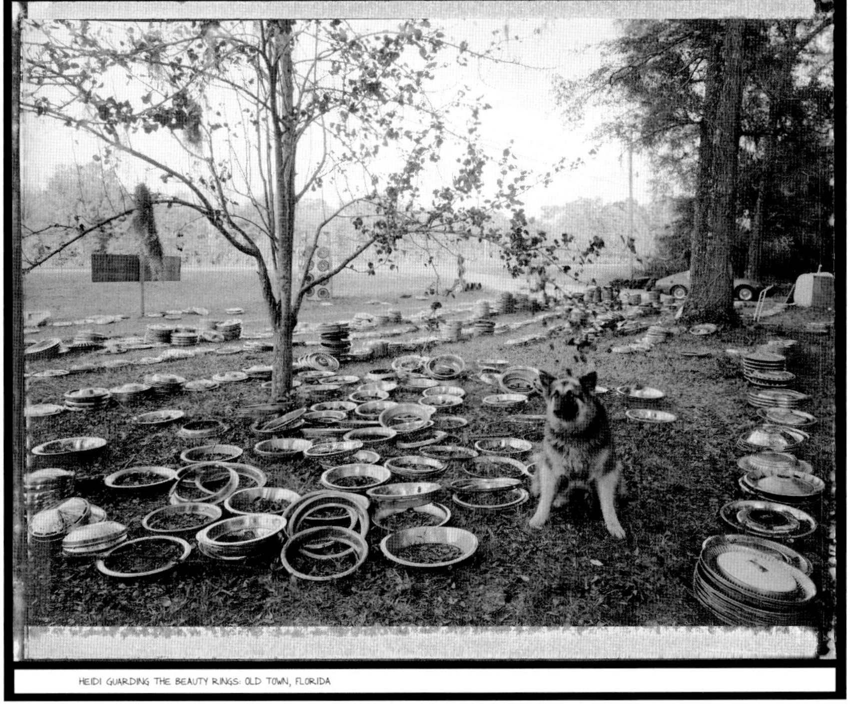

HEIDI GUARDING THE BEAUTY RINGS: OLD TOWN, FLORIDA

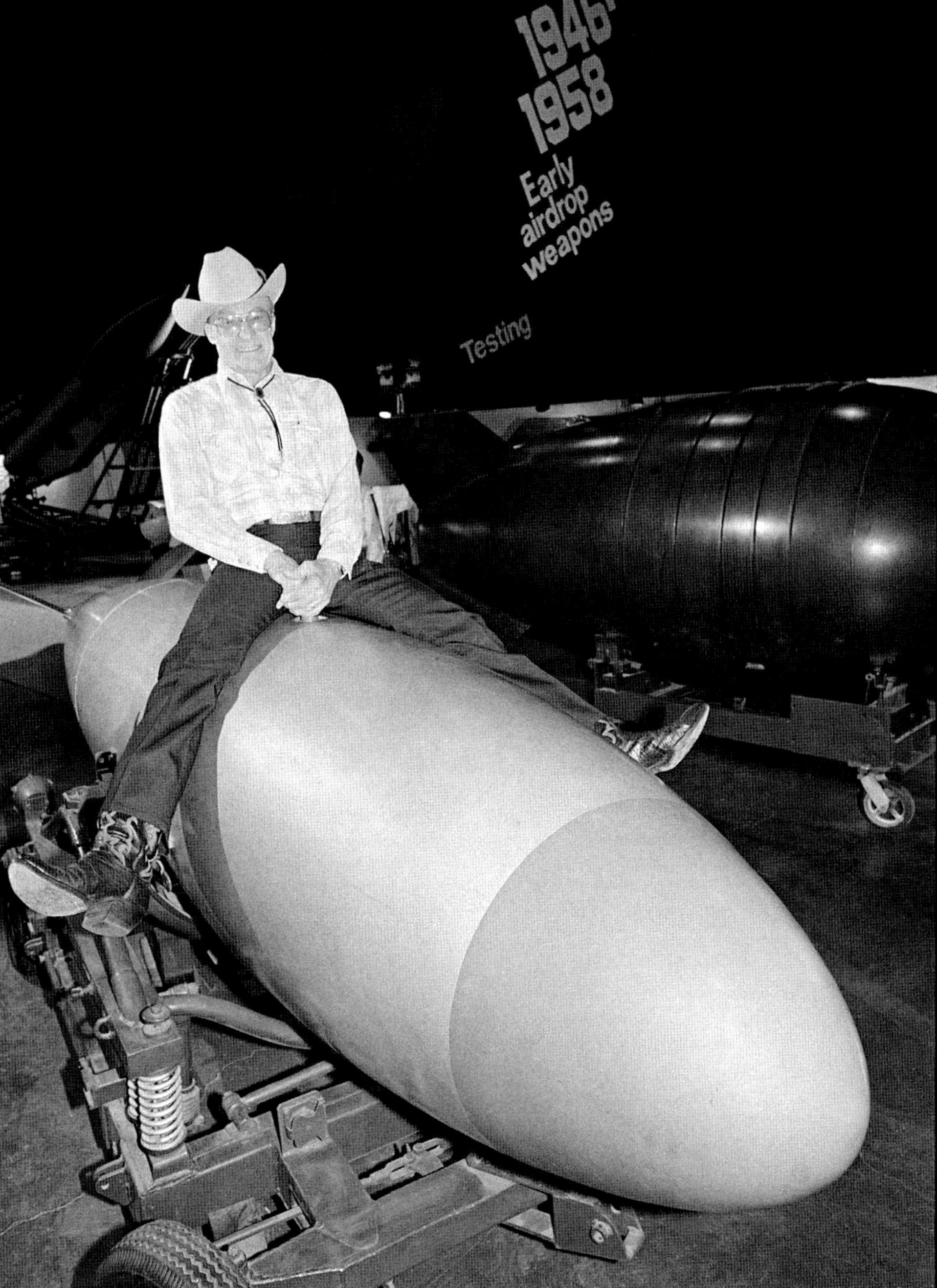
1946-
1958
Early
airdrop
weapons

Testing

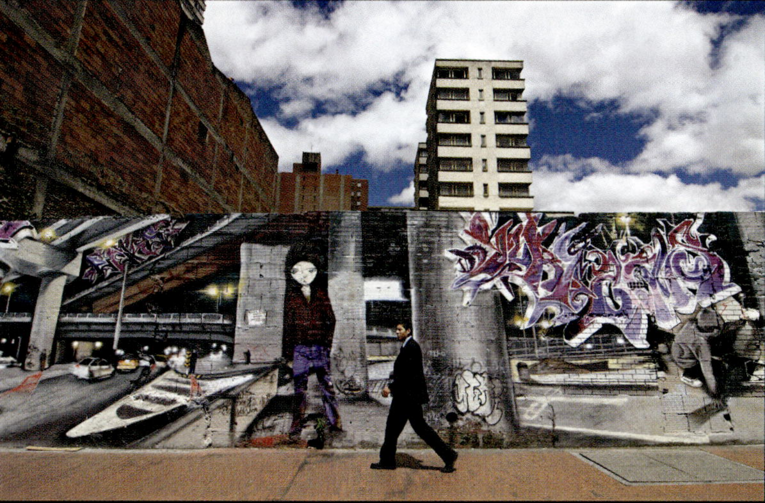

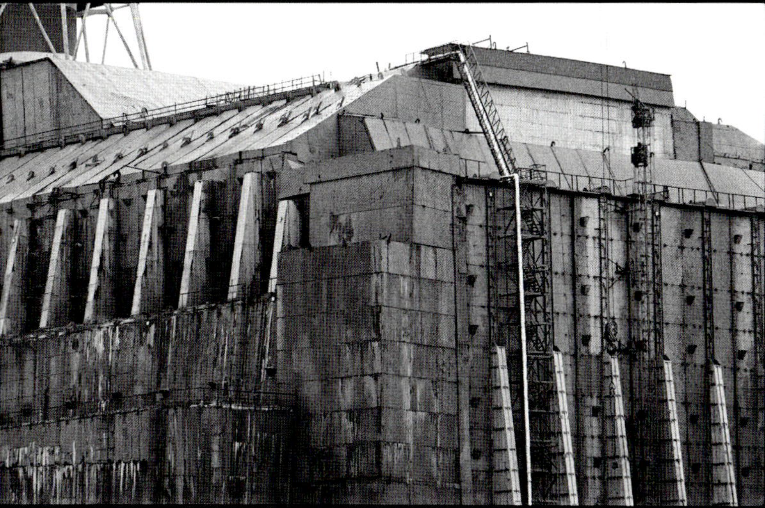

James Lerager
Major Hank Henry Rides the Bomb (National Atomic Museum, Albuquerque, New Mexico, 1986)
Gelitin silver prints

Graffiti, Bogotá, Colombia, 2007
Archival lightjet prints

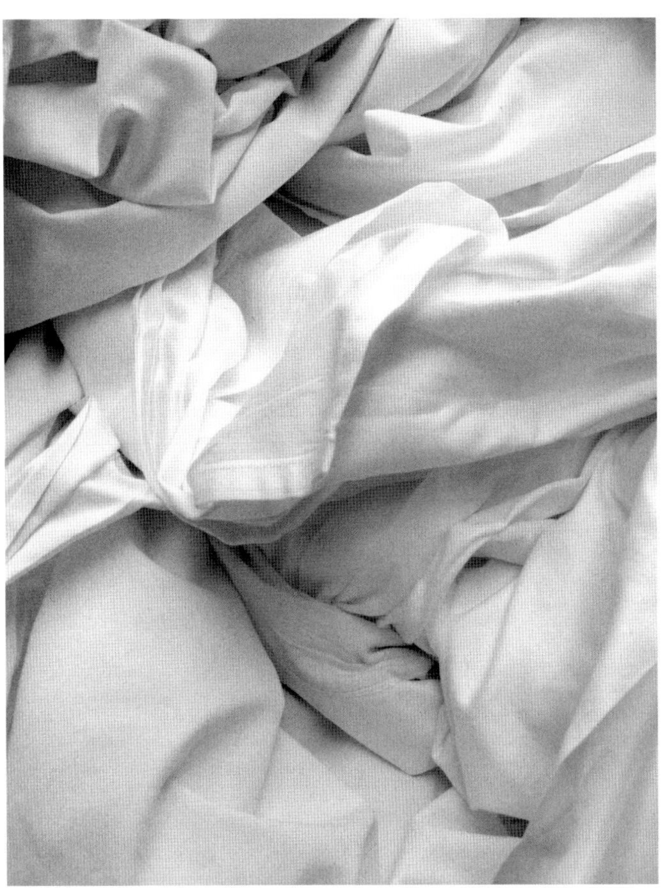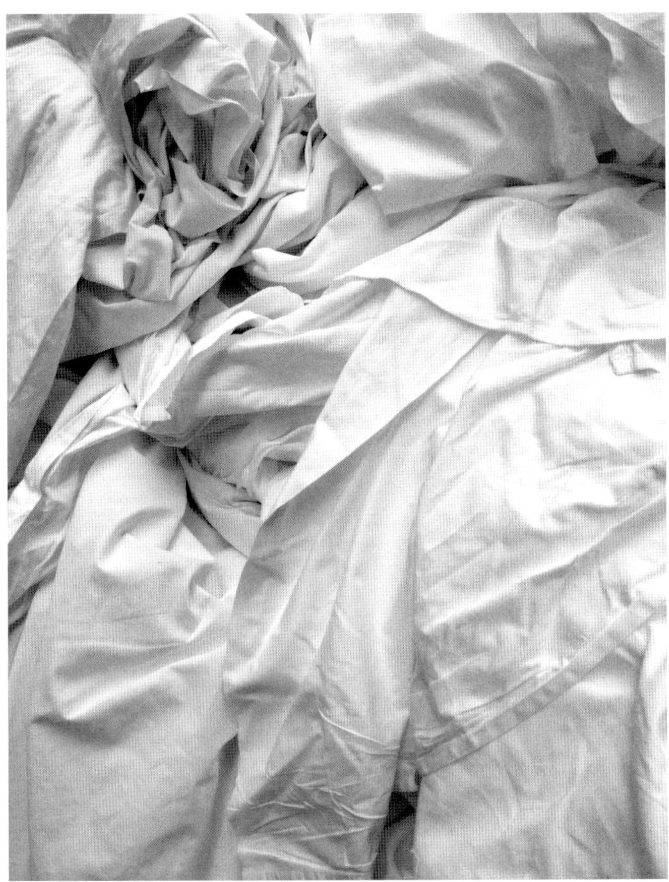

Suda House
Untitled #1 and #7 Sanctuary, 2009
Ultrachrome digital ink prints on polysilk fabric, draped in frames.

Leda from the Aqueous Myths, 1986
Dye -destruction-Cibachrome print
Courtesy of the artist

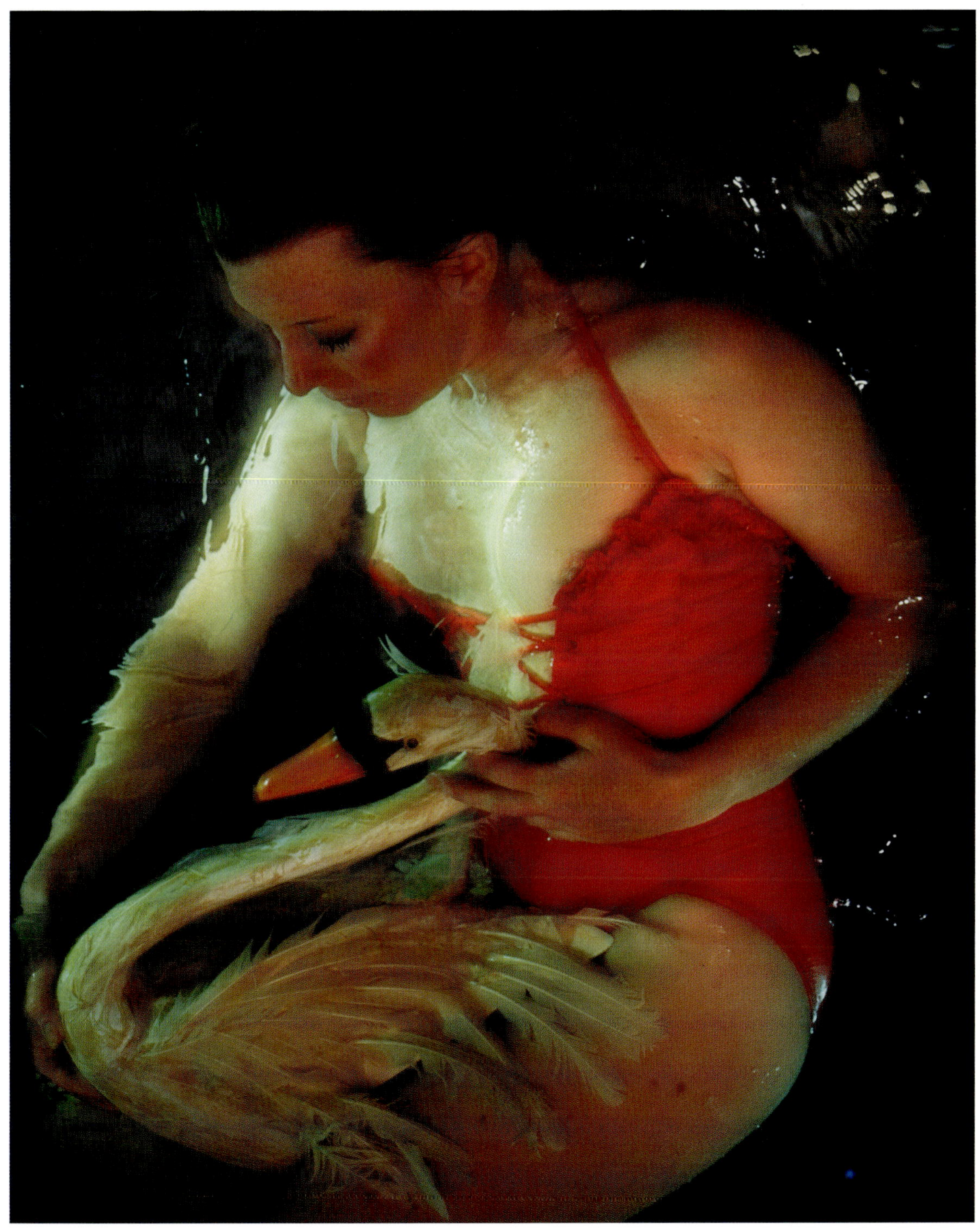

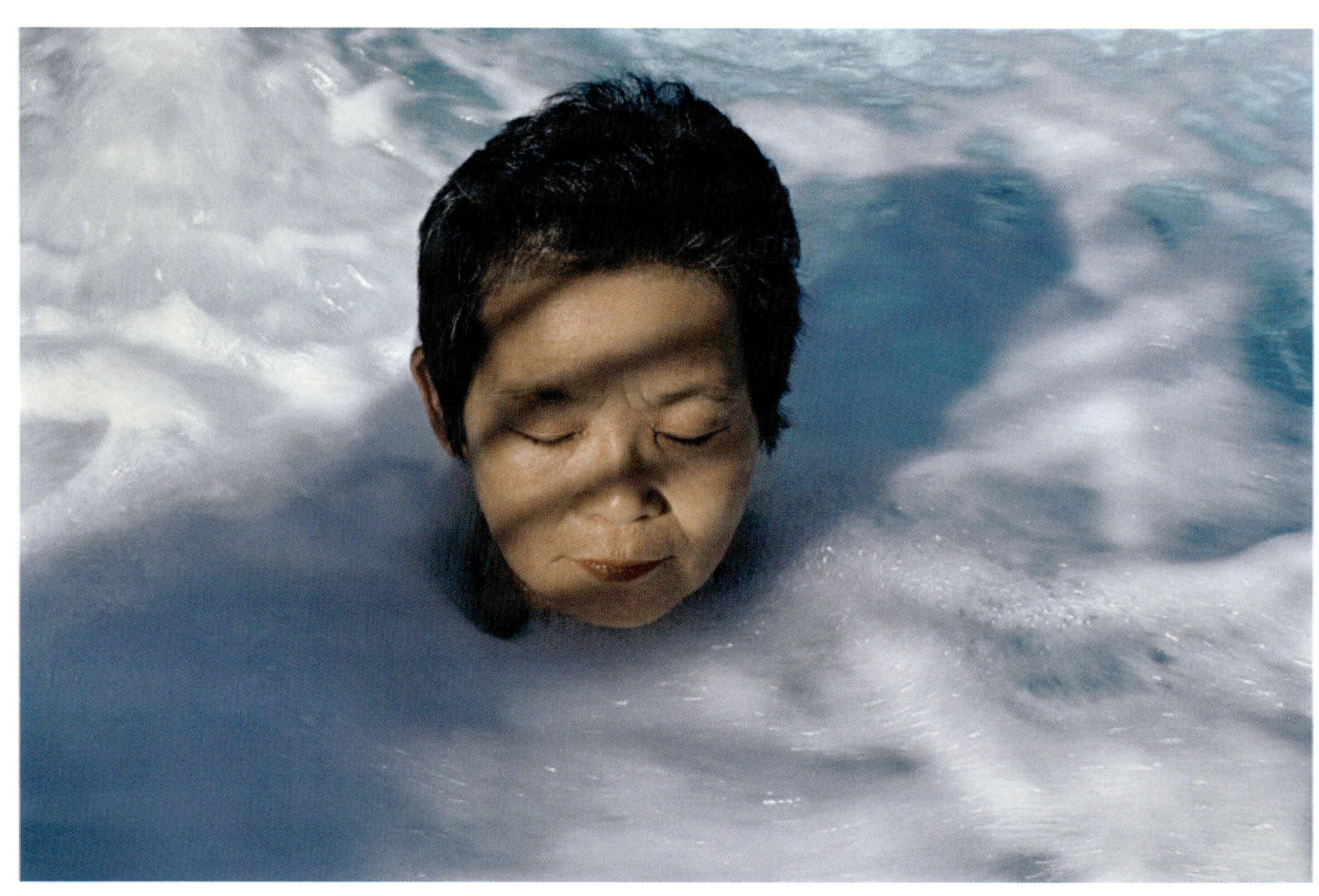

Mihoko Yamagata
from the portfolio Akiko, 2007
Image above, 1986
Chromogenic print

Image right, 1992
Chromogenic print
Courtesy of the artist

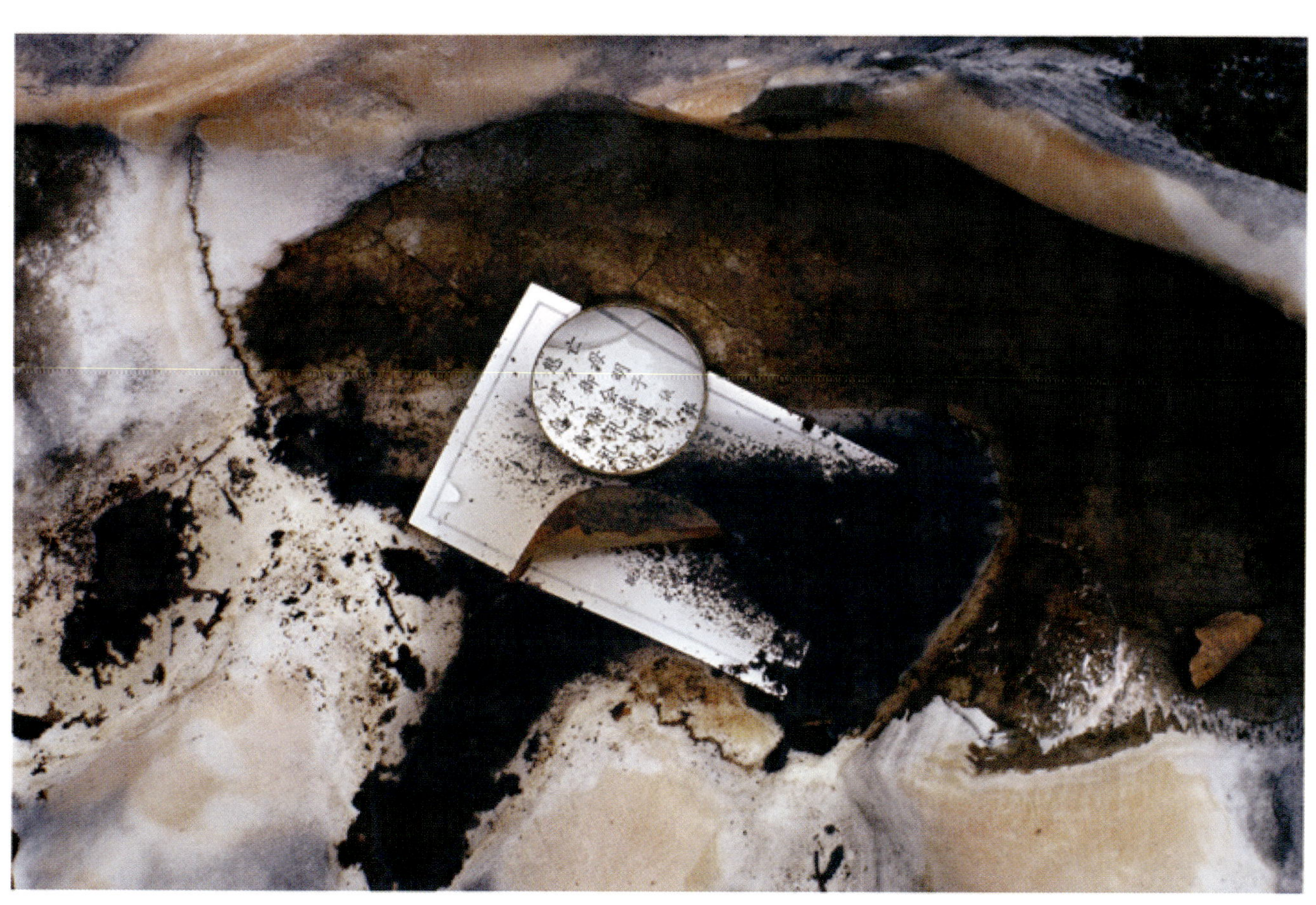

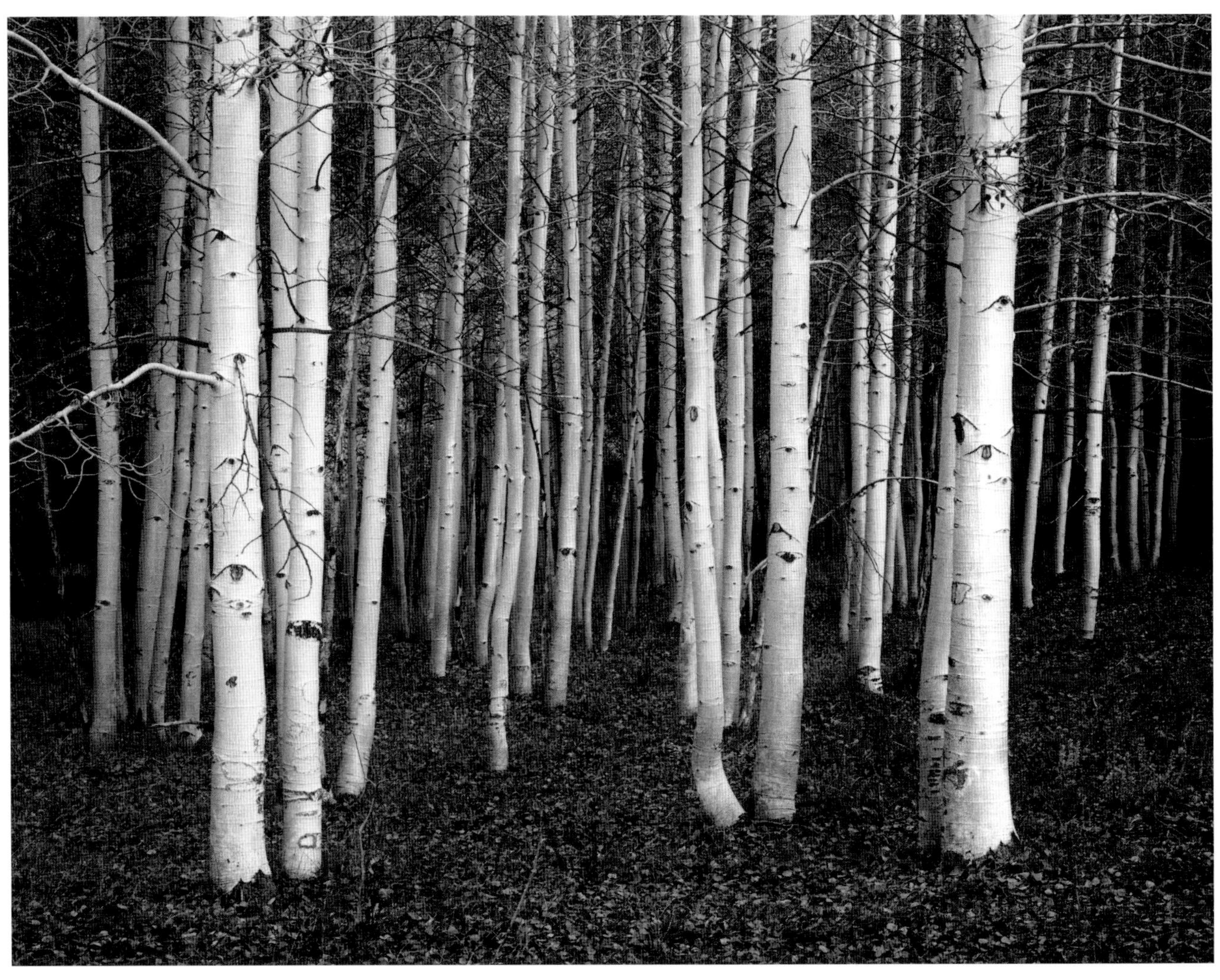

John Sexton
Aspen Dusk, 1984
Selenium toned silver gelatin photographic print
10-1/2 x 13-1/2 inches
Courtesy of Artist
©1984 John Sexton. All rights reserved

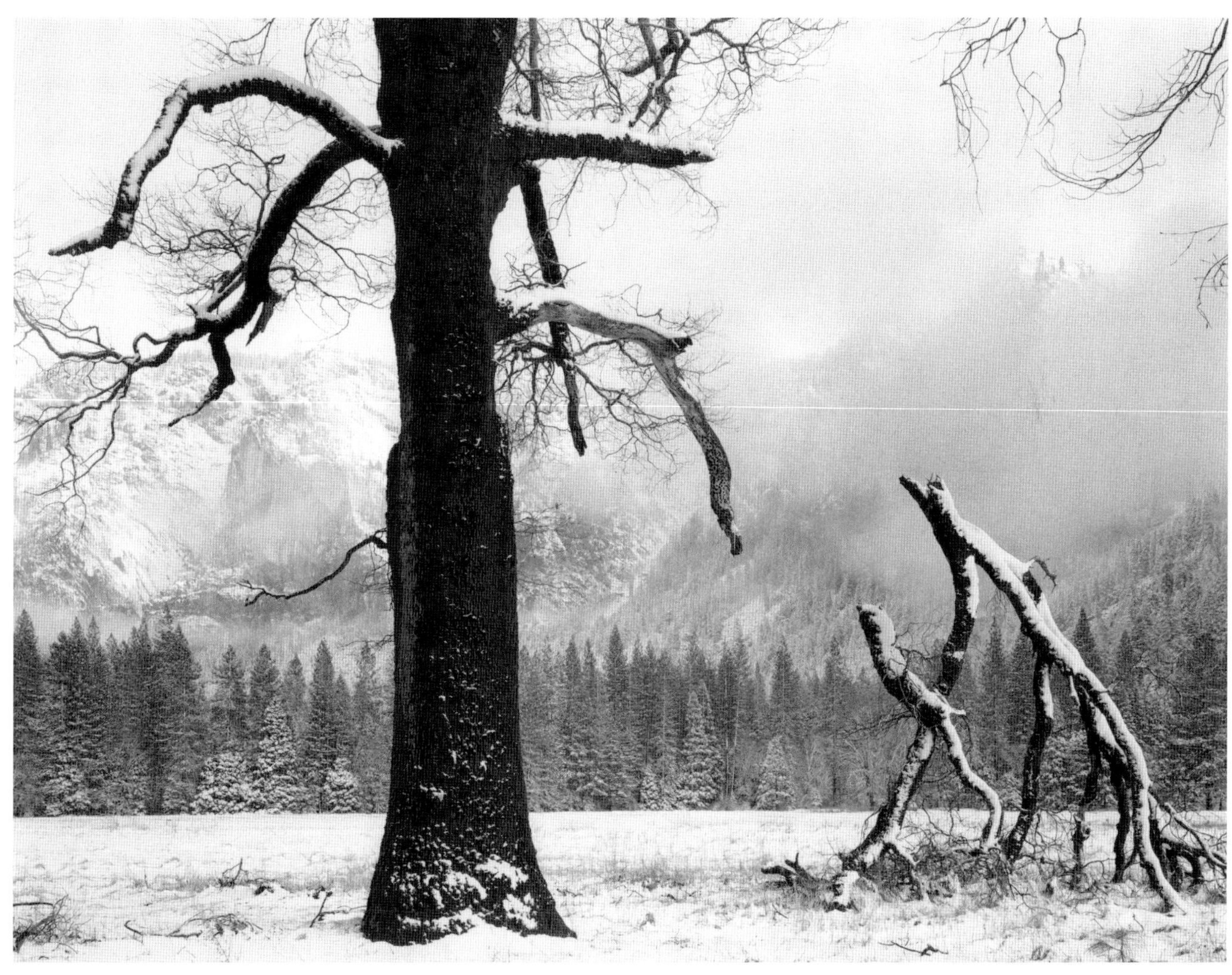

John Sexton
Black Oak, Fallen Branches, Yosemite Valley, California, 1984
Selenium toned silver gelatin photographic print
10-1/2 x 13-1/2 inches
Courtesy of Artist
©1984 John Sexton. All rights reserved

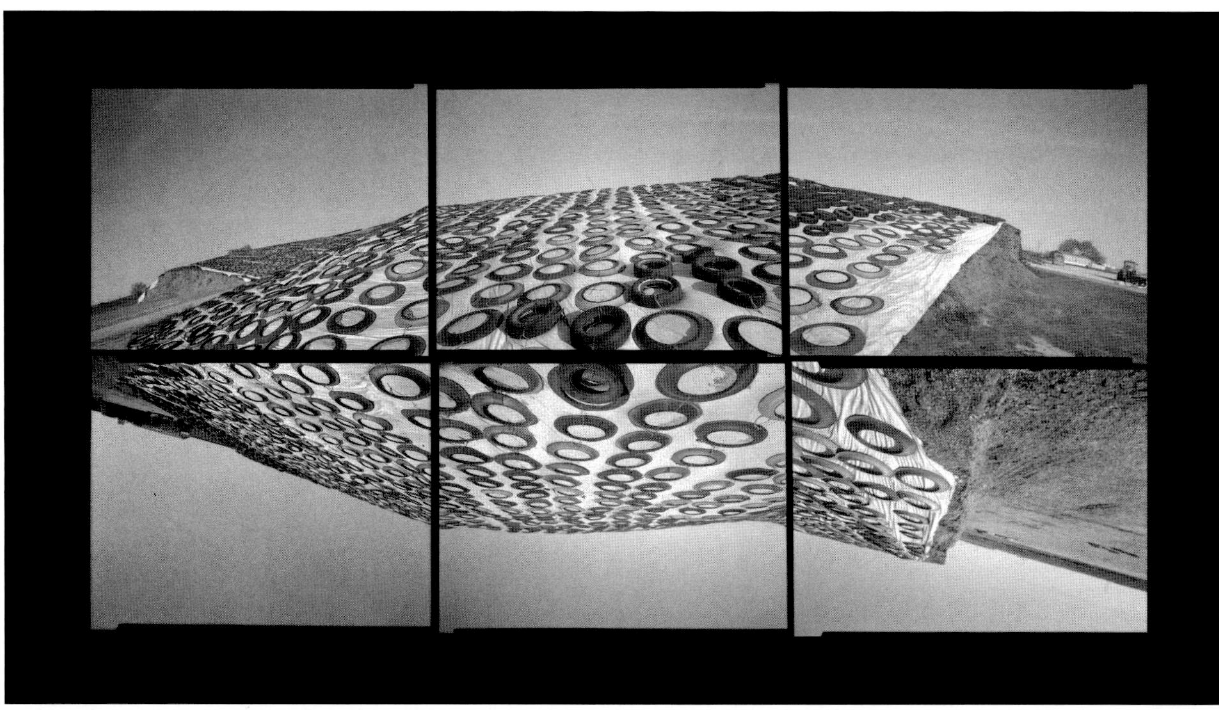

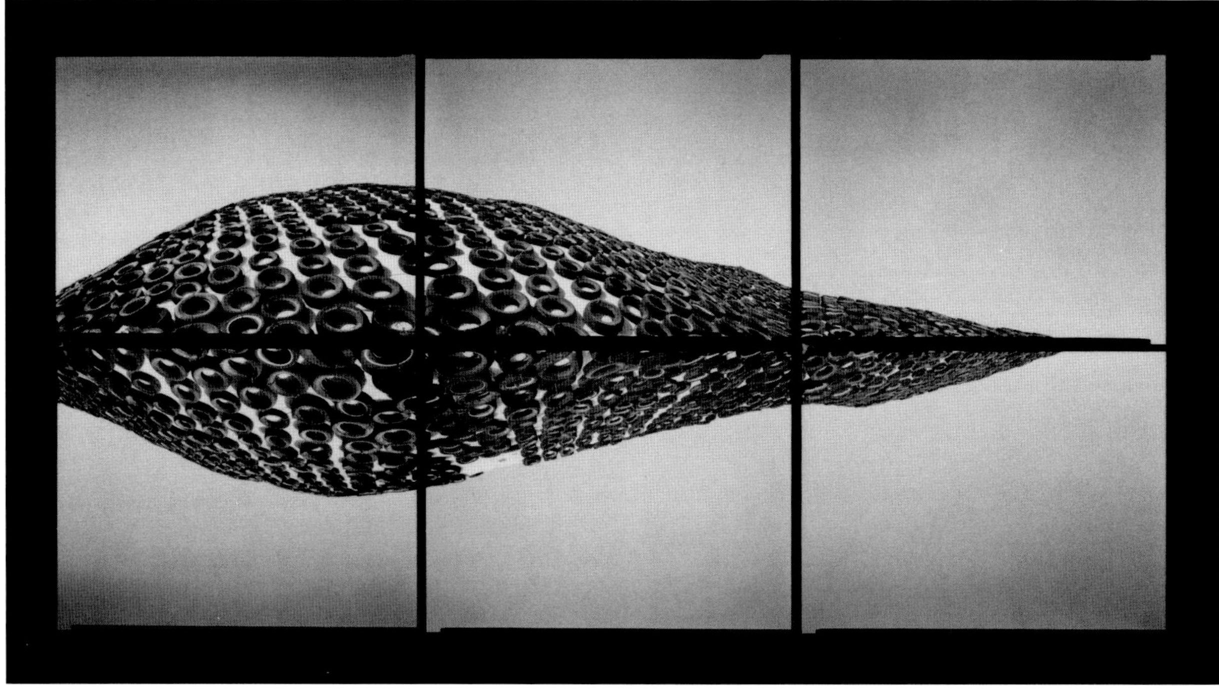

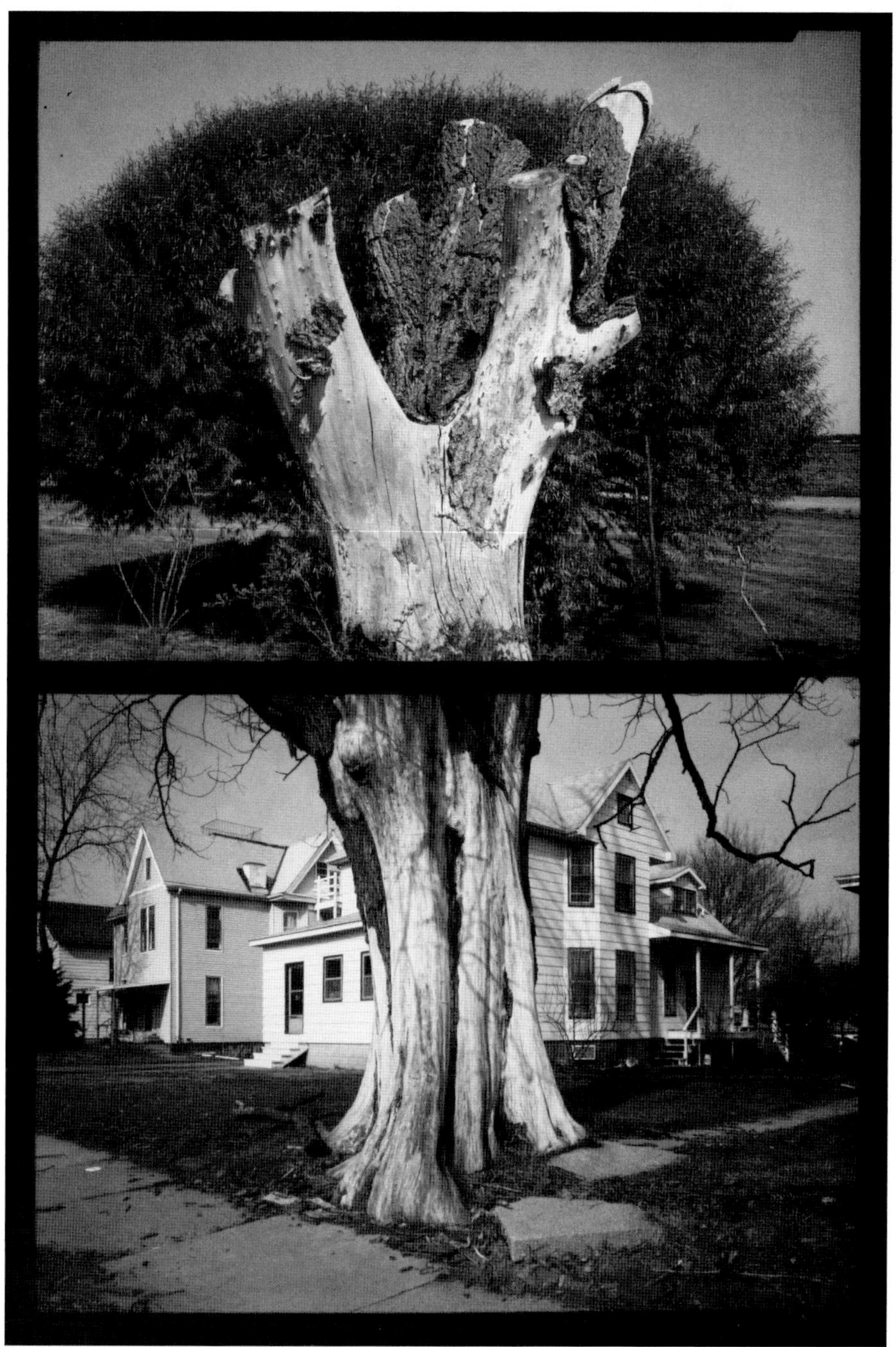

Greg Erf
Untitled 1 and 2, 1989
Gelatin Silver Print
Courtesy of the artist

Untitled, 1984
Gelatin Silver Print
Courtesy of BC Space

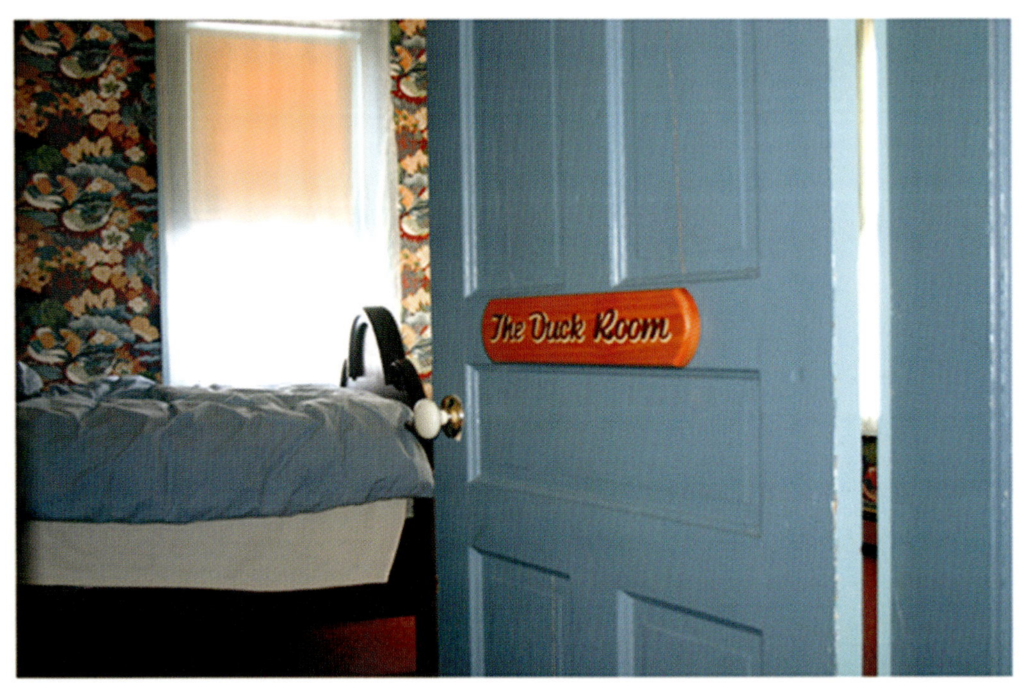

The Duck Room

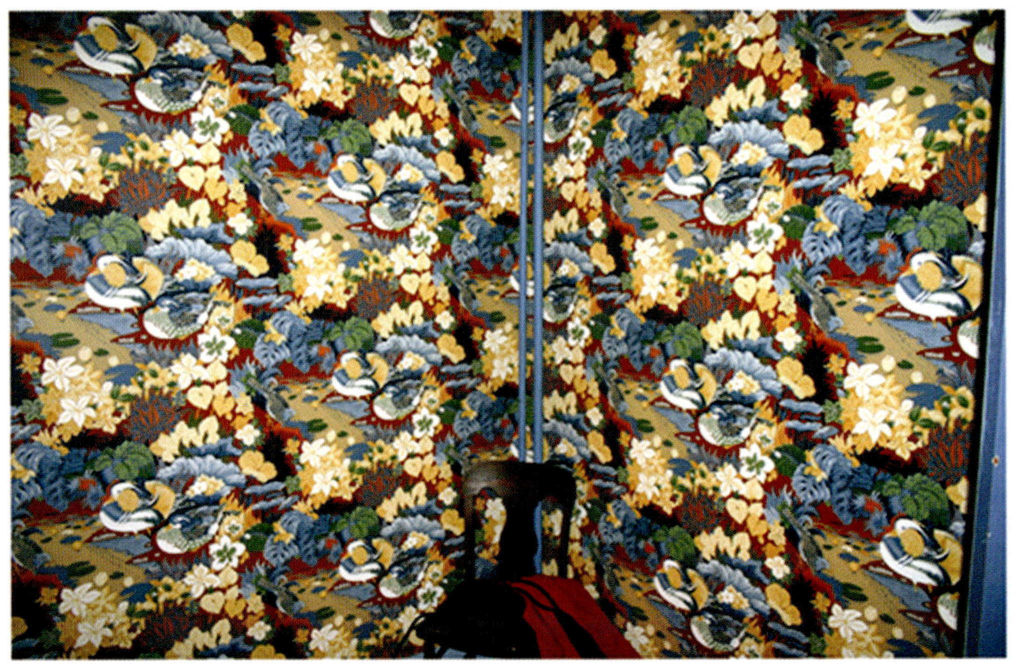

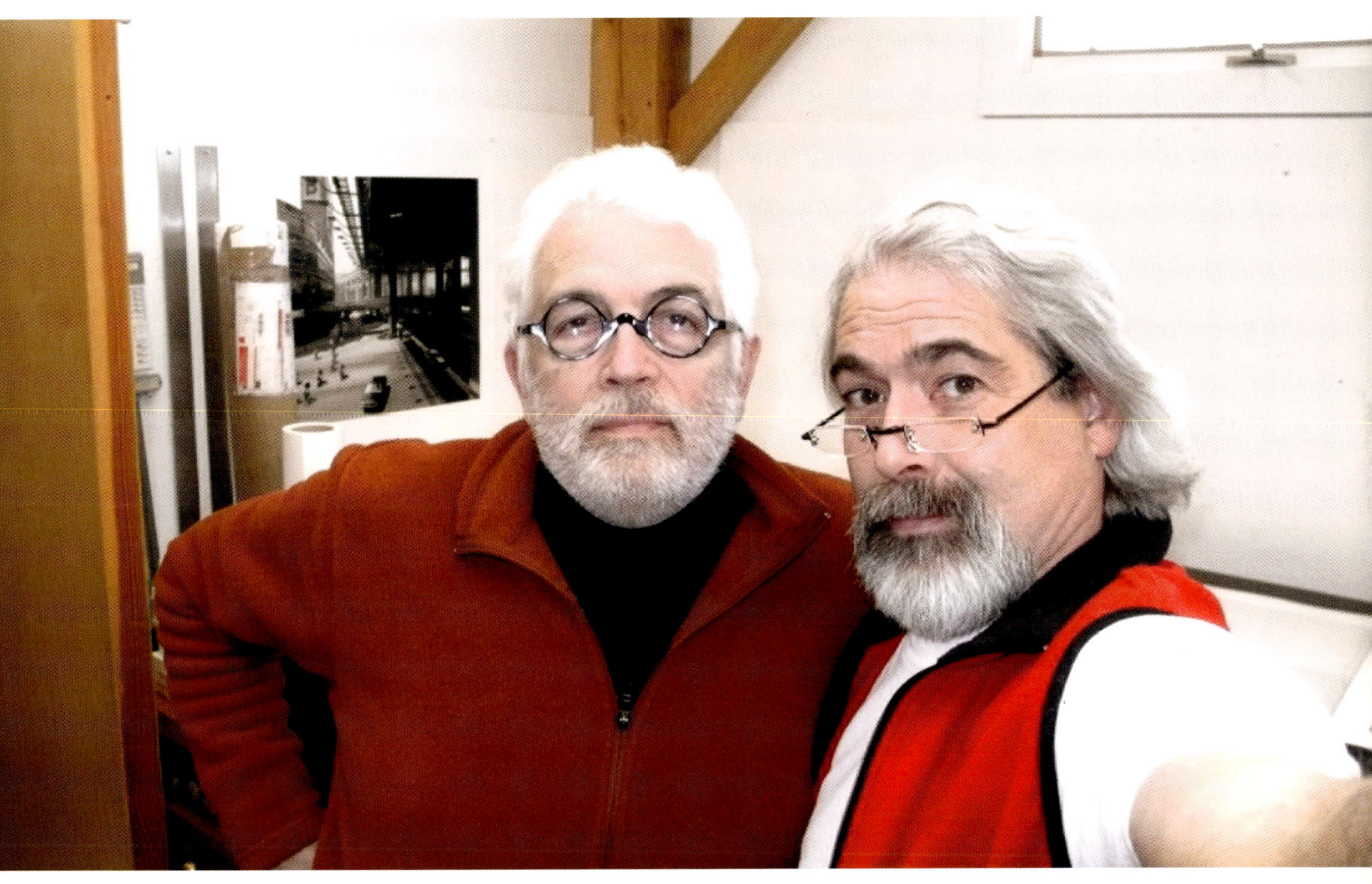

Mark Johnstone
Duck Room, East Topsham, Vermont, 2008
Ink jet print

Self Portrait with Joe Deal, Visiting Cone Editions, 2008
East Topsham, Vermont
Ink jet print
Courtesy of the artist

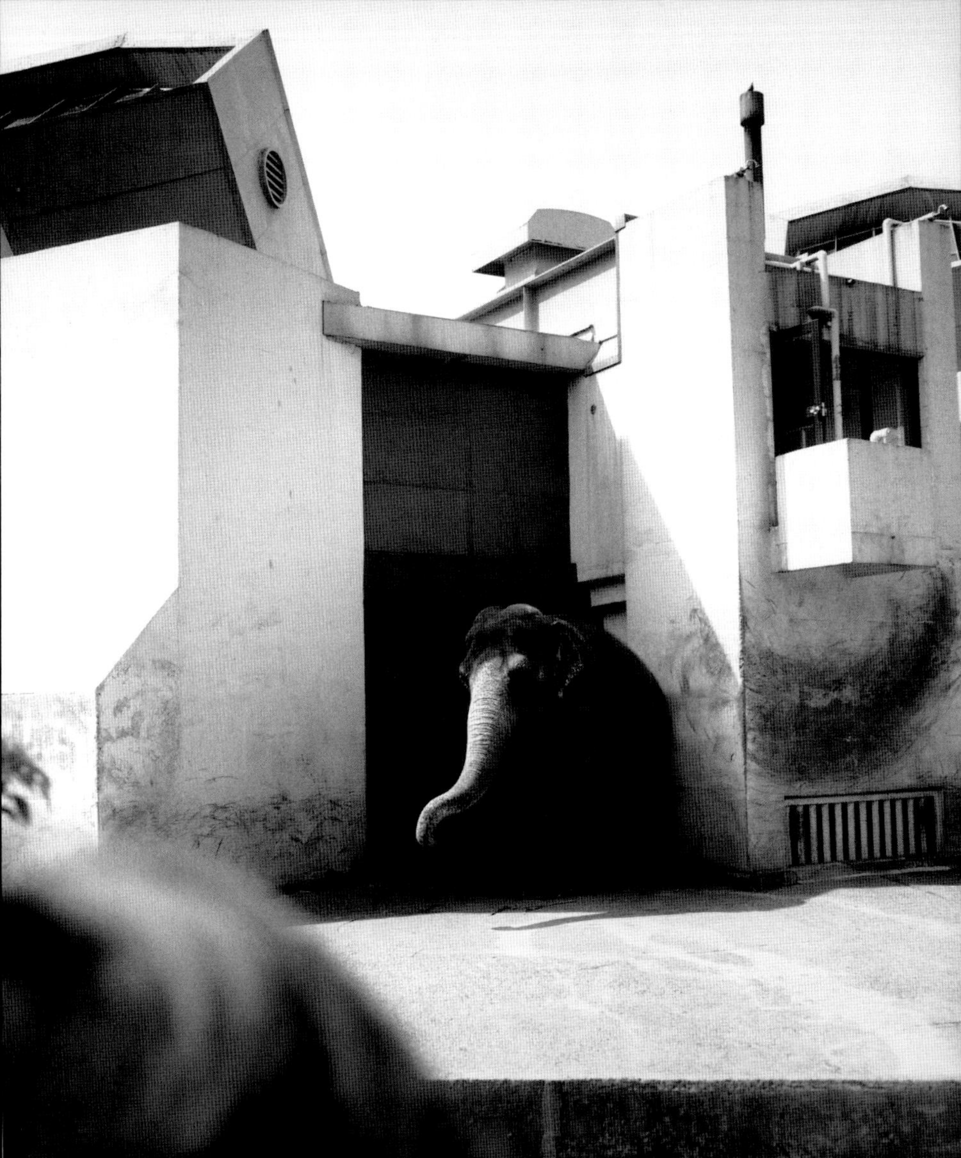

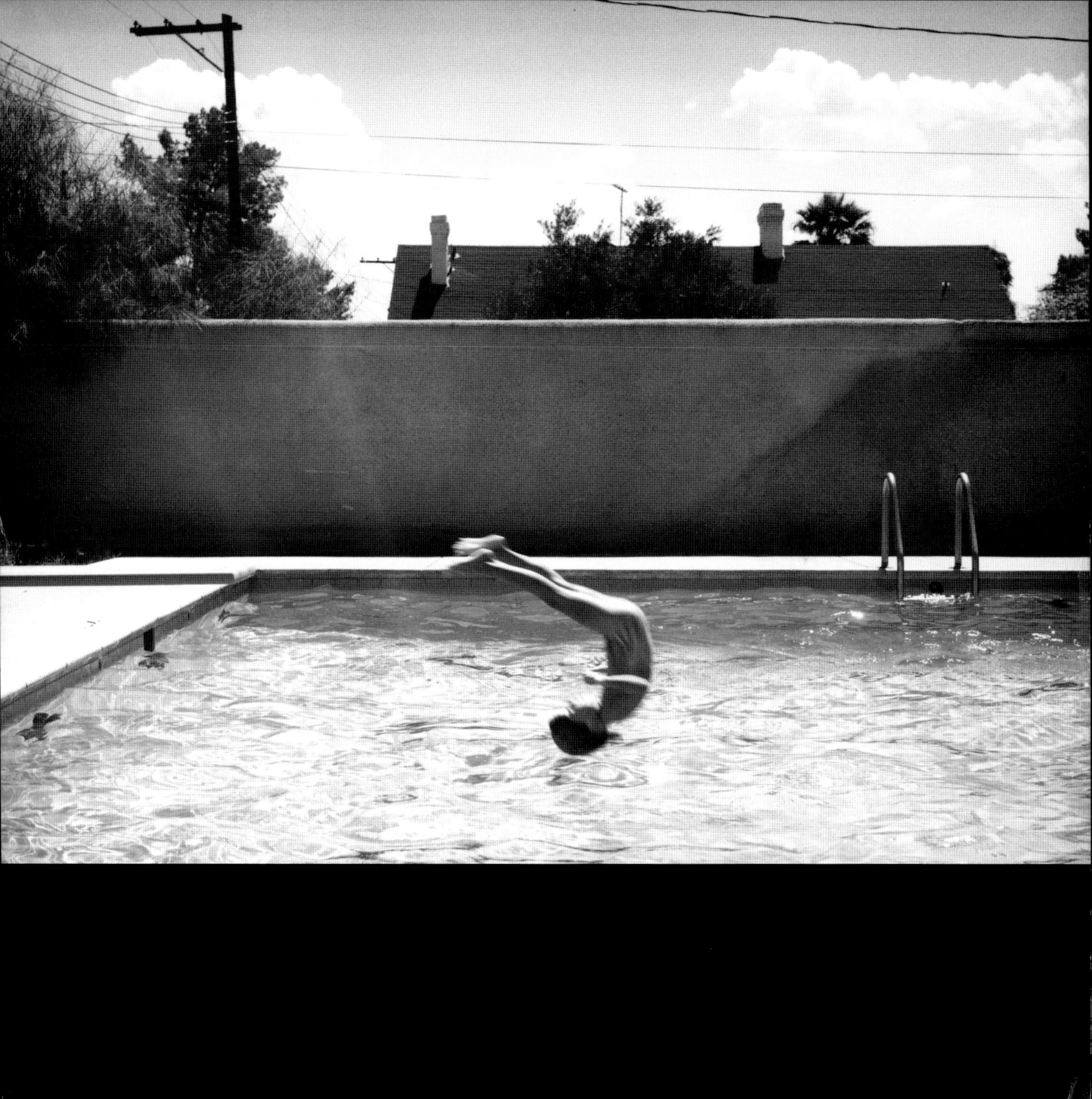

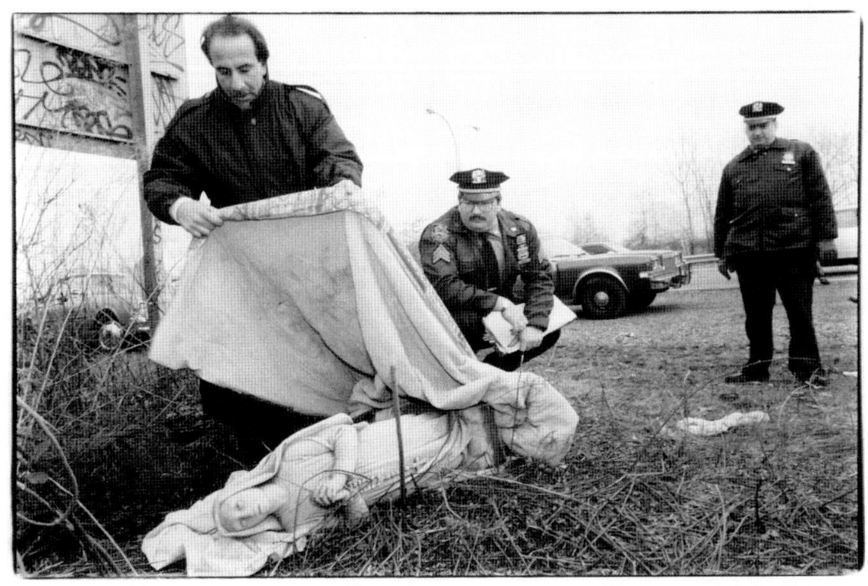

STOLEN FROM A BROOKLYN CHURCH ON CHRISTMAS — SAINT BERNADETTE WAS FOUND DUMPED NEAR THE BELT PARKWAY.

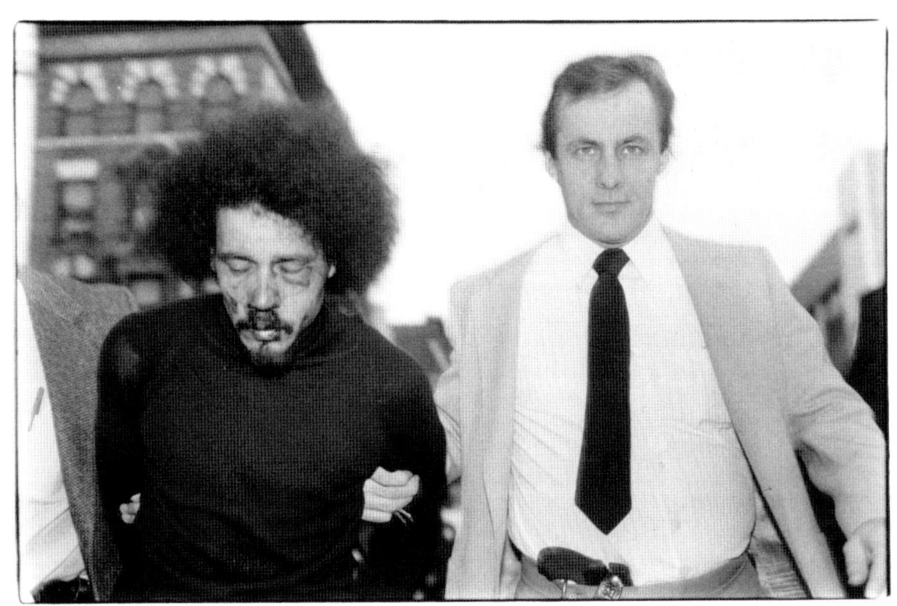

COP SHOOTING — SUSPECT TAKEN IN FOR QUESTIONING

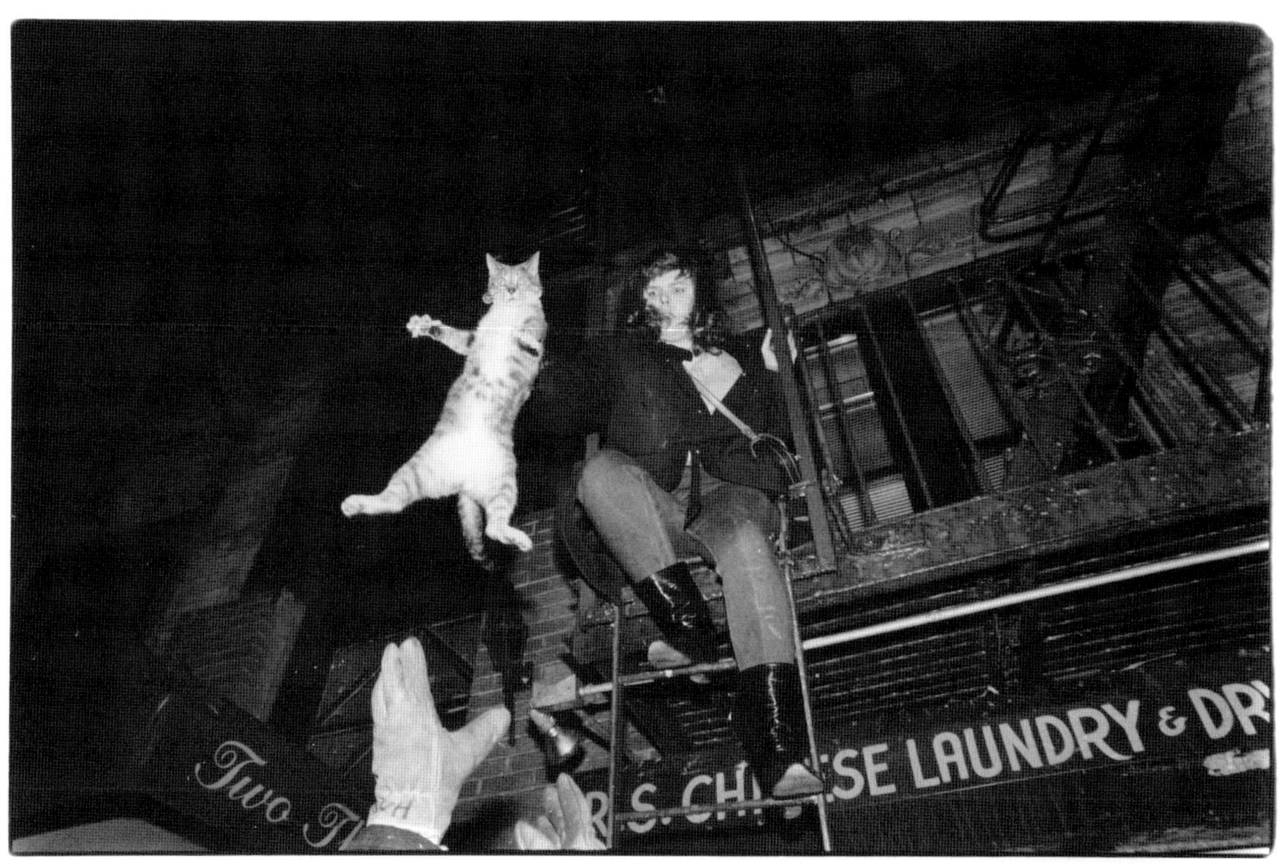

Andrew Savulich
Stolen from a Brooklyn Church on Christmas
Saint Bernadette was Found Dumped near the Beit Parkway, c. 1999
Silver gelatin print

Cop Shooting - Suspect Taken in for Questioning, c. 1999
Silver gelatin print

Four Alarm Fire- Midtown, c. 1999
Silver gelatin print
Courtesy of Mark Chamberlain

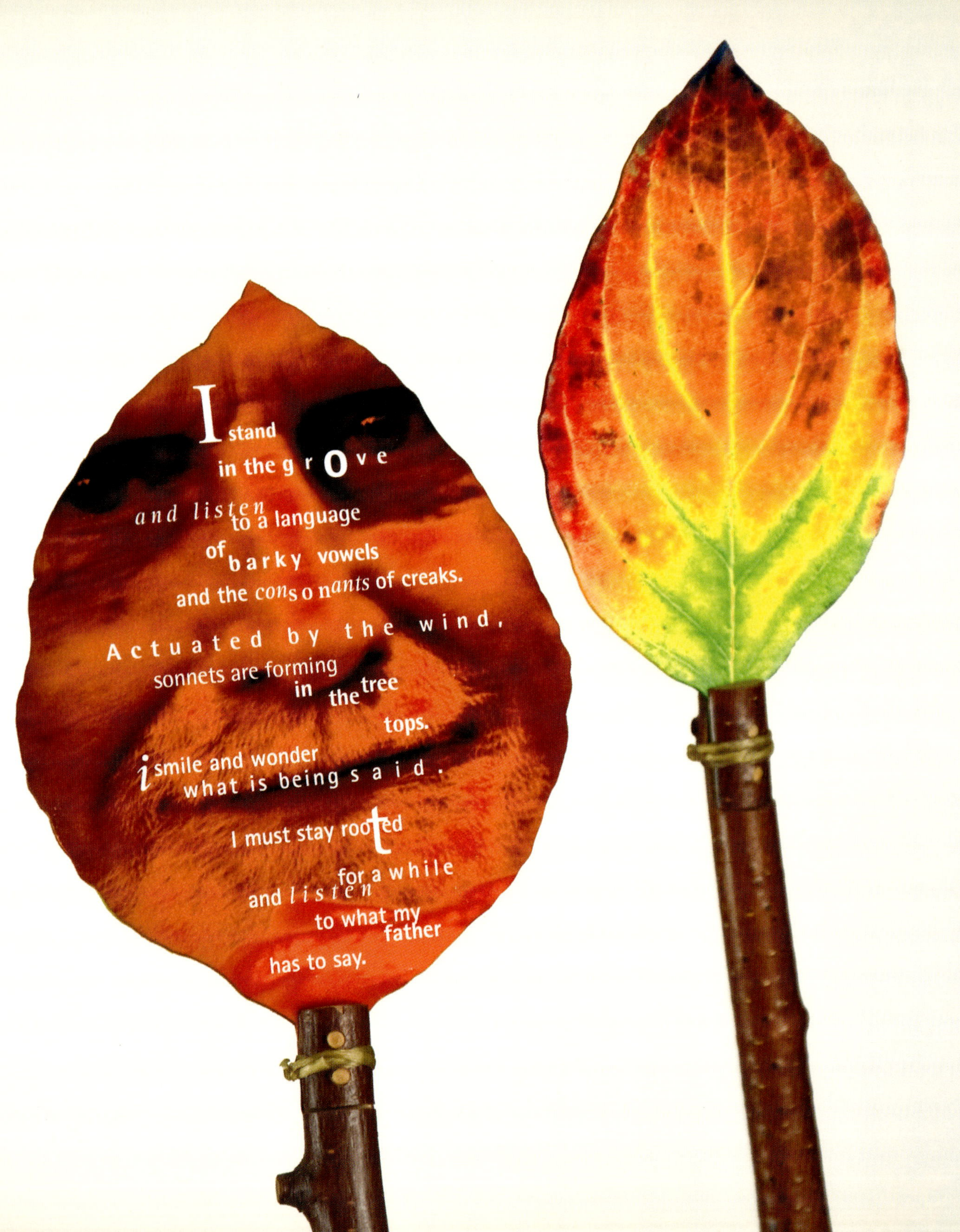

I stand
in the grOve
and listen to a language
of barky vowels
and the consonants of creaks.
Actuated by the wind,
sonnets are forming
in the tree
tops.
i smile and wonder
what is being said.
I must stay rooted
for a while
and listen
to what my father
has to say.

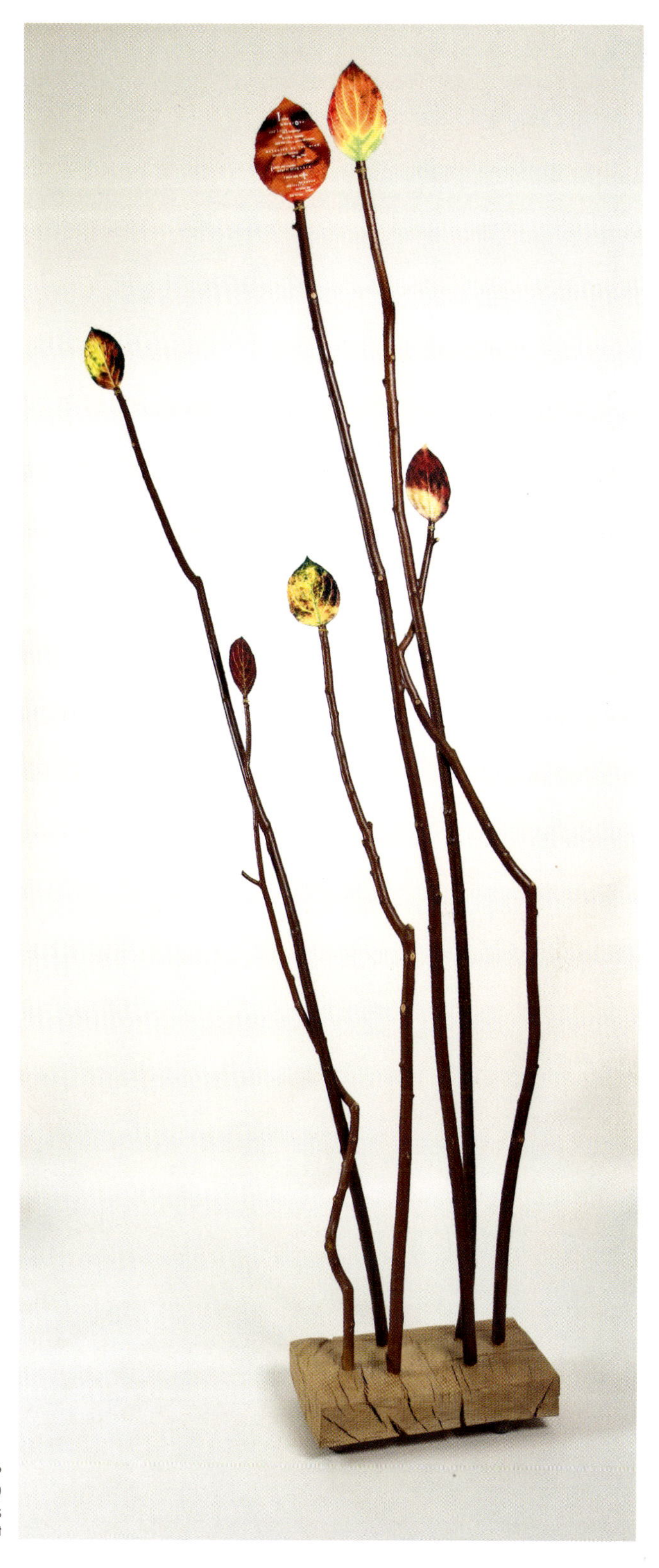

Jim Cukus
I Stand in the Grove, 2009
Giclee prints, waxed linen thread, birch branches, wood and river stones
Courtesy of the artist

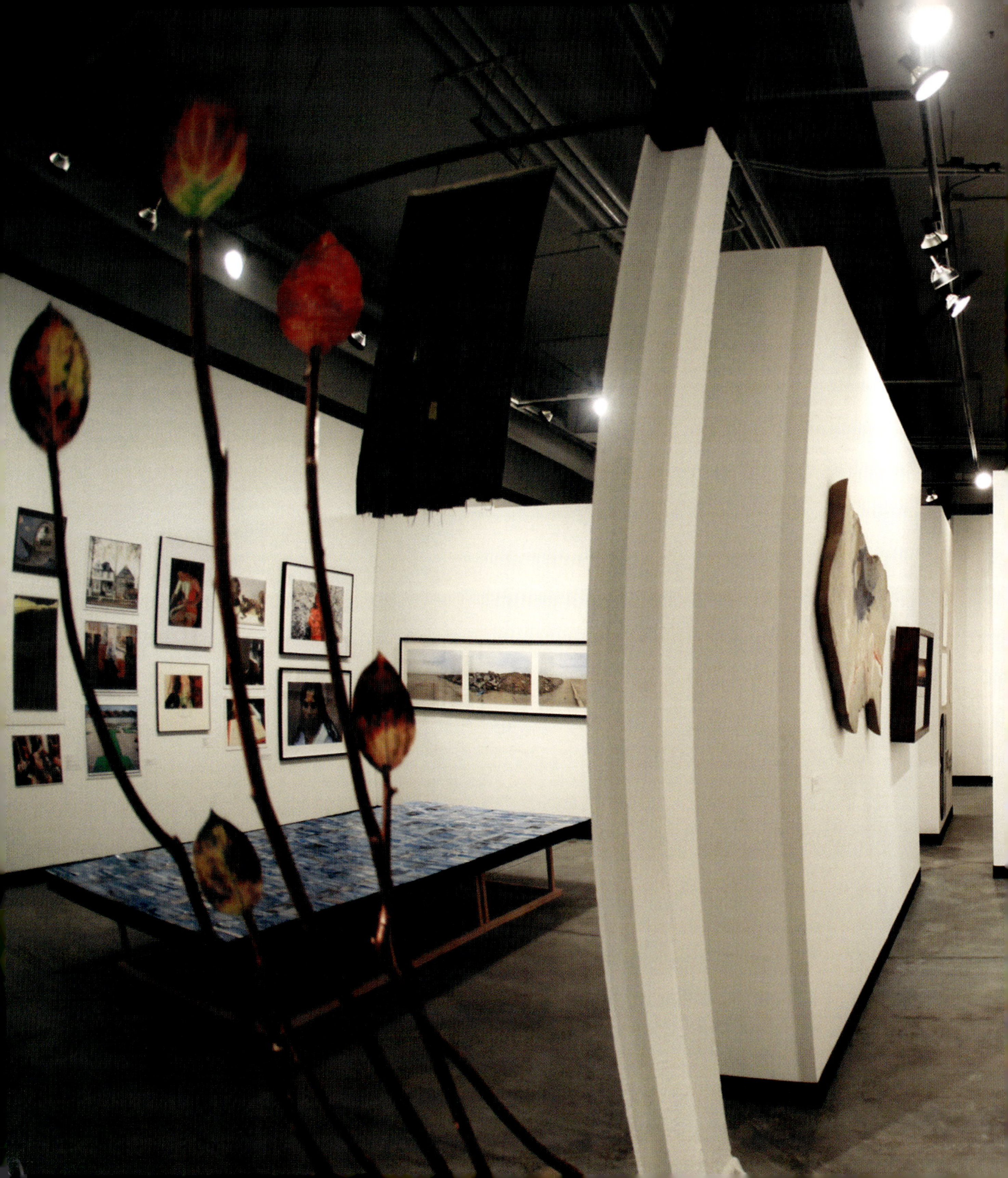

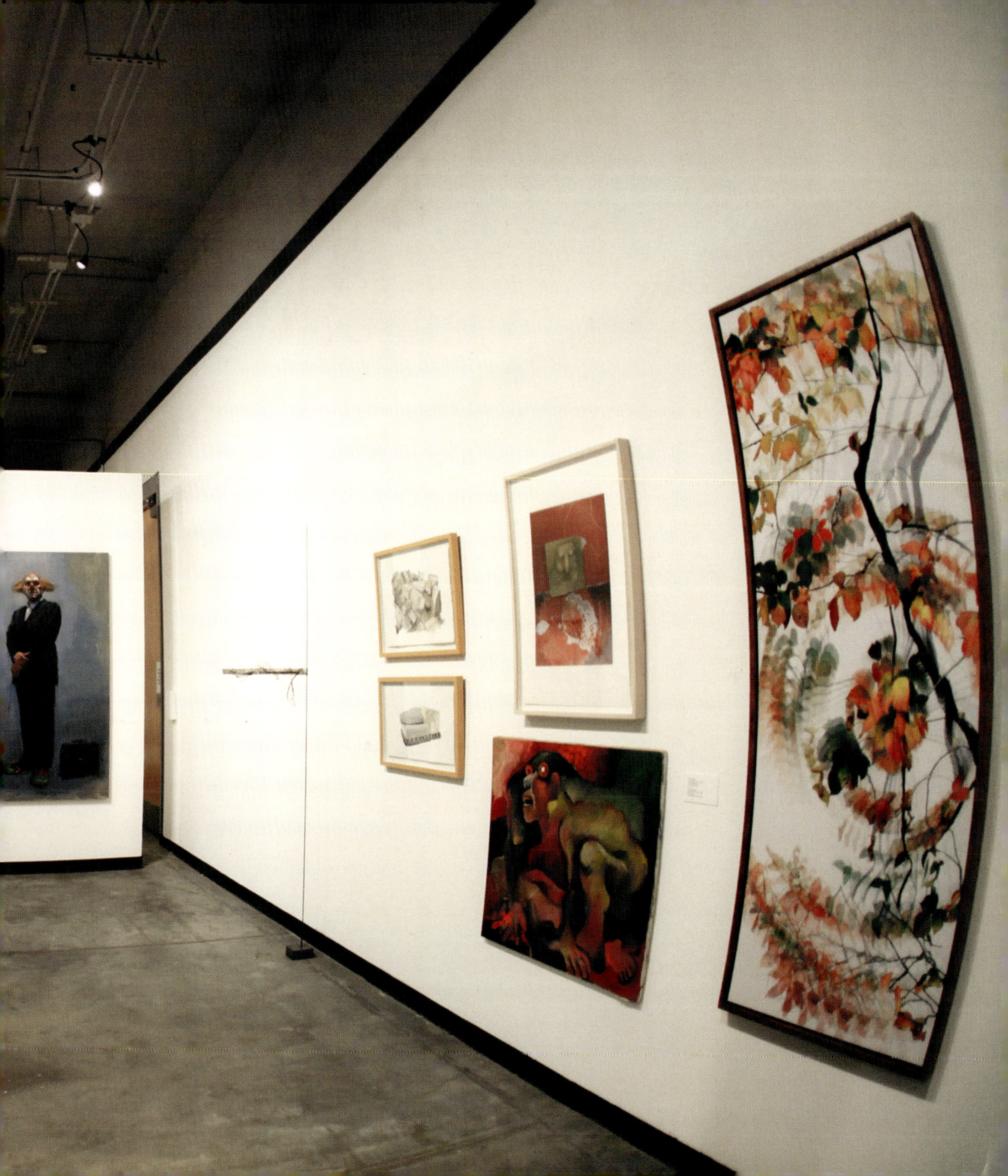

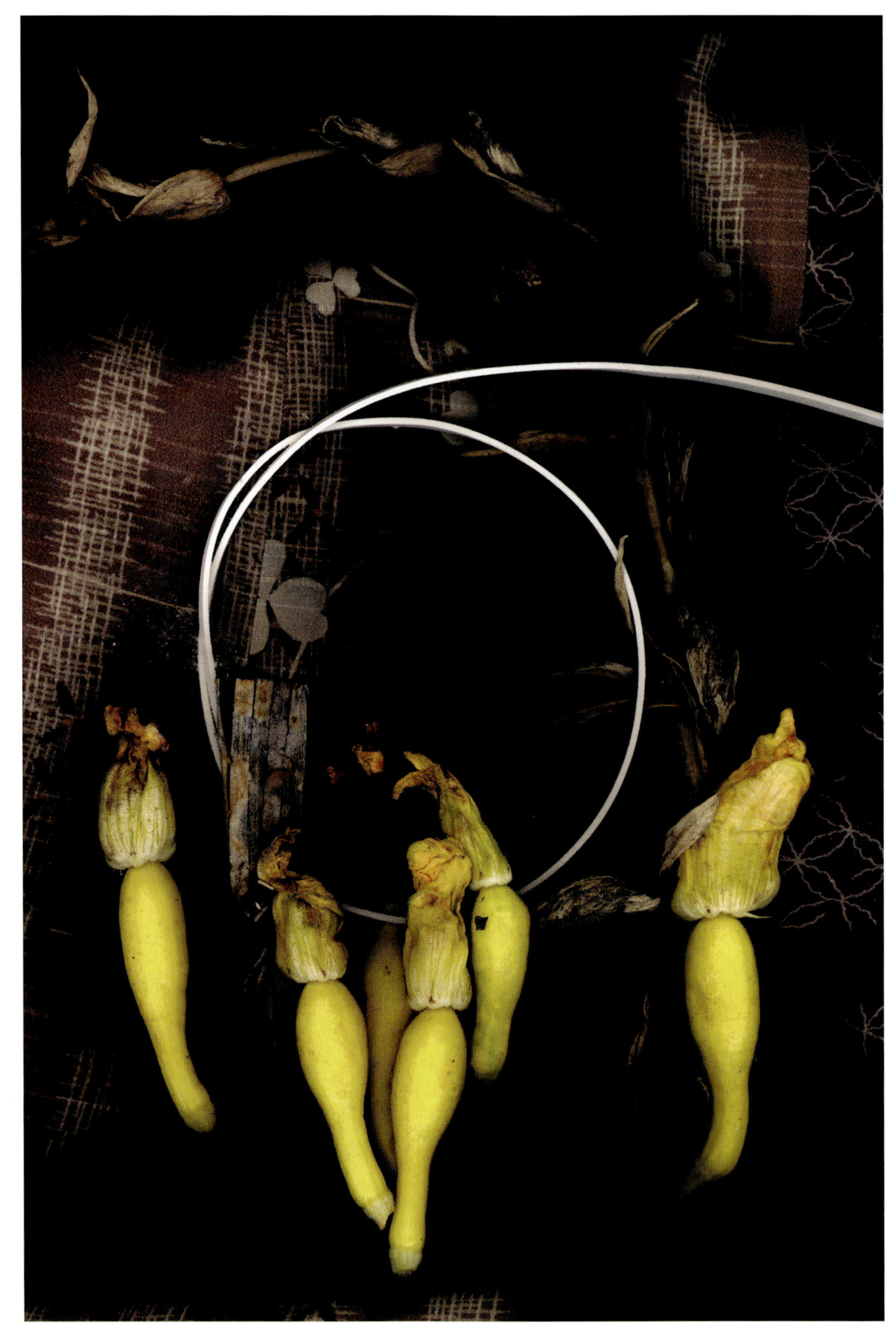

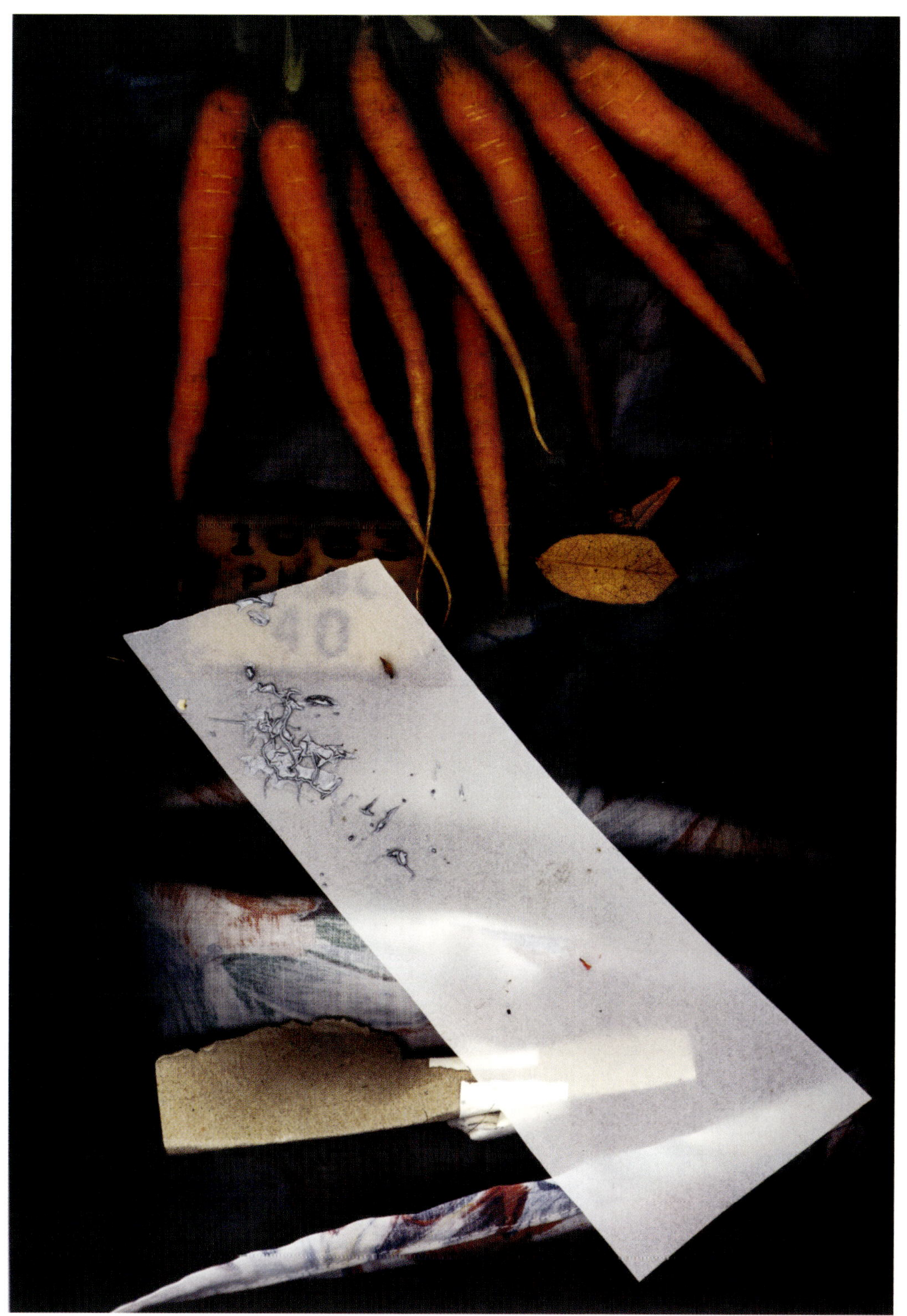

Darryl Curran
Five Squach Blossoms, 1996
Digital pigment print

Carrotid Scan, 1996
Digital pigment print
Courtesy of the artist

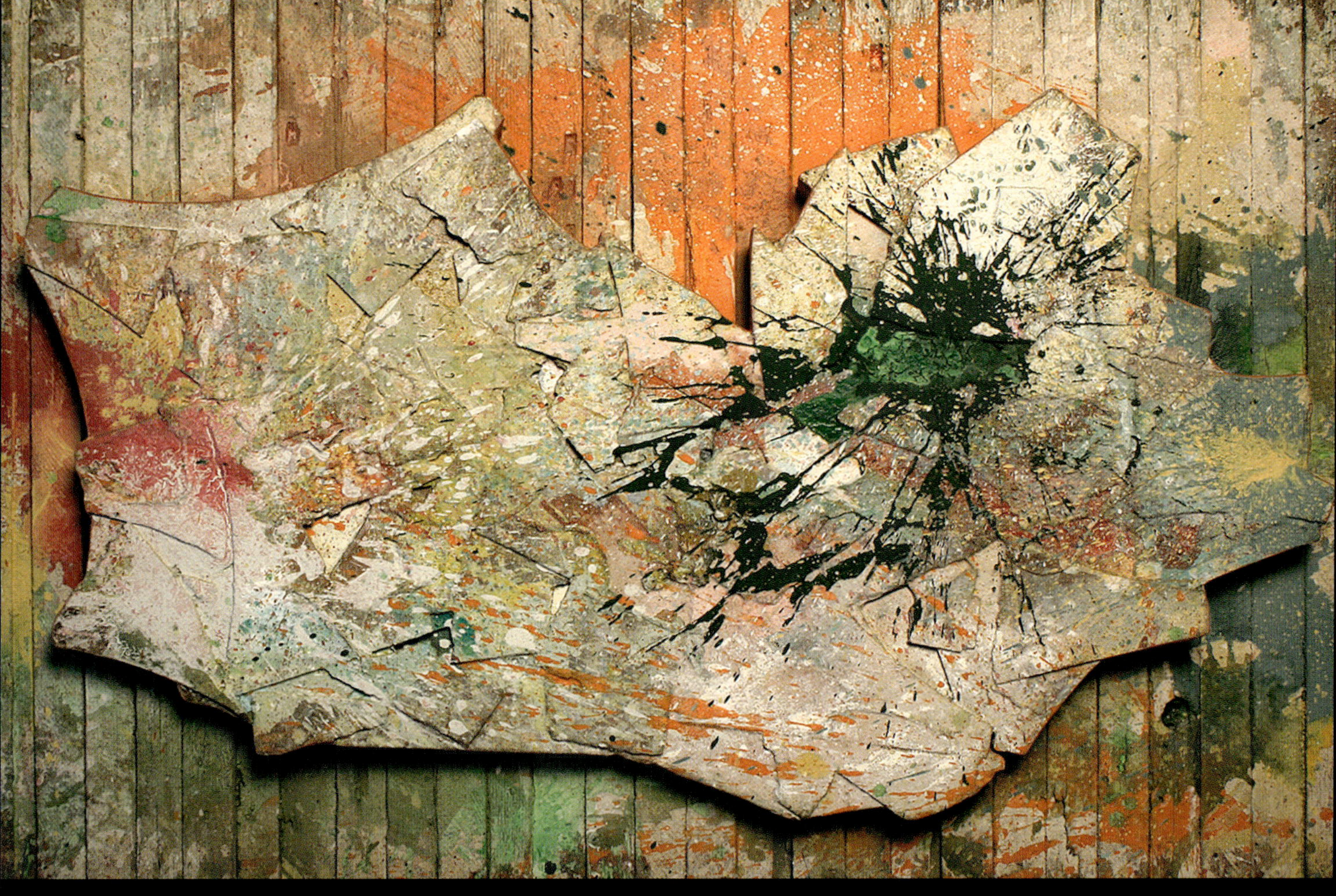

Andy Wing
US Say (Buffalo Hog), c. 1960-2000
Mixed media
Photo courtesy of BC Space

Roger Armstrong
Fait of the Beast Within, 1968
Oil on canvas

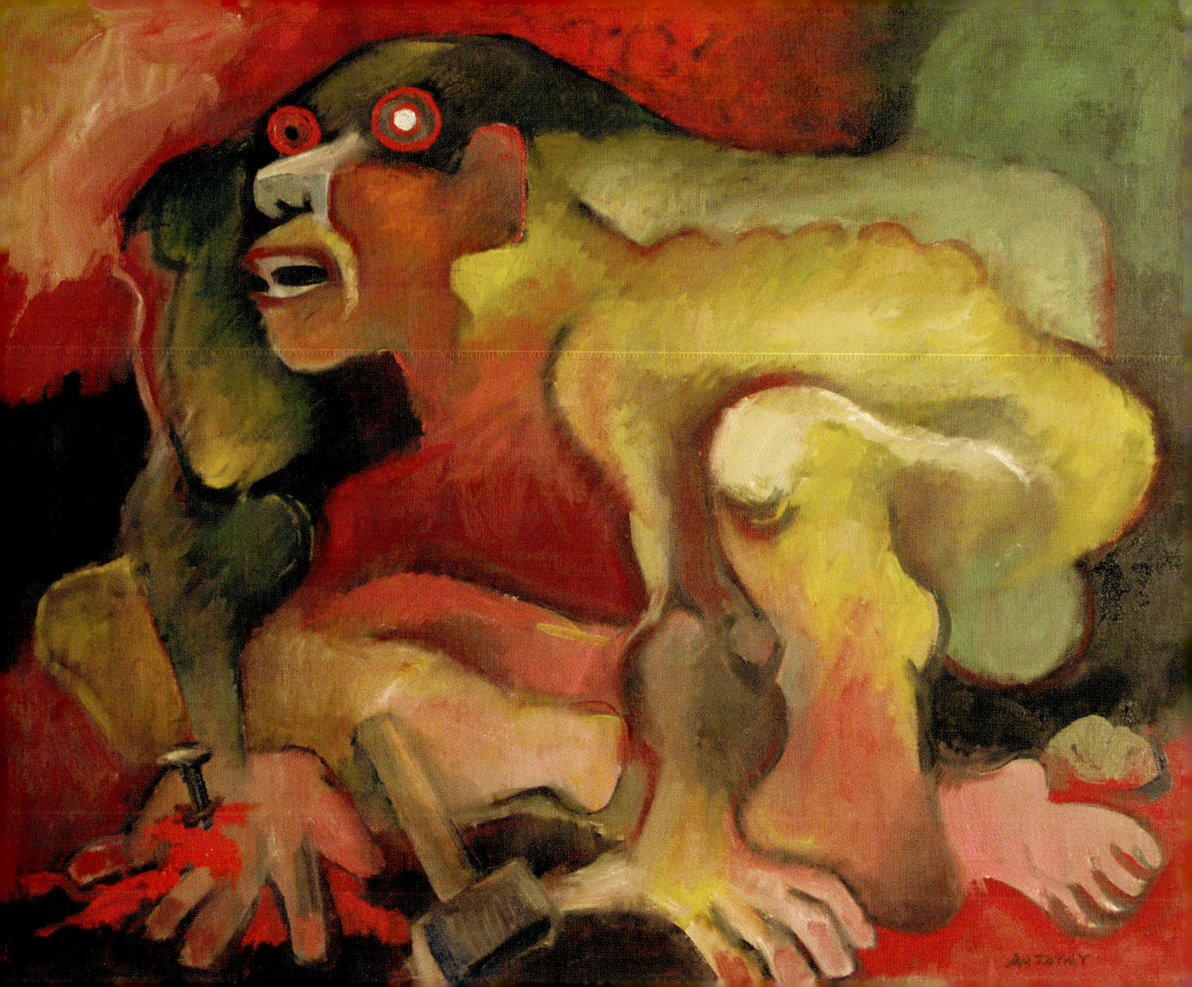

ANTONY

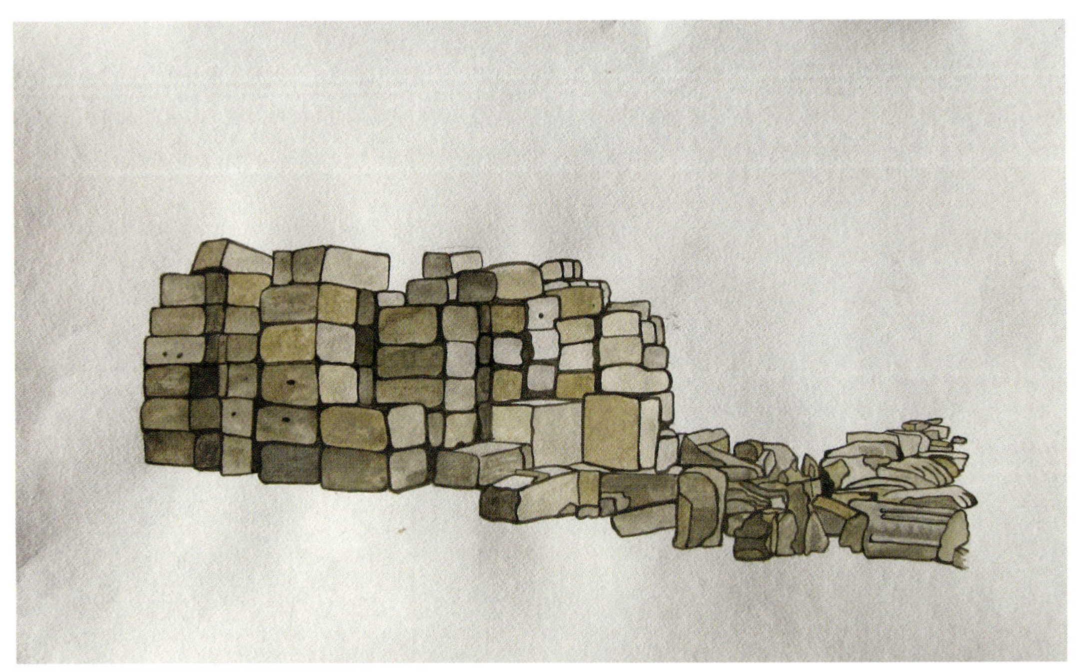

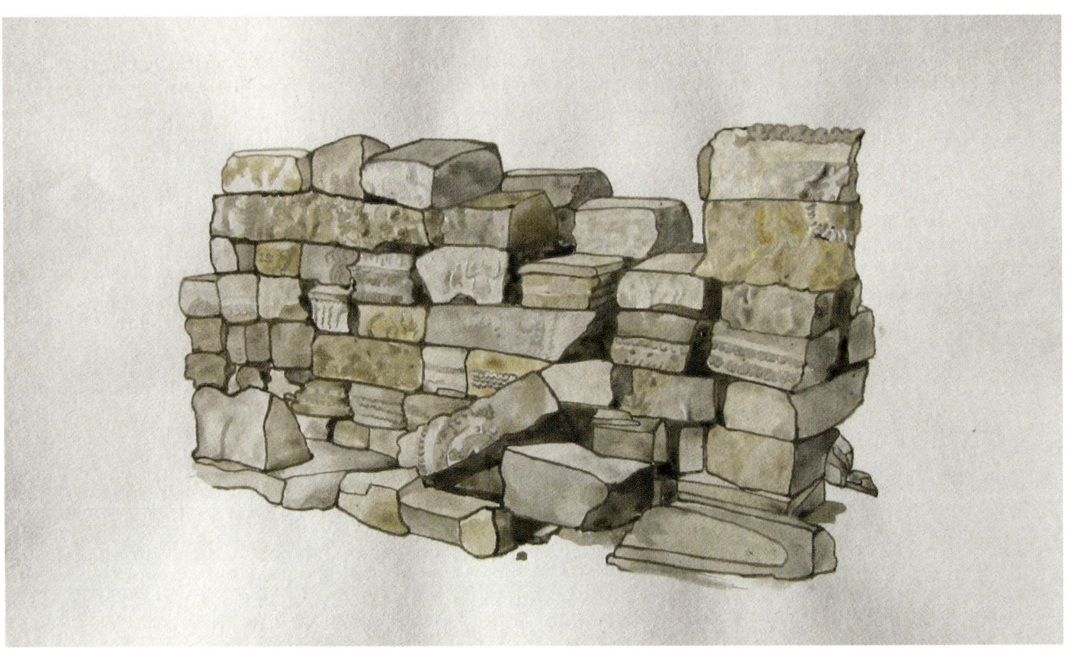

Richard Turner
See Angkor and Die, 2009
Water based media
Courtesy of the artist

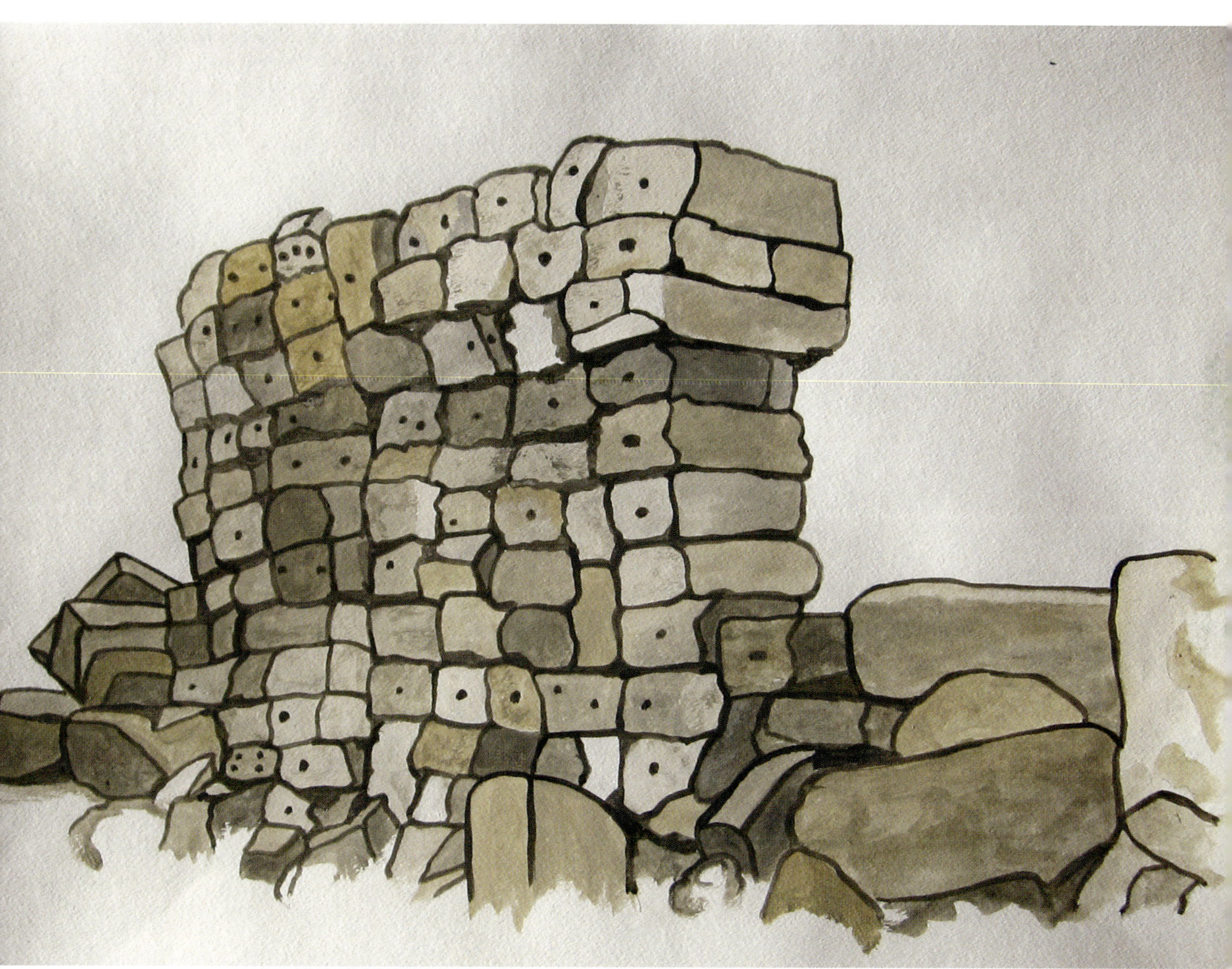

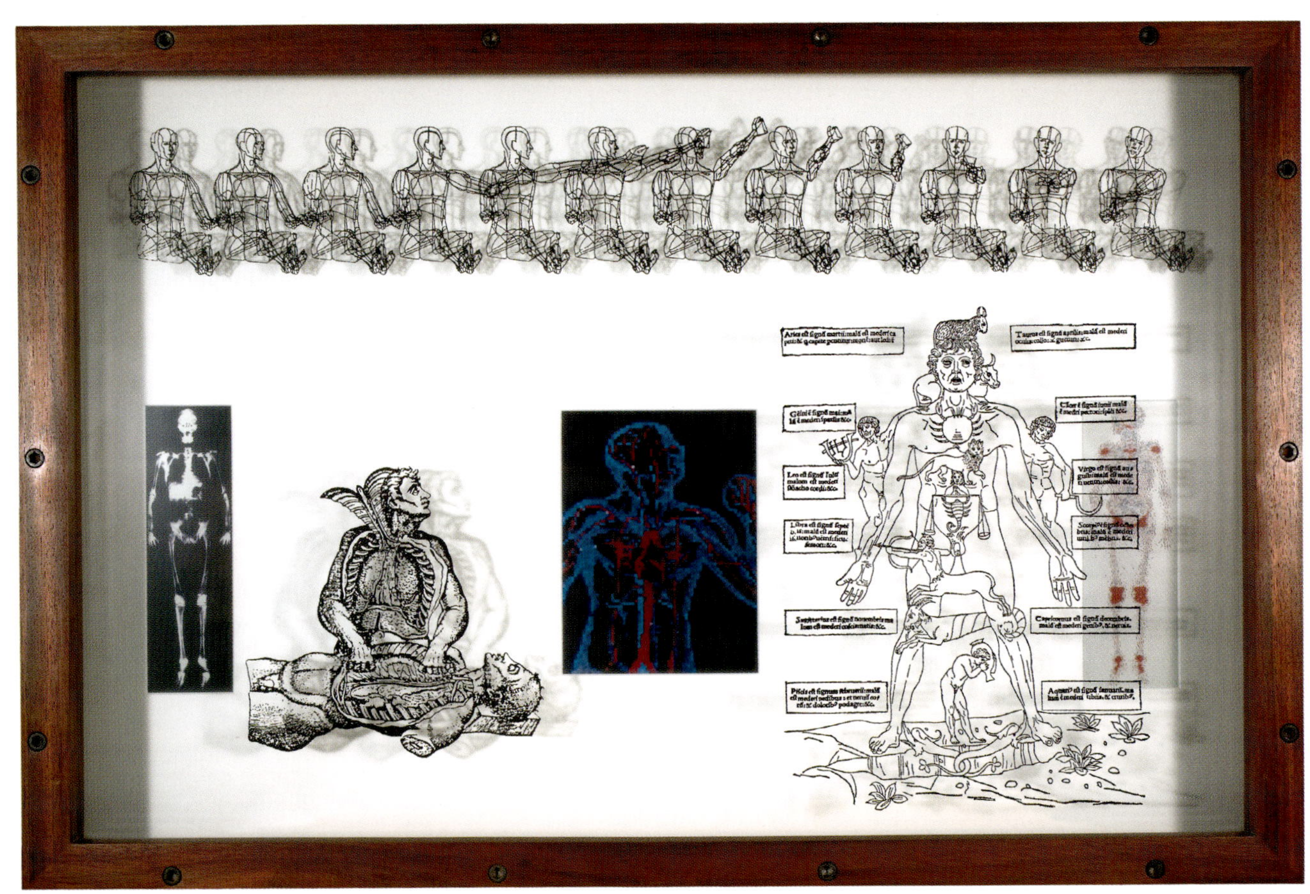

Clayton Spada
Magic Anatomy, 1995
Color dye destruction photographic prints on polyester, silkscreen on glass,
three panels and rare wood casing

Gridlocked XVI, 2000
Color dye destruction photographic print on plyester
Courtesy of the artist

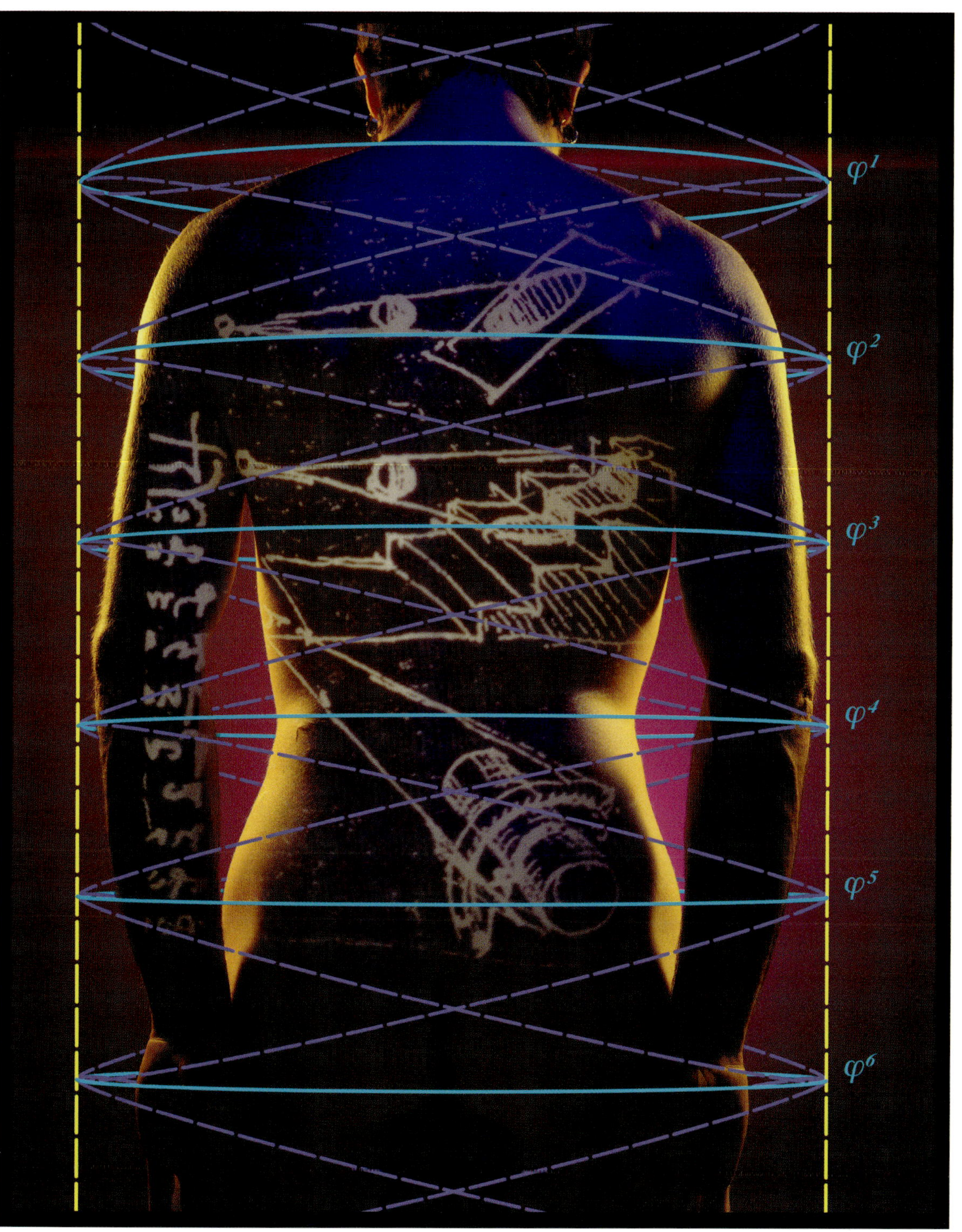

φ¹
φ²
φ³
φ⁴
φ⁵
φ⁶

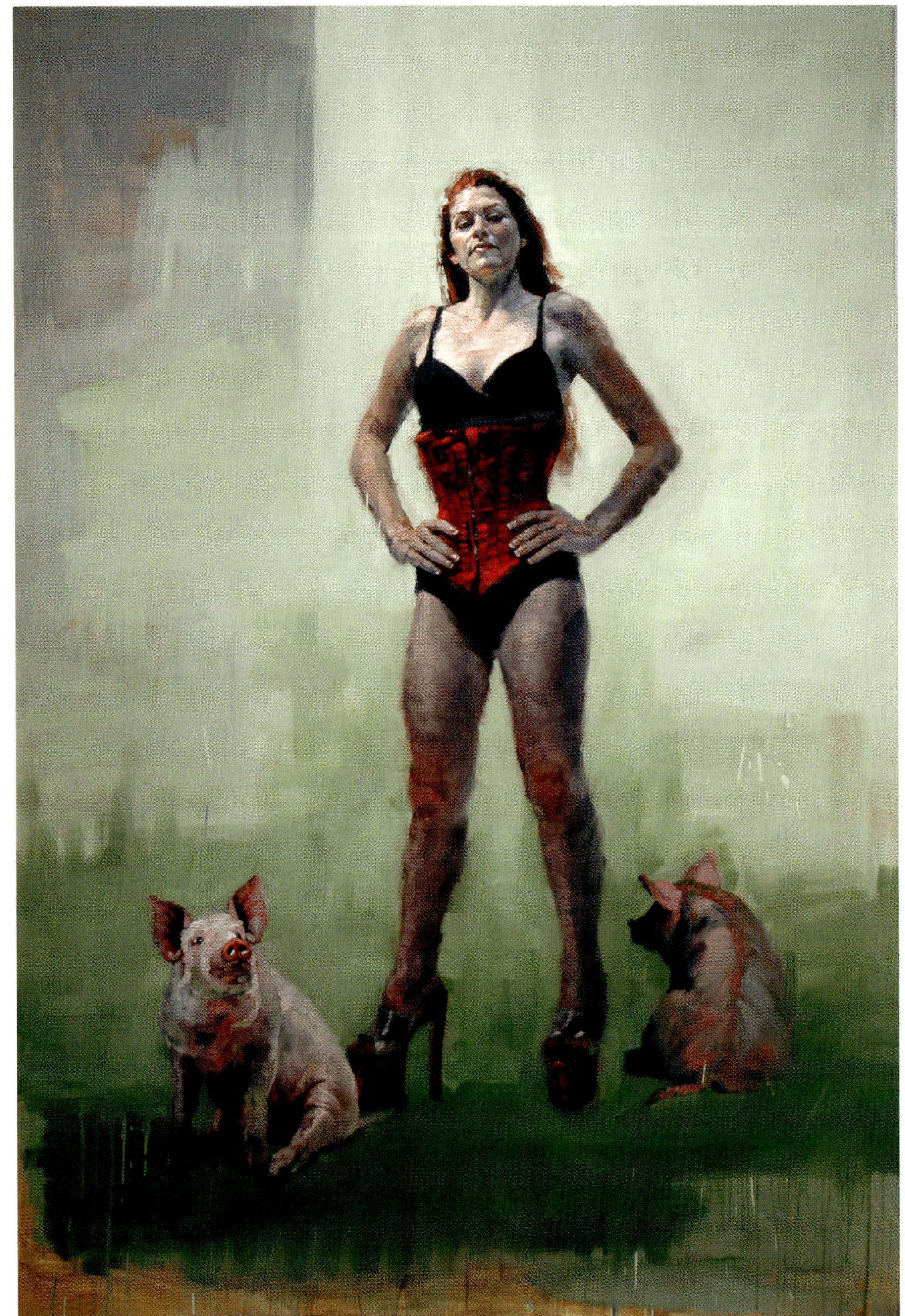

Jorg Dubin
Command and Control, 2008
Oil on linen

Sandman, 2008
Oil on linen
Courtesy of the artist

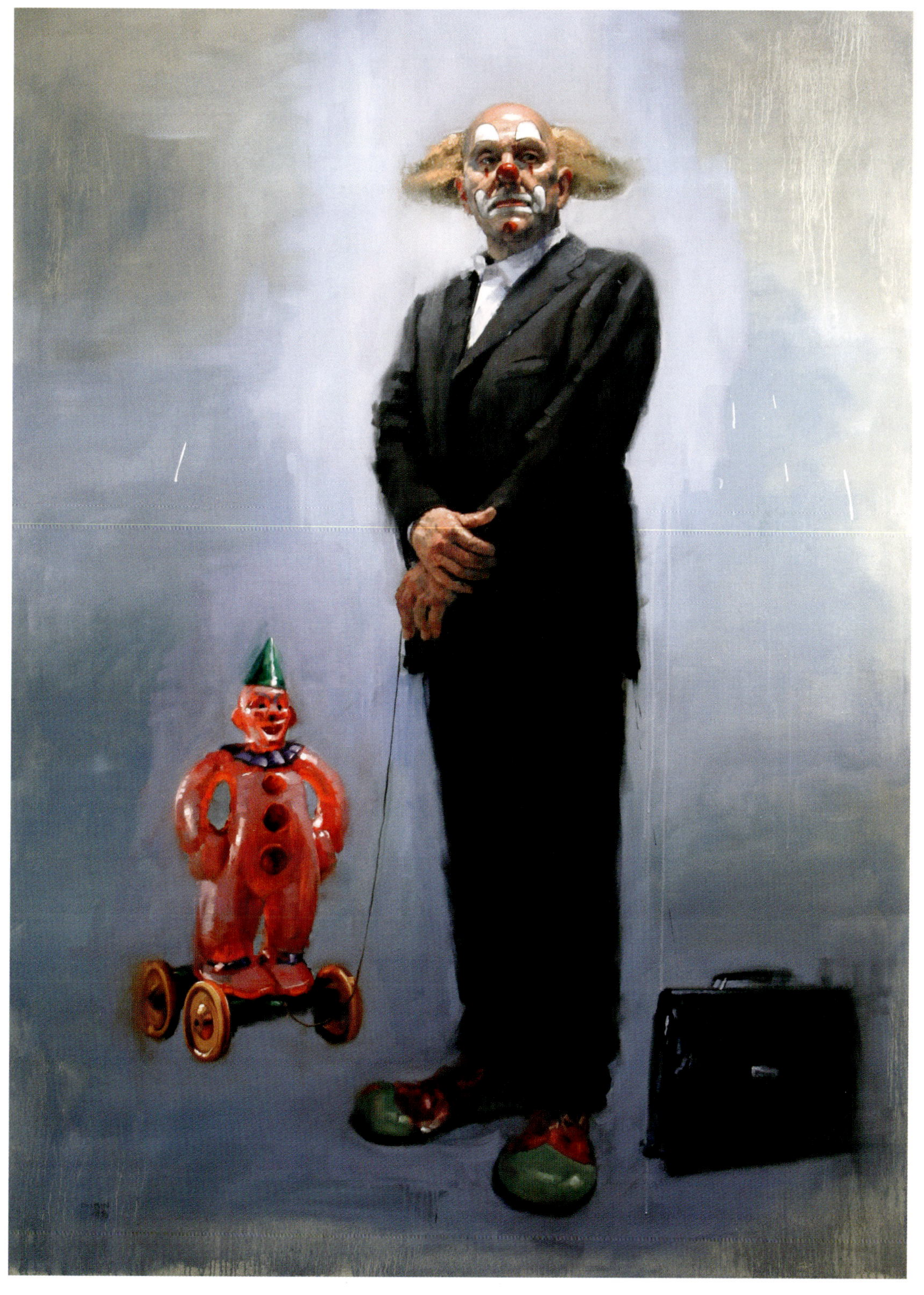

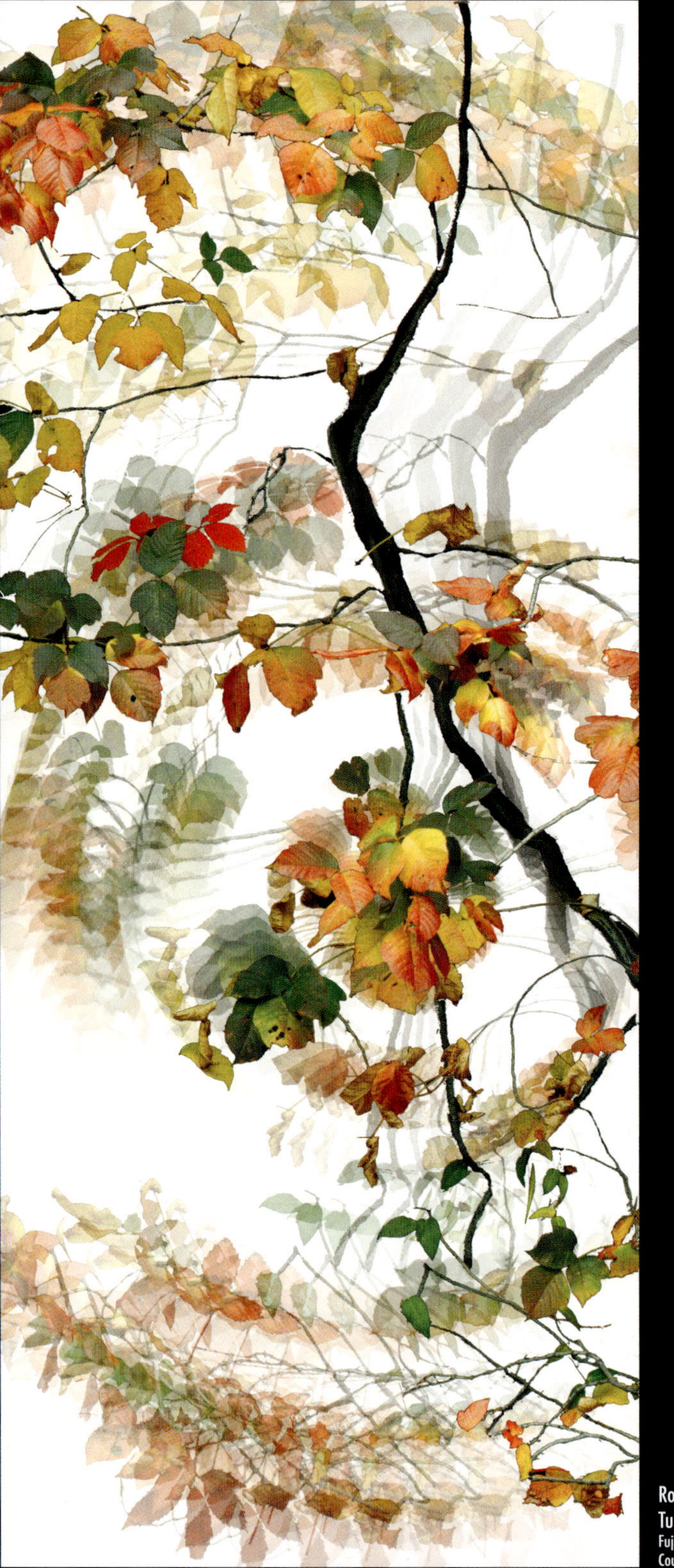

Robert Glenn Ketchum
Turn, Turn, Turn, 2001
Fuji crystal archive print (chromogenic)
Courtesy of the artist

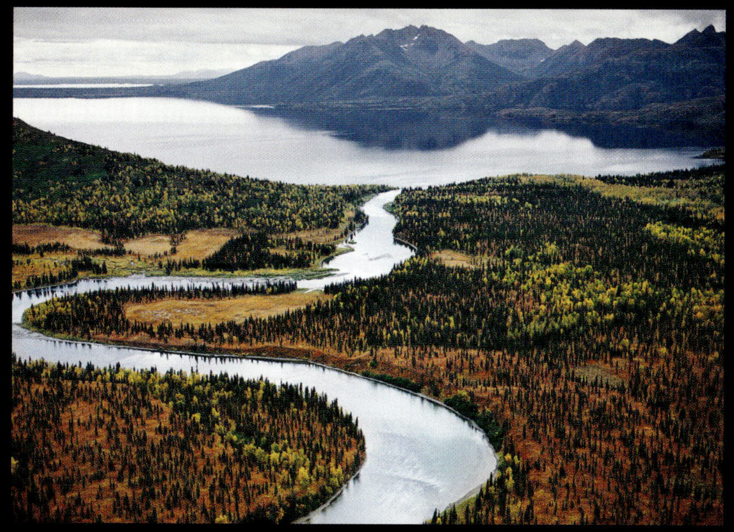

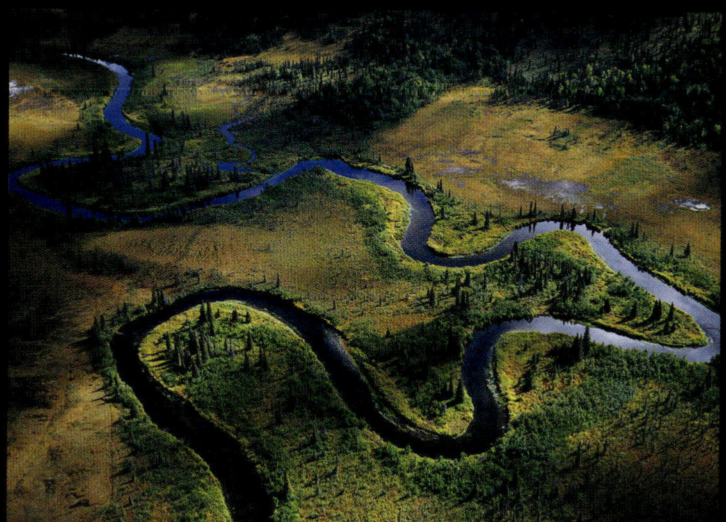

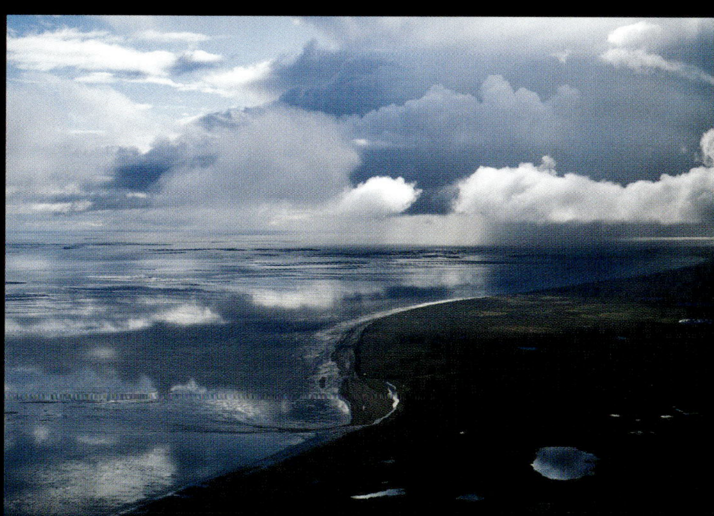

Robert Glenn Ketchum
The Allen River Enters Lake Chauekukli, 2001
Fuji crystal archive print (chromogenic)

Rat Creek, Wood-Tikchik State Park, 1999
Fuji crystal archive print (chromogenic)

Clearing Weather, Kvichak Mouth, 1998
Fuji crystal archive print (chromogenic)
Courtesy of the artist

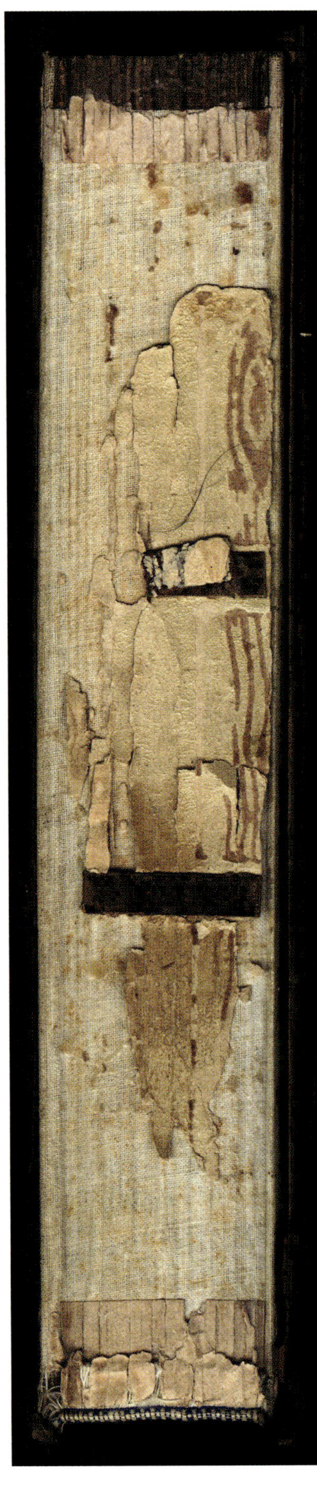

Joyce Neimanas
Book Spine, 2009
Archival ink jet on German etching paper

Yellow Paper Tablet, 2009
Archival ink jet on German etching paper
Courtesy of the artist

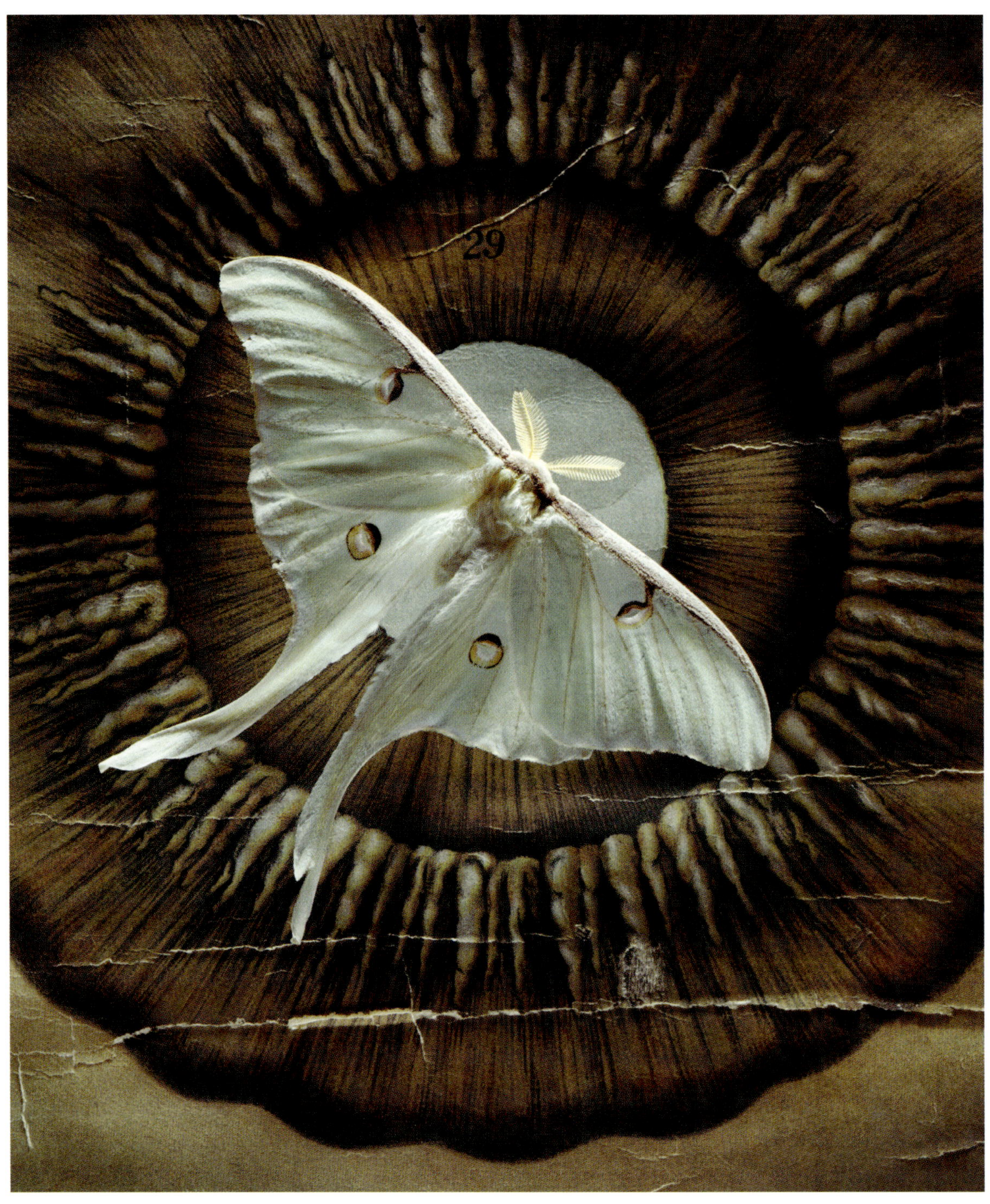

29

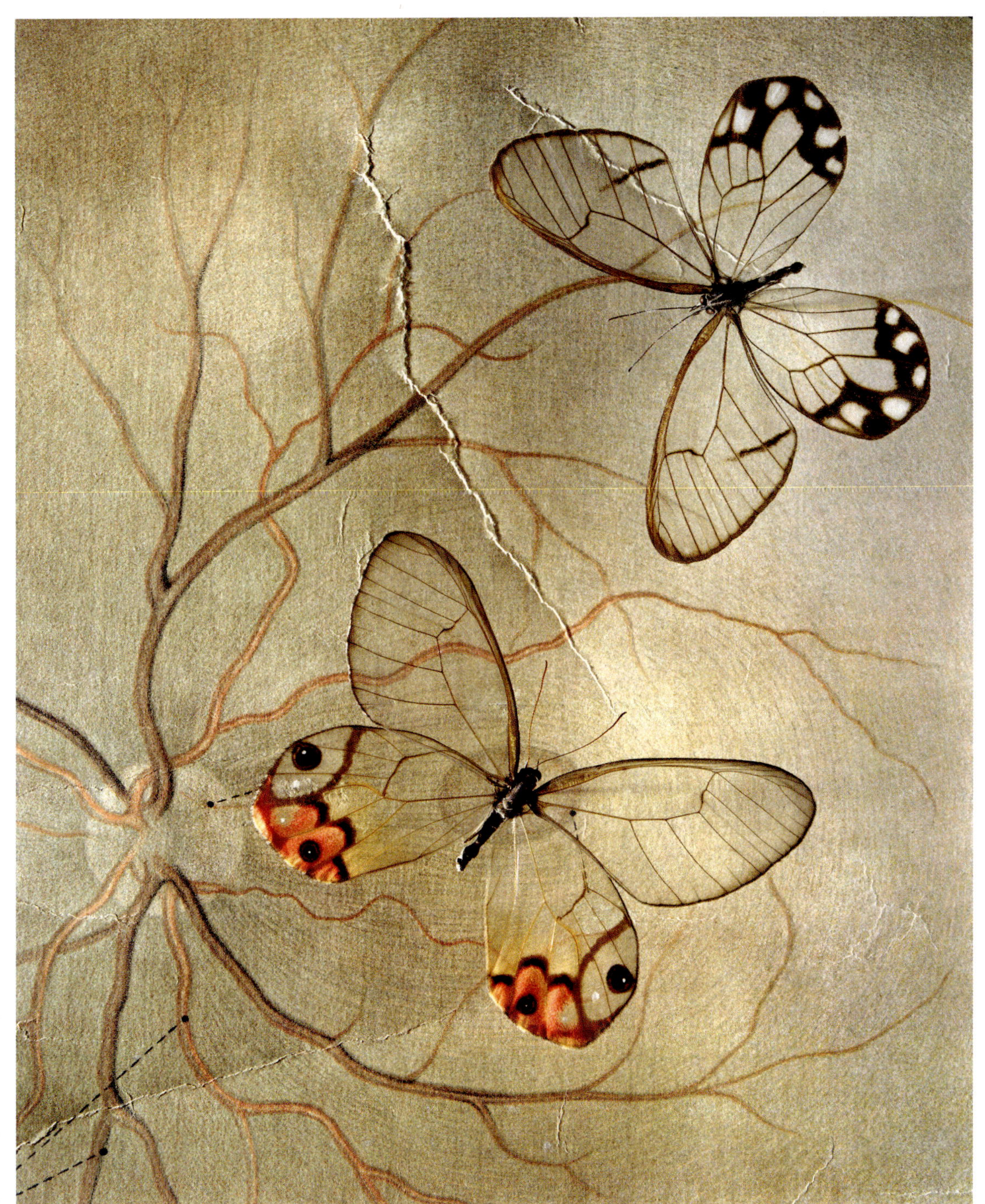

Jo Whaley
Tropea Luna, 2000
Printed, 2009
4x5 color negative
Archival pigment photograph

Cithaerias, 2000
Printed, 2009
4x5 color negative
Archival pigment photograph
Courtesy of the artist

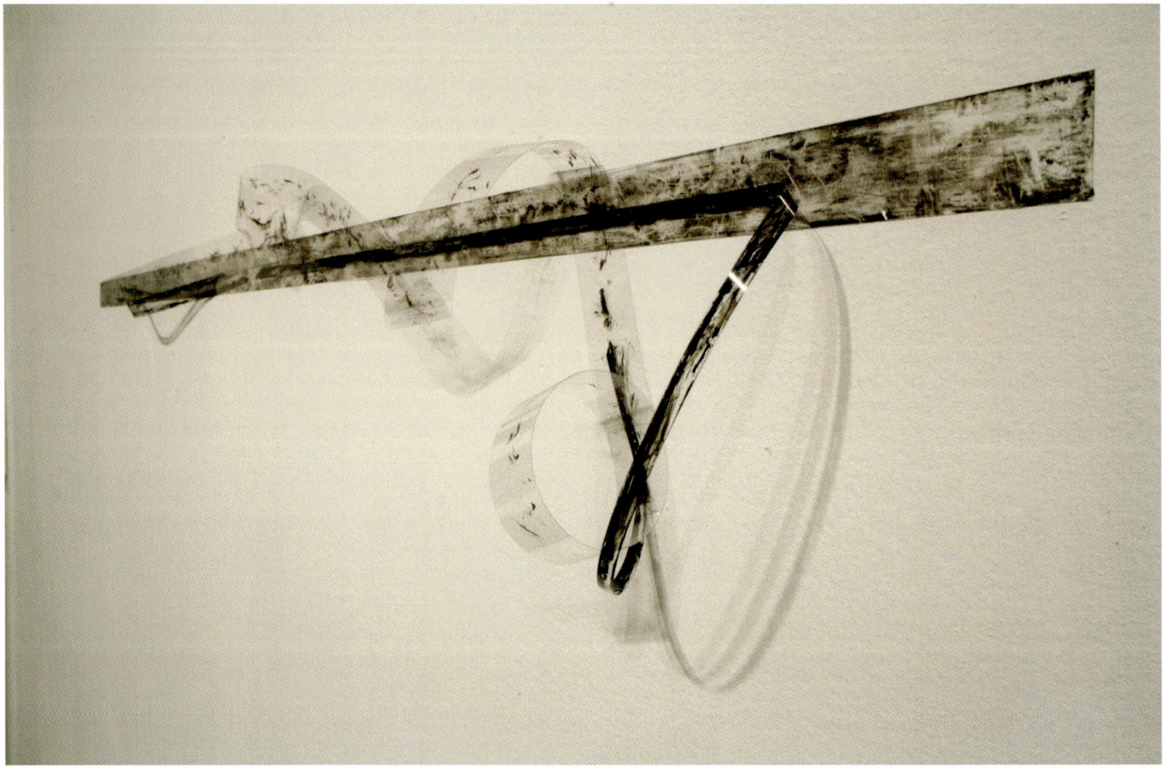

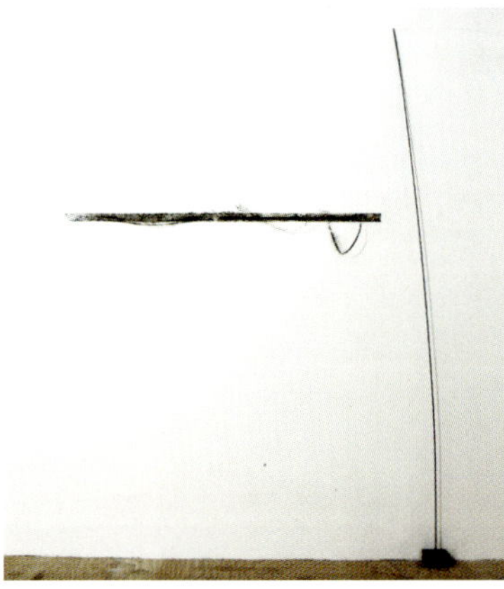

Angie Bray
Drawing New Drawing (detail)
Photo by Mark Chamberlain

Drawing New Drawing, 2009
Duralar, india ink, basswood, graphite, lead and motor
Courtesy of the artist

Installation CSUF Grand Central Art Center, 2009

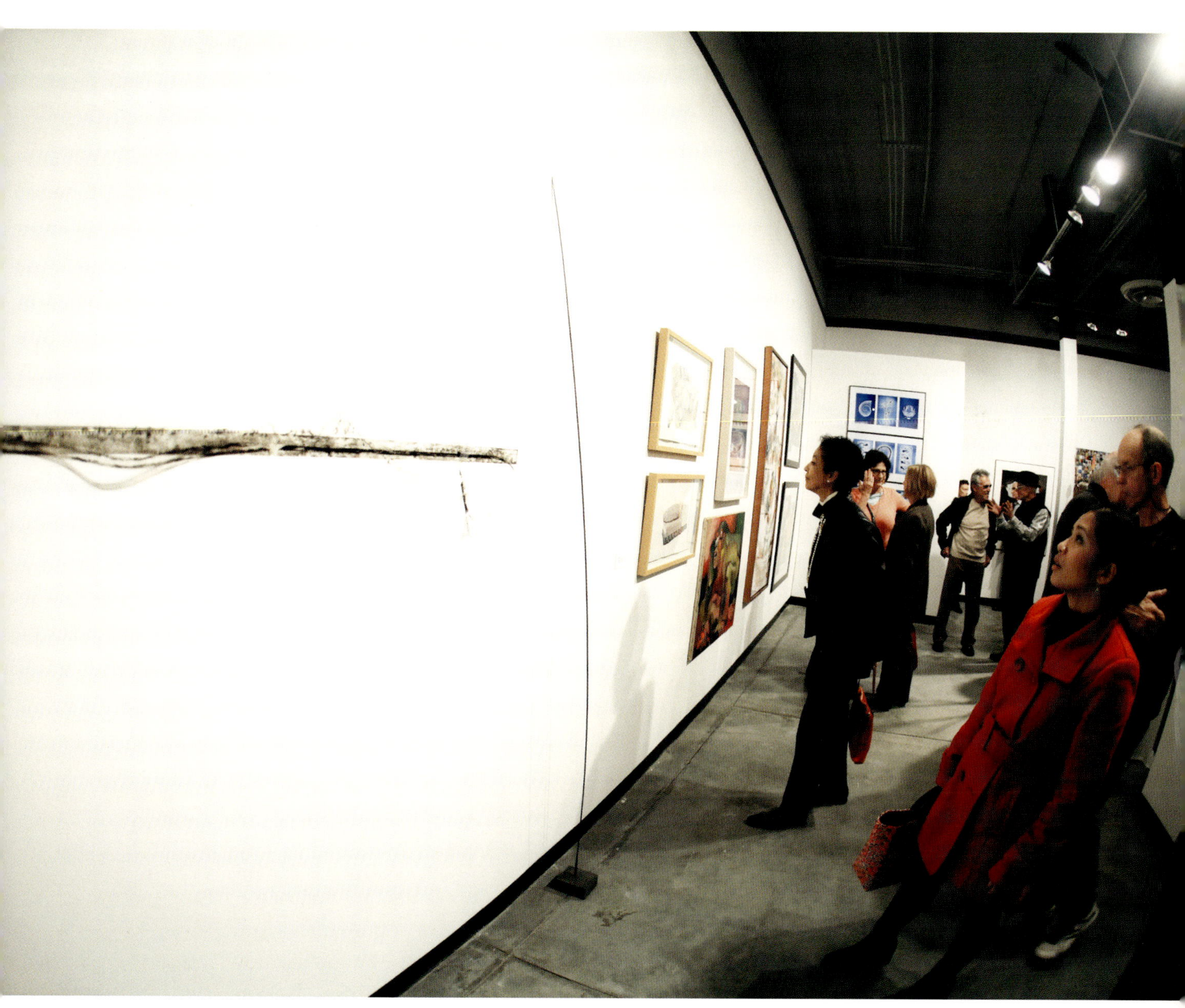

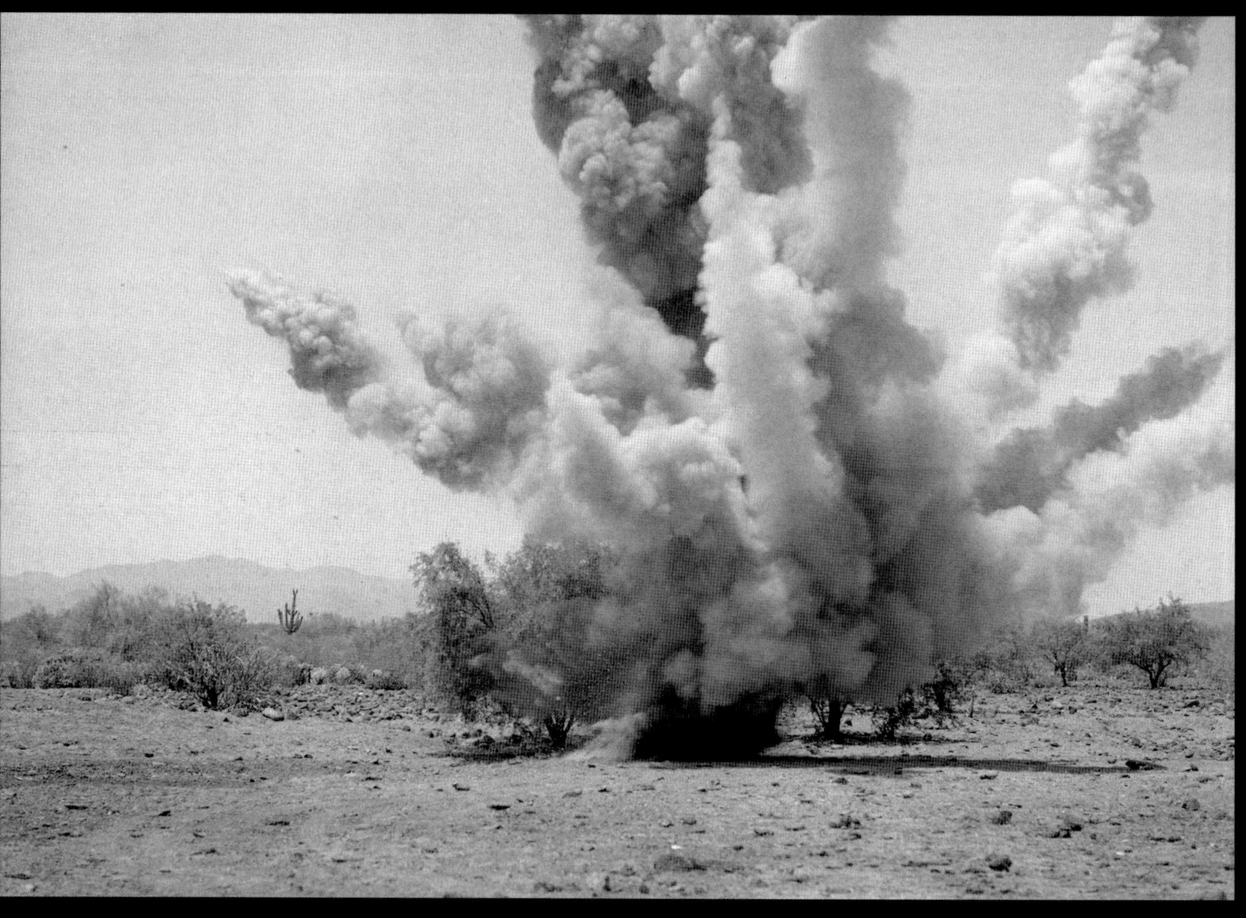

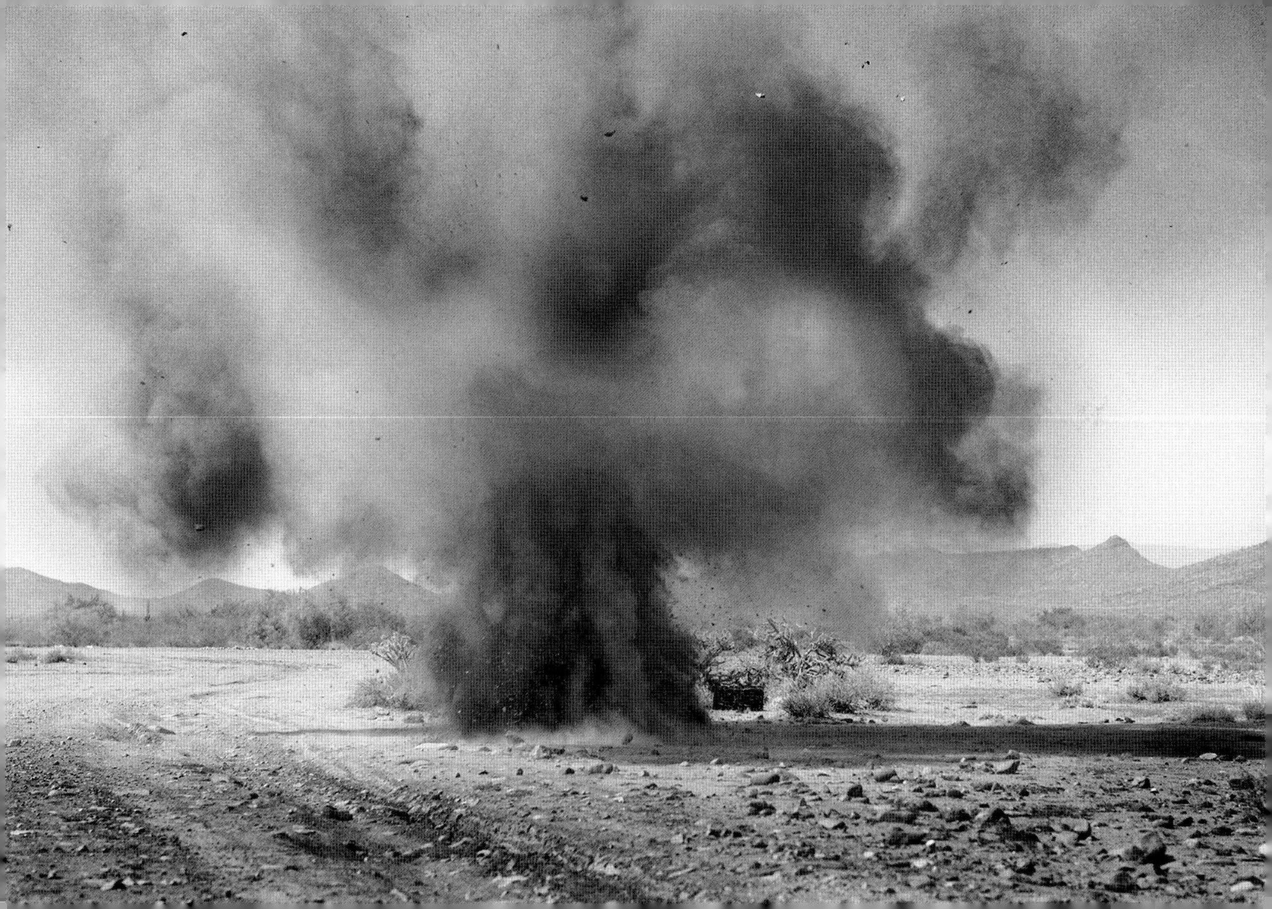

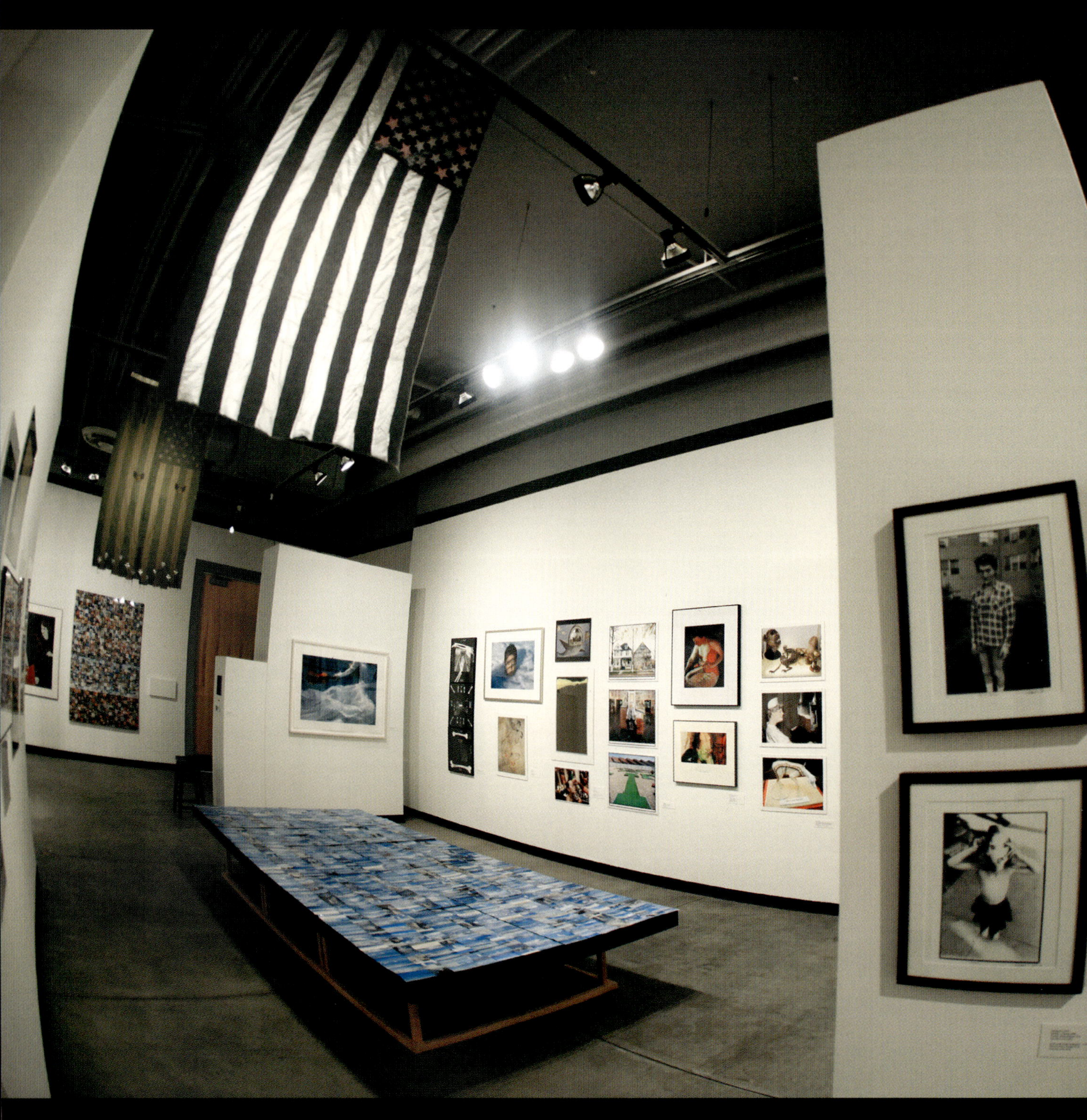

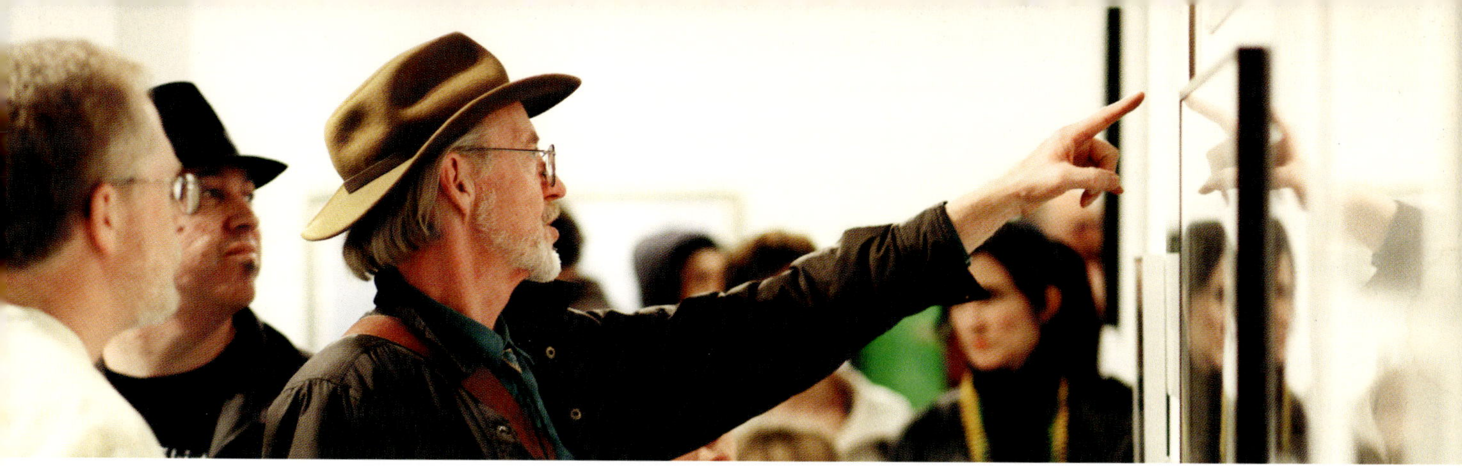

On behalf of Jerry and myself, I would also like to thank the artists who shared the journey over so many years and so enthusiastically participated once again. It was their passion and creativity that has nurtured, crafted, and sustained the mission of BC for all this time. It has been a real joy to be engaged with these generous and talented spirits in a way that we could help each other pursue our passions.

Special thanks are also due Peter Clothier for his generous writings on the art part of BC Space. Peter, himself, is a model of the persistence he writes about. And many thanks to Liz Goldner for her diligence, necessary nudging while still nurturing, and great patience in making a long and sometimes tortuous tale understandable.

I thank Cal State Fullerton and Grand Central Art Center for the opportunity to present this overview of the history of BC Space, with very special thanks to Mike McGee and Andrea Harris for conceiving of such an exhibition and bringing this wonderful book to fruition.

I also thank my art partner, Jerry, for being willing to engage in such an absurdly idealistic enterprise at a crucial time, and for becoming the brother I always wished for. I am most thankful for Jerry's unflagging eagerness to engage in big dreams and always look over the horizon, while having the extraordinary ability to make hard work a three letter word, and the journey a joy.

Dream on, my brother, and I will continue to do the same.

Mark C bc

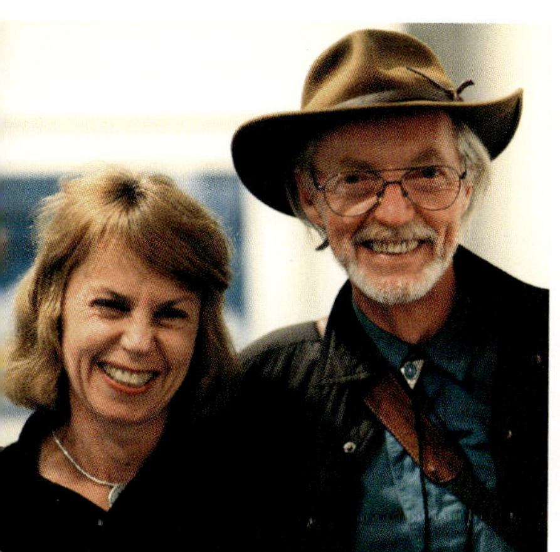

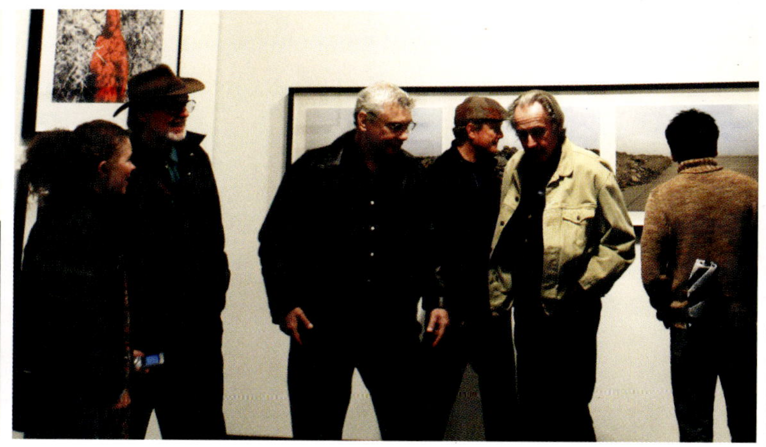

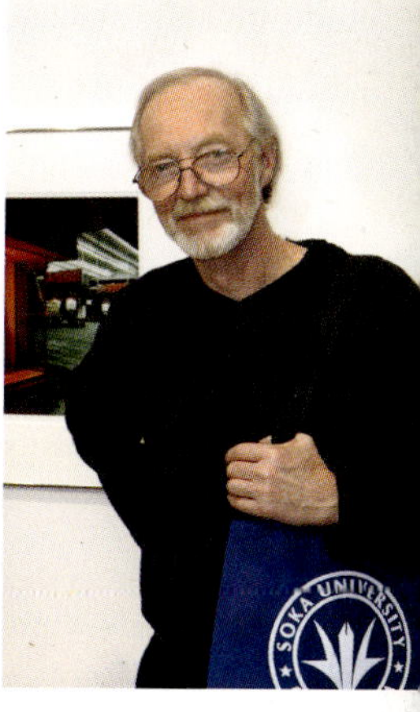

BC SPACE: MATURATION OF A CONTEMPORARY PIONEERING EFFORT

Copyright ©1984 by the Los Angeles Center for
Photographic Studies.
Published in Obscura, Photography in the Los Angeles Area.
By Linda Bellon

Although the words "contemporary" and "pioneer" evoke
opposing ideas, they well describe Jerry Burchfield and
Mark Chamberlain, co-owners and directors of BC Space
Gallery in Laguna Beach. Like Steiglitz, nearly a century
before them, Burchfield and Chamberlain are devoted to
the promotion and public acceptance of photography as a
fine art form.

Steiglitz fought his battle well, but photography, as all art
media and forms, requires a new battle with each gen-
eration for its acceptance. Burchfield and Chamberlain
contributed much energy to this battle at a time when photographs were not always accepted by the art establishment;
and photography which crossed boundaries into painting,
sculpture and conceptual art was not always acceptable to
the photography establishment.

In 1971, Mark Chamberlain convinced Laguna Beach
Art Festival officials, who were skeptical of photography's
artistic value, to allow two eight-foot pegboard panels for
exhibiting the dubious medium. Jerry Burchfield answered
a local newspaper ad placed by Chamberlain to solicit
photographs for the Art Festival. As a result of their meeting,
Burchfield became enthusiastically involved in the exhibit.

They obtained two Outerbridge prints from Lois Outerbridge. Having no idea of their value, they displayed them
along with the other prints. The outdoor, pegboard exhibit of
photographs, with the prints unprotected by glass in foggy,
February weather, began the Burchfield-Chamberlain partnership, a partnership, which continued to initiate photography
exhibitions at local art establishments.

Realizing the need for a center to serve as a focal point for
local photographic energy, Chamberlain later proposed
co-ownership of a commercial lab, which would support
this type of endeavor. Thinking it was merely talk, Burchfield
agreed and was later surprised when he received a call from
Chamberlain who had just rented a space. The space was
on the second floor of an architecturally intriguing building,
which formerly served as the local Masonic Temple.

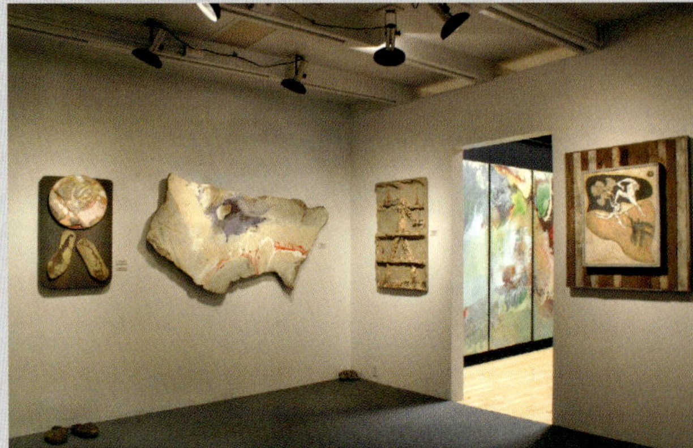

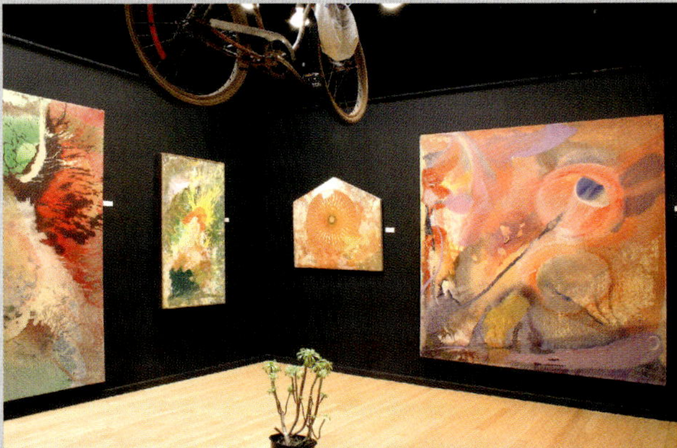

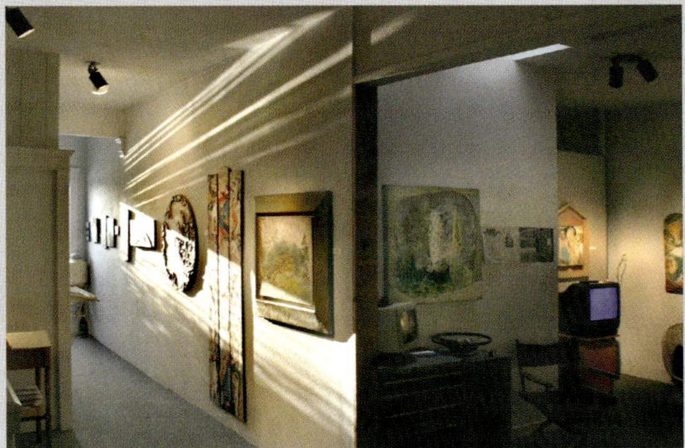

Homage to Andy Wing, 2004
Courtesy of BC Space
Laguna Beach, CA

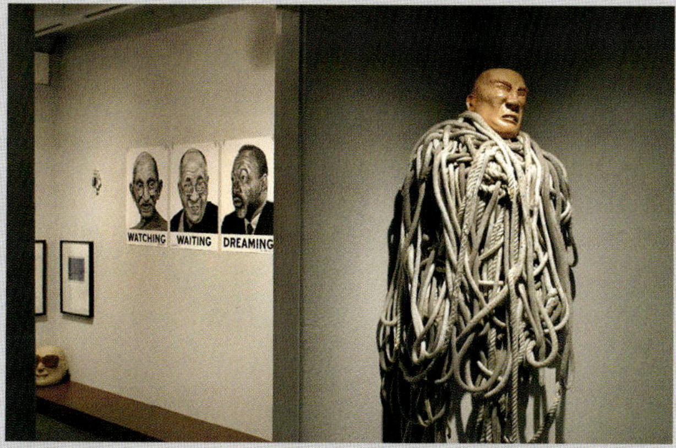

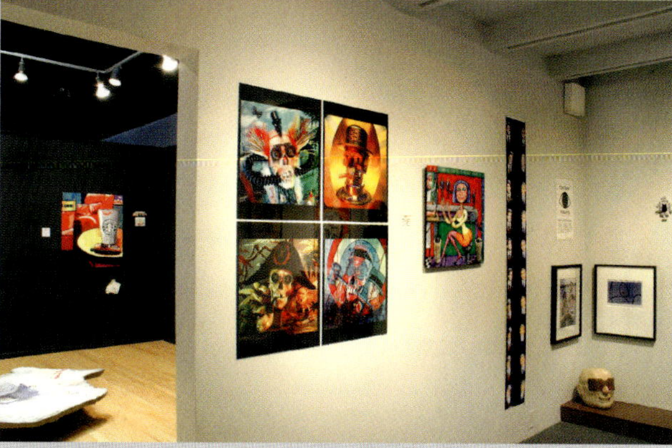

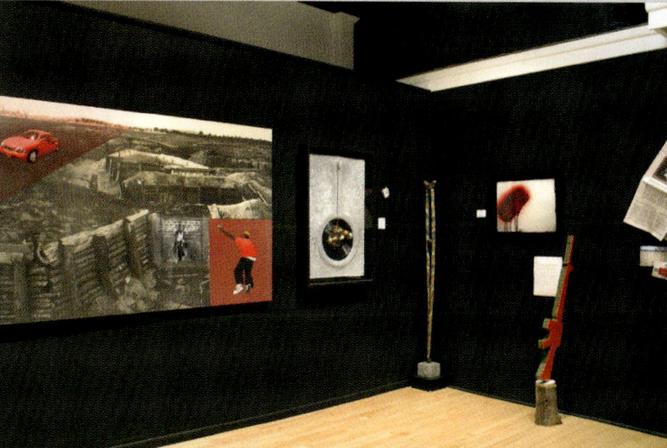

Means Times Back at Home, 2004
Group exhibition
Courtesy of BC Space
Laguna Beach, CA.

On April Fools Day, 1973, against much well meaning advice, BC Space opened for business. Neither partner was aware of the other's lack of interest in the commercial side of their endeavor. Burchfield, who had been employed as a commercial photographer, was growing increasingly interested in his art photography and, in fact, soon returned to school for his master's degree in art. Chamberlain, who held a master's degree in business administration, had long since decided that the artistic side of photography, not the business side, was his main interest. However, the lab provided the ideal situation. It supported the photographers' artwork and began to serve the photography community in an unplanned way.

Ten years ago, contemporary photography had little patronage. Museums were unwilling to test its artistic and monetary value and neither G. Ray Hawkins nor Susan Spiritus Galleries existed. Realizing the local photographers' need for exhibition space, Burchfield and Chamberlain began inviting artists to exhibit photographs in their foyer. Eventually they came to view their pioneering efforts as insufficient. Because BC Space was not a gallery, publications would list its exhibitions only when works by more well known artists such as Darryl Curran and Victor Landweber, were exhibited. Emerging artists' work was not listed. Also, large photographs, such as those shown by Laurie Brown and Mark Chamberlain, could not be properly viewed in the foyer.

By 1978, BC Space Lab had grown lucrative enough to support the addition of a gallery. Because Burchfield and Chamberlain felt that a gallery's main role was to educate, they continued to exhibit the work of many photographers who had not had much exposure. Although BC Space exhibited, and continues to exhibit, established artists, it gained a reputation for exhibiting work by local artists, such as Patrick Nagatani, Michael Levine, and Sheila Pinkel, before the work received widespread attention.

Burchfield and Chamberlain also contributed to local photography's growth by presenting workshops and lectures, reviewing portfolios whenever possible, and being supportive and helpful toward amateur, student, and emerging photographers. They felt that having a space to exhibit gives an artist the impetus to carry through an idea.

Often, Burchfield and Chamberlain have committed the space to an artist as a show of support before the work was actually finished. By creating the unique situation of a commercial lab that supports a gallery, Burchfield and Chamberlain were free to exhibit work chosen solely for its artistic value, without consideration of marketability. Toward the end of 1980, the partners were not certain of the gallery's viability. It demanded much of their time and exhibition attendance seemed low. By this time, contemporary photography was not only exhibited elsewhere, but it was exhibited in more aesthetic atmospheres than was financially feasible at BC Space.

Concerned that their efforts were no longer needed, Burchfield and Chamberlain decided to keep the gallery only if they could improve it. They planned an auction to support the building of a second gallery room. The auction's success was dependent on the photographers enlisted to donate prints.

In response to Burchfield and Chamberlain's request, 260 pieces by 150 artists from across the country arrived at BC Space! The support from the photography community was overwhelming. The gallery was virtually converted into a museum where visitors spent three to four hours viewing prints by Matthew Brady, Imogen Cunningham, George Hurrel, Philippe Halsman, Andre Kertez and Helmut Newton, as well as work by young artists from California.

A tremendous amount of hard work, artist support, and volunteer help secured the auction's success and financed the second gallery room. Burchfield and Chamberlain were assured of the photographic community's support and interest. They have since improved invitations and mailers, created a new filing system for reference slides, renovated the gallery, and hired a fulltime assistant. The exhibits usually include three photographers: two local artists and one from outside the Los Angeles area. The openings now approximate 200 people.

The opening reception for the ten-year anniversary celebration and the exhibit entitled "Ooparts the Uncategorical," which followed April Fools Day 1983, again provided local artist support.

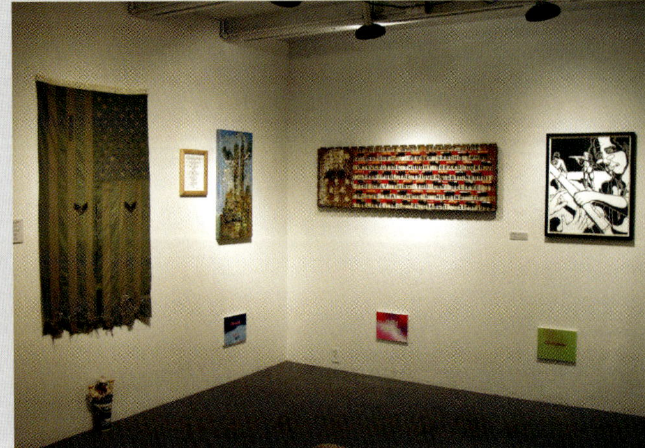

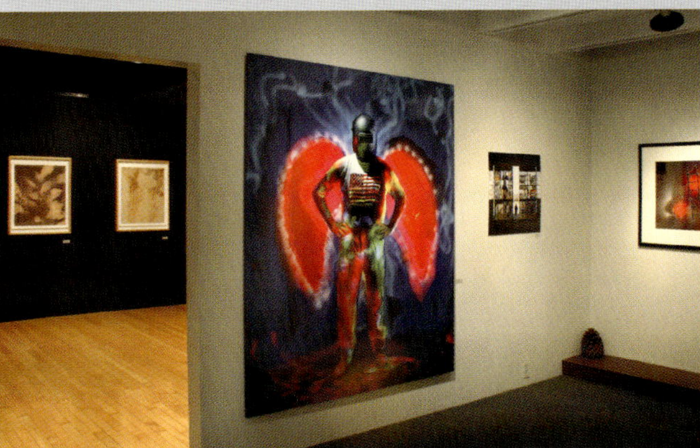

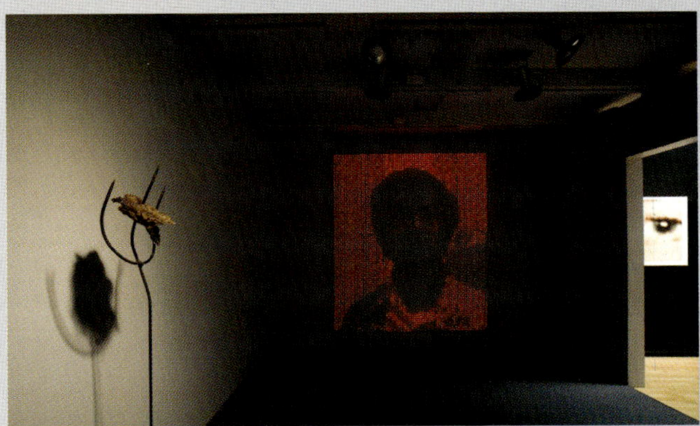

Pretty Lies Dirty Truth, 2003
Courtesy of BC Space

Requium for a Brother, 2009
Courtesy of BC Space

Skin Deep, 2009
Dao Nguyen and Richard Hutter
Courtesy of BC Space

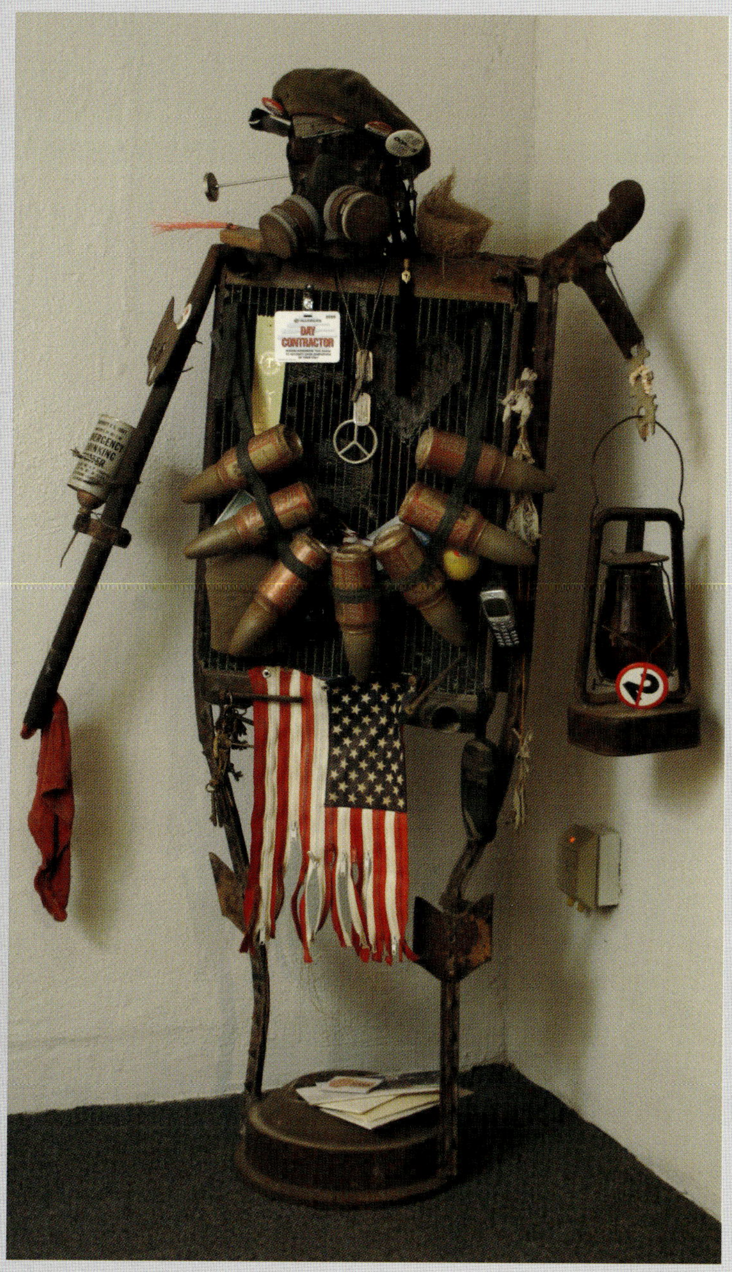

Mark Chamberlain
Private Property Goes To War
1989 to present
Work in progress
Courtesy of BC Space

The exciting and unusual exhibition which featured the "ooparts" (visions, artifacts and technologies that are unconnected to the time period of their discovery and/or are unable to fit into any previously established categories of classification) of 55 previous BC Space exhibitors was attended by 300 people on opening night. "Ooparts the Uncategorical" continued to attract a large audience throughout the duration of the exhibit.

The positive response to their activities has caused the partners to feel even more responsibility toward the local photography community. Because commercial galleries have become overextended by the number of photographers they represent, and because the present economic atmosphere has caused these galleries to cut the number of contemporary photographers that they represent, in September of 1983, BC Space began to represent the following 12 artists: Johnny Alterman, Jerry Burchfield, Jack Butler, Mark Chamberlain, Joe Deal, Suda House, Harold Jones, Michael Levine, Sheila Pinkel, Susan Rankaitis, Arthur Taussig and Mihoko Yamagata.

Burchfield and Chamberlain have elected to represent a limited number of artists in order to devote sufficient time to these artists. The artists' work is available for viewing and purchase in the back room, while the front gallery will continue to feature changing exhibitions of other contemporary photographers.

The partners are pleased with the growing artistic energy in Orange County. They are hopeful that Laguna Museum visitors will cross the street to BC Space to discover that contemporary photography is not only every bit as vital as other contemporary media, but also often defies categorization. They hope to bridge the gaps and break classifications that keep photography separate today, decades after Stieglitz's struggle. However, unlike Steiglitz, who himself became convinced of the superior vitality of traditional art media, Burchfield and Chamberlain remain enthusiastically committed to photography. Indeed they are contemporary pioneers.

BC Space Mything in Action was published in collaboration with the exhibition presented at CSUF Grand Central Art Center, February 6th through April 11th, 2010

All rights are reserved for the participating artists and publisher. No part of this publication can be reproduced without the concent of the artists and publisher

BC Space Mything in Action © 2013 - Produced 2010-2013

Curated by Mike McGee and Andrea Harris
GCAC Director during this exhibition: Dennis Cubbage
Current GCAC Director/Curator: John D. Spiak
Associate Director: Tracey Gayer
Chief Preparator: Matthew William Miller
Gallery Assistant: Yevgeniya Mikhailik
Preparator: Angelica Perez
Building Maintenance: Tony Pedraza

California State University Fullerton
Dean, School of the Arts: Dr. Joe Arnold
Grand Central Art Center Founder: Mike McGee
Assistant to the Director CSUF Begovich Gallery: Jacqueline Bunge
Executive Director of ASC: Frank Mumford

Grand Central Art Forum
Julie Perlin-Lee, President
Jon Gothold, Chairman
Wendy Sherman, Secretary
Robert Redding, Treasurer
Members: Greg Escalante, Mitchell DeJarnett, Diana Donaldson
James Hill, Mary Ellen Houseal, G. Ray Kerciu, Dennis Lluy
Shelley Liberto, Mike McGee, Joanna Roche, John Webb, C.W. West

Book Design: Andrea Harris
Editor: Sue Henger
Photography unless otherwise stated is by Mark Chamberlain
Eric Stoner and Andrea Harris
Font: Future TT Light, Medium and Consensed Light
Printed in China by Prolong Printing Limited

California State University Fullerton
Grand Central Art Center
125 N. Broadway
Santa Ana, CA 92706
fullerton.edu
grandcentralartcenter.wordpress.com
grandcentralartcenter.com
bcspace.com

Special Thanks to:
Our featured artists, Mark Chamberlain and Jerry Burchfield
Liz Goldner, Peter Clothier, all the collectors and galleries that graciously
loaned artworks, Marilyn Moore, Dennis Cubbage, Martin Lorigan
CSUF graduate exhibition design students, Nancy Wing, Tracey Gayer
Alyssa Cordova and Bill Axline Jr. and Sr.

This exhibition highlights the forty year history of BC Space. As much a mental space as it is a physical space, BC representing the initials of founders Jerry Burchfield and Mark Chamberlain is one of the oldest established galleries in Orange County. Located on the second floor above a commercial storefront on Forest Avenue in downtown Laguna Beach. BC Space began as a commercial photo lab and studio. Through the dedication of Chamberlain and Burchfield, this high quality photo lab soon transformed into a scarcely-for-profit art gallery, performance hall, public meeting place and a headquarters for community documentation projects and social activism. The most famous project to emerge from BC Space is the 15 phase, three decade long Laguna Canyon Project - which garnered national media attention including Life magazine and national TV coverage, involved thousands of Southern California residents, and ultimately saved the canyon from development.

-Mike McGee, co-curator

This book was a stop and start...stop and start again labor of love. Sometimes great projects take time. I feel so proud to have been part of this process. Thank you to all for your support.

-Andrea Harris, co-curator

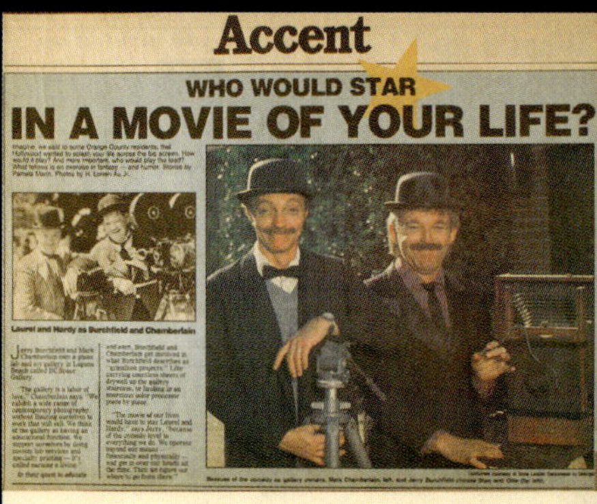

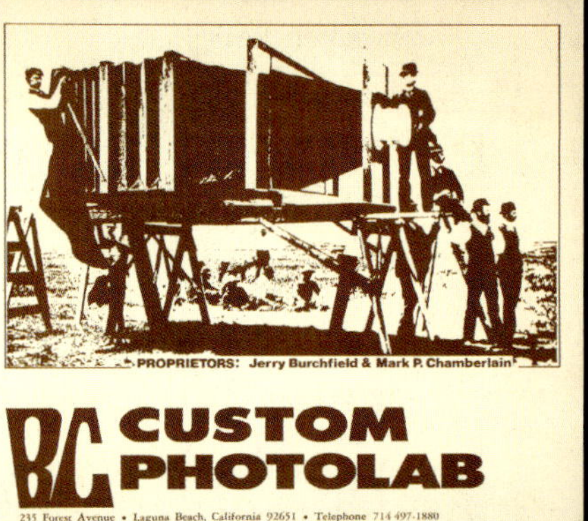